LEGAL DIRECTIVES AND PRACTICAL REASONS

Legal Directives and Practical Reasons

NOAM GUR

OXFORD
UNIVERSITY PRESS

OXFORD
UNIVERSITY PRESS

Great Clarendon Street, Oxford, OX2 6DP,
United Kingdom

Oxford University Press is a department of the University of Oxford.
It furthers the University's objective of excellence in research, scholarship,
and education by publishing worldwide. Oxford is a registered trade mark of
Oxford University Press in the UK and in certain other countries

Published in the United States of America by Oxford University Press
198 Madison Avenue, New York, NY 10016, United States of America

British Library Cataloguing in Publication Data
Data available

Library of Congress Control Number: 2018934173

ISBN 978–0–19–965987–6

For Sarah

Acknowledgements

I have incurred multiple debts of gratitude in the course of forming and developing the ideas put forward in this book. These begin in the period of my doctoral work under the supervision of Julie Dickson, who has provided me with invaluable feedback and advice, and has been a source of unwavering support for which I remain thoroughly grateful. Other beneficial feedback on early work that informed the book was given by colleagues and friends in different forms, such as written comments on papers, questions following presentations of my work, and informal conversations. For such inputs I wish to thank Sarah Chapman, Maks Del Mar, Anthony Duff, Richard Ekins, John Finnis, John Gardner, Leslie Green, Michael Griebe, Mickey Hyman, Maris Köpcke Tinturé, Anne van Mulligen, Christian Piller, Dan Priel, Meredith Root-Bernstein, Fred Schauer, Stefan Sciaraffa, Nigel Simmonds, Nicos Stavropoulos, and Bas van der Vossen. OUP's anonymous referees provided me with further penetrating comments that highlighted and led me to address some important objections to my position.

I owe special thanks to my friend Björn Alexander Düben for stimulating conversations that assisted my deliberation on the book and for his ever thoughtful and helpful advice.

I also thank Denise Lim for her diligent assistance with citations formatting, as well as Wendy Toole and Stephen Pigney for their careful proofreading at different stages of the work, and, in Stephen's case, also for his valuable assistance with indexing. At the publisher's end, a dexterous and responsive editorial team that included Natasha Flemming, Elinor Shields, and Eve Ryle-Hodges has been remarkably helpful and a pleasure to work with.

I am deeply grateful to my family for their patience, love, and support. My two young daughters Amalia and Elinor—who have had little interest in this book save for using my drafts as drawing paper—have helped me keep a sense of perspective about my work. And, finally, my partner Sarah has made an immeasurable contribution to the fruition of this book, not only by enabling me to devote the required time but also through her discerning comments and ceaseless encouragement. I have been fortunate to have her by my side.

The following papers are drawn upon in the book:

'Legal Directives in the Realm of Practical Reason: A Challenge to the Pre-emption Thesis' (2007) 52 American Journal of Jurisprudence 159—a revised version is incorporated in chapters 2–4.

'Normative Weighing and Legal Guidance of Conduct' (2012) 25 Canadian Journal of Law and Jurisprudence 359—a revised version comprises chapter 6.

Contents

III The Dispositional Model

1

Introduction

Reasons are fundamental to our self-understanding as human agents, and to the way we relate to our actions. When acting intentionally, we normally take ourselves to be acting for some reason;[1] and we regularly invoke reasons by way of explaining, recommending, requiring, justifying, evaluating, or criticizing actions, among other purposes.[2] At the same time, our operation in many spheres of life is subject to *legal* requirements—which are intended to direct and shape our behaviour. But, precisely because our self-understanding as agents is bound up with reasons in the fundamental way just indicated, it is plausible to suppose—as many legal philosophers have—that law's conduct-guiding operation typically involves some sort of appeal to our reasons; and that law's function as a guide to conduct cannot be fully or adequately understood without insight into law's ability to interact with our reasons. To put it differently, the domain of reasons provides what seems to be an important, and perhaps essential, medium between law and our actions. This last statement brings into focus the principal topic of this book: the way in which law bears (or can bear) on our reasons.

This initial statement of my topic requires significant refinement and limitation. That is part of what I will do in this introductory chapter, along with clarifying relevant notions and premises, and introducing some candidate answers that will be examined in later chapters. I start with the following three clarifications. First, my ultimate objective is not the identification of a normative quality shared by all systems or institutions that might be called legal, however iniquitous, corrupt, unreasonable, or thoroughly defective in other normatively significant ways they might be (if any such shared normative

---

[1] I say 'normally' to allow for some instances that can plausibly be understood as involving intentional action done for no perceived reason. This will be fleshed out in ch 9, where a thesis akin to the statement in the body text will be discussed. That thesis, known as the 'guise of the good' thesis, has been advocated by an illustrious series of thinkers that includes, inter alia, Aristotle, St Thomas Aquinas, Immanuel Kant, Elizabeth Anscombe, Donald Davidson, and Joseph Raz.

[2] The list is partial, not only because there are other action-focused invocations of reasons, but also because reasons are frequently invoked with regard to other things, such as beliefs and other attitudes.

Legal Directives and Practical Reasons. Noam Gur. © Noam Gur 2018. Published 2018 by Oxford University Press.

quality exists).[3] Indeed, much of the discussion, including the thesis I will eventually put forward, will focus on legal systems and lawmakers that satisfy certain prerequisites, or pass some minimum threshold level, in terms of relevant qualities, such as lawmakers being reasonably fit to exercise moral and equitable judgement and reasonably informed about matters germane to their decisions. Thus, my focal question is somewhat more accurately defined as a question about law's *potential* bearing on our reasons, namely as the question of how it bears on our reasons when it meets those prerequisites, which will be further specified in due course. That said, it should be added by way of qualification that parts of the discussion will revolve around cases of objectionable directives which are *less likely* to emerge under reasonably just and judicious legislatures than under legislatures that fall below this standard. But it is one thing to say that such cases are *less likely* to emerge under reasonably just and judicious legislatures, and quite another to say that they *cannot* or *never do*. And precisely because it would be false to say the latter, those cases remain relevant to my inquiry.

Second, the term 'reasons', as used in my initial topic description, warrants some explanatory comments. While I largely leave these to Section 1.2, one comment is apposite at this point. This book is not concerned with *any* reasons, but with reasons that relate in some relevant and significant way to our *actions*.[4] That I direct my attention to such reasons in a book focused on law should hardly come as a surprise—for law is after all a practical affair, a social practice primarily concerned with our actions.[5] But a question might follow here: am I referring to essentially the same thing that philosophers call *practical* reasons? The answer is: in large part yes, but not exclusively. When philosophers speak of practical reasons, they normally mean reasons for action: a term of art usually intended to include reasons in favour of or against an action,[6] such as, for example, the reason for you to set your alarm

---

[3] I say in the body text above 'might be called legal', but I should add, of course, that, from the perspective of natural law theories, defects of the types mentioned above may undercut the legality of a system, or may render it a peripheral instance of law (John M Finnis, *Natural Law and Natural Rights* (2nd edn, Clarendon Press 2011) 9–11, 363–66), or may mean that it is a legally (not only morally) defective system (Mark C Murphy, *Natural Law in Jurisprudence and Politics* (CUP 2006) *passim*, esp 10–12). See further, Jonathan Crowe, 'Clarifying the Natural Law Thesis' (2012) 37 Australian Journal of Legal Philosophy 159.

[4] These words are not meant to signify anything like a category with fixed and sharp boundaries determined in an a priori fashion. I wish to retain a relatively open-ended field of vision in this respect, so as to be able to pick up different types of reason that might emerge through substantive analysis as significant mediators between law and our actions.

[5] The qualifier 'primarily' is used above, inter alia, because legal responsibility sometimes depends in part on mental elements, such as *mens rea* in criminal offences.

[6] Though this or closely related terms have also been used in more inclusive ways. I am thinking particularly of Joseph Raz who, in his seminal book *Practical Reason and Norms*, introduced the

clock to 7.00 a.m. (e.g. that otherwise you would be late to work), or, say, your reasons not to order the whole boiled lobster at a business lunch (e.g. it would be messy to crack and eat and would consume your entire attention). The law does not tell us at what time to wake up or what to order for lunch, but reasons with the above type of structure and function—that is, reasons that militate for or against an action—have central relevance to this inquiry. However, to confine the inquiry to those reasons alone would, I believe, be unduly restrictive. It would prematurely preclude the possibility that at least part of law's potential normative significance is to be understood in terms of reasons that, although not reasons for action themselves, have indirect pertinence to our actions. One such type of reason, for example, could be reasons for belief (sometimes referred to as theoretical or epistemic reasons) that, in turn, *inform* our assessment of reasons for action. And there are other reasons that, although not reasons for action in the paradigmatic sense or arguably in any sense, have potential significance for our actions—one of which reasons, as will become clearer in Part III, is central to the position I will ultimately advocate. More will be said about this in due course. I should only add here, as a terminological point, that when referring to the book's topic or question I will nonetheless frequently opt for the term 'practical reasons',[7] it being a compact term that approximates reasonably well the range of reasons with which I am concerned. But this is a choice of convenience made without intention to preclude from consideration potentially relevant reasons that do not, or do not squarely, fall within the term's standard meaning.

A third clarification may help provide a still more accurate idea of the question addressed in this book. There are different facets to the question of law's bearing on practical reasons, and different angles from which it can be approached. My primary focus here will be a *modal* or *structural* aspect of this puzzle, which can be encapsulated in the following question: what is law's mode of operation in the domain of practical reasons? Or, what is the modus operandi of its interaction with practical reasons? At the centre of attention in the first two parts of this book will be two competing answers to this question. The first contends that, when law meets certain prerequisites that endow it with legitimate authority,[8] its normative mode of operation is

---

notion of second-order reasons, i.e. reasons to act for a reason or to refrain from acting for a reason (Joseph Raz, *Practical Reason and Norms* (2nd edn, Princeton University Press 1990) 39). The relevant aspects of Raz's theory will be expounded and discussed at length in this book.

[7] As I have done in the book's title.

[8] That is, 'legitimate' not in the sense of how it is perceived by people, but in the sense that it satisfies certain justificatory conditions. On the distinction between these two senses, see, e.g., Fabienne Peter, 'Political Legitimacy' in Edward N Zalta (ed), *Stanford Encyclopedia of Philosophy* (2017) s 1 <https://plato.stanford.edu/entries/legitimacy/> accessed 15 December 2017.

pre-emptive—namely, it constitutes reasons for action that *exclude and take the place of* some of the reasons that otherwise bear on what we ought to do.[9] The second answer contends that, rather than excluding otherwise applicable reasons, law can only give rise to reasons for action that compete with opposing ones in terms of their comparative weight.[10] In the third part of the book, I will put forward and advocate a third position, which explains the normative force of reasonably just and well-functioning legal systems in terms of reasons to adopt a certain attitude which reflects a middle course between pre-emption and weighing, an attitude that will be characterized more specifically in Chapter 7.[11]

1.1. Law—Preliminaries

1.1.1. A Comment on Legal Validity

My inquiry revolves around the relationship between law and practical reasons, but each of the two constituents of this relationship is the subject of philosophical disputes in its own right. Focusing momentarily on the former,[12] there are, as readers of this book are likely to be well aware, wide-ranging disagreements over the question of what law is. This question, needless to explain, cannot be addressed within the confines of this book. But should I, nonetheless, adopt by way of stipulation any one specific conception of law among the jurisprudential contenders? I think it would be neither necessary nor advisable to do so, at least not on a general basis. This is because

---

[9] This answer derives from Joseph Raz's pre-emption thesis (Joseph Raz, *The Morality of Freedom* (Clarendon Press 1986) 46). I will describe it more fully in Section 1.3.

[10] This answer is espoused (explicitly or implicitly) by several of Raz's critics cited in n 61. It will be presented in further detail in Section 1.3.

[11] Two additional qualifications as to the scope of this inquiry should be added. First, my focus will be mandatory legal norms, rather than norms such as power-conferring and permission-granting norms. My primary interest here is law's operation in practical reason when and insofar as it *requires compliance*—and the paradigmatic sense in which it requires compliance occurs where it mandates behaviour. Furthermore, past discourse on our subject matter has tended to revolve around this type of norm, and, by way of engaging with past discourse, it would make sense for us to focus on the same object. For some exceptions, wherein other types of norm are discussed from a reason-focused perspective, see, e.g., Raz, *Practical Reason and Norms* (n 6) ch 3; Nigel E Simmonds, *Central Issues in Jurisprudence: Justice, Law and Rights* (Sweet and Maxwell 2002) 256–63, 298–304. Second, I will focus primarily on the interface between the law and non-legal actors, rather than on intra-legal methods of reasoning employed by officials, e.g. judges. Legal reasoning will feature in the discussion only instrumentally to my primary objectives. The specific characteristics of legal reasoning mean that including it as a primary topic here, first, would result in a substantially different book than that which I set out to write, and, second, could not fit in this book's scope along with my present objectives.

[12] As regards the latter, some comments will be offered in Section 1.2.1.

much of what I will argue here in addressing the particular question at hand may hold good under more than one conception of law, and because of the obvious advantages to keeping the inquiry's presuppositions as inclusive as possible. I will thus refrain from tying the inquiry wholesale to any particular jurisprudential outlook. Specific indication of whether any of my arguments presuppose contested jurisprudential assumptions is something that, insofar as needed, will be given in the course of substantive discussion.

One exception to the statement just made, however, is the following comment. According to one of the principal positions I will consider, that of Joseph Raz, the directives of a legitimate authority constitute 'pre-emptive reasons'.[13] Apart from its direct relevance to the question of this book, this position is indirectly linked to another central theme in jurisprudence: the grounds or sources of legal validity.[14] The link is compound, but most pertinent at this point is its following facet. The possibility of pre-emptive normative force in the legal context is clearly incompatible with certain conceptions of legal validity, which we may call non-positivist conceptions: namely, those which treat evaluative reasoning about the purpose and content of a directive as an essential part of the test for determining its legal validity.[15] This sort of evaluative reasoning involves recourse to the very same reasons for action that (as will be explicated at later points)[16] pre-emptive reasons are thought to exclude.[17] So if this sort of reasoning were essential to the identification of a directive as legally valid, the possibility for the law to operate as a pre-emptive reason would be undercut.[18]

---

[13] Raz, *The Morality of Freedom* (n 9) 42, 46. The term 'directives', as will be used throughout this book, is intended to include different kinds of prescriptions, such as rules, decrees, orders, and judicial rulings.

[14] Or, as it is sometimes referred to, the truth conditions of propositions of law.

[15] Ronald Dworkin's approach is a classic example, though he does not express it in the above terms (Ronald Dworkin, *Taking Rights Seriously* (rev paperback edn with a reply to critics, Duckworth 1978) chs 2–4; Ronald Dworkin, *Law's Empire* (Fontana 1986)). See related positions in Mark Greenberg, 'How Facts Make Law' in Scott Hershowitz (ed), *Exploring Law's Empire: The Jurisprudence of Ronald Dworkin* (OUP 2006) 225–64; and Nicos E Stavropoulos, 'Why Principles?' (2007) Oxford Legal Studies Research Paper 28/2007 <https://papers.ssrn.com/sol3/papers.cfm?abstract_id=1023758> accessed 5 September 2017.

[16] Sections 1.3 and 1.4; and p 58.

[17] Cf similar point in Dimitrios Kyritsis, *Where Our Protection Lies: Separation of Powers and Constitutional Review* (OUP 2017) 109.

[18] I am somewhat less certain as to whether the version of positivism known as inclusive or soft positivism can be reconciled, or partially reconciled, with the pre-emption thesis. Raz, for one, claims that inclusive positivism 'is incompatible with the authoritative nature of law' (which, on his understanding, implicates the idea of pre-emption) (Joseph Raz, *Ethics in the Public Domain: Essays in the Morality of Law and Politics* (rev paperback edn, Clarendon Press 1995) 227). See contra, e.g., WJ Waluchow, 'Authority and the Practical Difference Thesis: A Defense of Inclusive Legal Positivism' (2000) 6 Legal Theory 45.

In light of this, it would make little sense for a critical examination of the pre-emption thesis to be premised on (unargued-for) non-positivist assumptions about legal validity. To thus proceed would, in effect, finish the discussion before it starts. Of course, one may offer or cite *arguments* in support of a non-positivist conception of legal validity, and count such arguments (insofar as they are cogent) as indirect evidence against the pre-emption thesis. But, since arguments of this type fall outside the compass of this book, it is not my intention to examine the pre-emption thesis from the perspective of non-positivist validity criteria. Now, does this render my discussion of the pre-emption thesis less relevant to those of a non-positivist persuasion about legal validity? I believe it does not. An attempt to directly engage with the pre-emption thesis is an exercise that has, I think, a strong claim to the attention of non-positivists. The reason is that, having offered independent arguments in support of the pre-emption thesis, Raz has famously turned to deploy the thesis as part of an argument for his brand of legal positivism—exclusive legal positivism—and against rival conceptions of legal validity.[19] His argumentative move need not be reiterated in detail here,[20] but it clearly illustrates that the pre-emption thesis has central dialectic relevance to the debate over the grounds of legal validity—which, in turn, means that direct arguments on the thesis's veracity may be of interest to non-positivists as much as to any other party in the debate.

1.1.2. A Comment on Authority

According to a notable strand of jurisprudential thought, which was mentioned in the previous section, every legal system, as part of its very nature as a system of *law*, makes a normative claim to legitimate *authority*,[21] or is held to possess it, or both.[22] Even those who do not share, or entirely share, this

---

[19] Raz, *Ethics in the Public Domain* (n 18) ch 10; Joseph Raz, *The Authority of Law: Essays on Law and Morality* (2nd edn, OUP 2009) 51–52. Can the pre-emption thesis both depend on the truth of positivism (as pointed out in the previous paragraph) *and* be used for advocating positivism (or a version thereof)? Yes: this need not be circular, in part because the grounds on which the pre-emption thesis itself has been argued for are independent of positivism.

[20] In a thumbnail sketch, the argument says that since it is in the very nature of law that legal systems claim to have legitimate authority, they must also (by their nature as law) have certain formal features that make them *capable* of having legitimate authority; and given certain truths about the role of legitimate authority—including its pre-emptive normative function—the above formal features must include, inter alia, the identifiability of legal directives without recourse to the underlying reasons on which those directives purport to adjudicate. For the full argument, see Raz, *Ethics in the Public Domain* (n 18) ch 10.

[21] Raz, *The Authority of Law* (n 19) 30. See also John Gardner, *Law as a Leap of Faith* (OUP 2012) 125–48; Julie Dickson, *Evaluation and Legal Theory* (Hart Publishing 2001) *passim*.

[22] Raz, *Ethics in the Public Domain* (n 18) 215.

view may find it hard to deny that law, and its normative operation, bear a close relationship to the idea of authority.[23] If this much is true, the question might be asked: what place do arguments on authority have in this inquiry? In part, this is a question I will address in the course of substantive discussion in places where it arises.[24] But it is appropriate briefly to indicate at this point how I plan to proceed. My approach will largely be this: I will treat arguments about authority as an essential resource for the purpose of this inquiry and will give them considerable attention, but at the same time I will avoid a general shift in the focus of my inquiry from law to authority, or a restriction of my purview to legal instantiations of authority only.

Thus, a significant part of the discussion will be devoted to normative arguments about the kind of reasons for action provided by a legitimate authority,[25] and to arguments about the phenomenology characteristic of our encounters with authorities.[26] But my recourse to such arguments will at all times remain instrumental and subordinate to the primary question I am addressing: a question about *law's* potential bearing on practical reasons. And the range of possible answers to this question will not be assumed from the outset to be strictly defined by, or confined to, what is or is not true of authority. To be clear, I do not rule out the possibility that arguments about authority (viz. about its concept, normative implications, justificatory grounds, etc.) will, in the end, turn out to contain all the insight we need for an adequate understanding of law's potential normative significance in terms of reasons. But nor do I wish to approach this inquiry in a way that effectively forecloses other possibilities, such as the possibility that, for all its pertinence to this inquiry, an authority-focused outlook cannot adequately capture the relevant normative picture.

1.2. Reasons—Preliminaries

1.2.1. Reasons for Action

It is essential to say more in clarification of a notion I will frequently be using: reasons for action. I begin with a terminological note. It was mentioned above that 'reasons for action' is a term of art normally intended by philosophers to include reasons in favour of or against a specific action—and that is also how I will be using the term here.[27] The explanations given in this section

---

[23] But see contra, e.g., Laurence Claus, *Law's Evolution and Human Understanding* (OUP 2012) esp ch 4.

[24] pp 75–76, 97–98.   [25] chs 2–4.   [26] ch 5.

[27] But when speaking of reasons in reference to '*an* action', '*the* action', or a specific action description, I will normally state whether the reasons concerned are for the action, against the action, or both.

regarding 'reasons for action', however, will focus on the former alternative, reasons in favour of an action, in the interest of brevity. But these explanations extend, *mutatis mutandis*, to reasons against an action.

The next point concerns an ambiguity in the notion of 'reasons for action': the notion can be understood in a normative sense or a motivational sense.[28] Some writers have responded to this ambiguity by distinguishing between 'normative reasons for action' and 'motivating reasons for action'.[29] Reasons for action in the first sense are what we typically invoke when making a statement of the form 'There is a reason for you to φ', or some variant thereof, as in: 'You should really try cycling to work, if not for health reasons, then simply because it would spare you the traffic jams.' Such statements point to factors that *speak in favour* of the action. Reasons for action in the second sense are what we typically invoke when making a statement of the form 'Her reason for φ-ing was ... ', or some variant thereof, as in: 'Her reason for calling an early election was the recent favourable opinion polls.' In a statement of this form, we intend to describe the motivation or consideration that made a difference to how the agent acted, or the purpose for which she did what she did. Now, how exactly the normative and motivational sense of reasons relate to one another is a philosophically contentious question extensively discussed in the relevant literature.[30] What is essential in the present context, however, is to forestall possible doubt or confusion about which of these two senses is the focus of this inquiry. It is the normative, rather than the motivating sense. For mine is not an inquiry into people's motivations to comply with or depart from legal requirements, but an inquiry into law's potential contribution to the set of reasons that normatively warrant acting this way or another. This is not to say that motivations for compliance or noncompliance are *entirely* irrelevant to this discussion. They have some relevance

---

[28] See, e.g., Michael Smith, *The Moral Problem* (Blackwell 1994) 94–98; Jonathan Dancy, *Practical Reality* (OUP 2003) 1–5, 20–25; Derek Parfit, 'Rationality and Reasons' in Dan Egonsson et al (eds), *Exploring Practical Philosophy* (Ashgate 2001) 17–39, at 17.

[29] See, e.g., Smith (n 28) 94–98; Dancy (n 28) 98–99 (using this terminology *arguendo*, but ultimately criticizing it); Parfit (n 28) 17. Other terms have been used in this connection, e.g. 'justifying' or 'grounding' instead of 'normative' reasons, and 'explanatory' instead of 'motivating' reasons. See, e.g., Joseph Raz, *From Normativity to Responsibility* (OUP 2011) 13–35, distinguishing between normative and explanatory reasons. Cf Maria Alvarez, *Kinds of Reasons: An Essay in the Philosophy of Action* (OUP 2010) ch 2. For jurisprudential references to the normative/motivating-reasons distinction, see, e.g., Jules Coleman, *The Practice of Principle* (OUP 2001) 71–72; David Enoch, 'Reason-Giving and the Law' in Leslie Green and Brian Leiter (eds), *Oxford Studies in Philosophy of Law*, vol 1 (OUP 2011) 1–38, at 15; Brian H Bix, 'The Nature of Law and Reasons for Action' (2011) 5 Problema 399, 413–14; Kenneth M Ehrenberg, *The Functions of Law* (OUP 2016) 150–52.

[30] On this question, contrast, e.g., Smith (n 28) chs 4–5, esp 94–98, with Dancy (n 28) 2, 98–99, 101, 103, and with Raz, *From Normativity to Responsibility* (n 29) 26–36. See also Ulrike Heuer, 'Reasons for Actions and Desires' (2004) 121 Philosophical Studies 43, esp 45.

and will feature in parts of the discussion.[31] But their relevance, which will be explained in due course, is indirect, and their role will only be subsidiary to my main purpose.

The preceding comment offers an essential disambiguation about reasons for action, but does not say much, at least not directly, about this concept. That is the subject of a large body of philosophical writings, wherein one finds several different stories about what it is for something to be a reason for action. I will now briefly state the core claims of one understanding of the concept, which I find generally intuitive—though, as will be further clarified below, I do not intend thereby to tie this inquiry in any restrictive way to that specific understanding. The understanding I am referring to can be encapsulated in this twofold statement: (1) Reasons for action are facts that count in favour of a certain action;[32] (2) Facts that constitute reasons for action are facts in virtue of which the action has some value (or its consequences do);[33] they are facts in virtue of which the action is, in some way, good or desirable.[34] By way of illustration, the fact that it is raining today is a reason for me to carry an umbrella. For that fact is part of what makes carrying an umbrella an act that will effectively contribute to a desirable condition, that is, my not being drenched (and there is a further explanation of why it is a desirable condition: otherwise I would be likelier to develop a cold, feel uncomfortable, have to waste time on changing clothes, etc.). A person may, directly or indirectly, refer to such a reason without fully stating why it is a reason, as when one says, simply: 'It's going to rain today. I'd better take an

---

[31] Particularly in Sections 8.2 and 8.5.

[32] On reasons as facts see, e.g., Raz, *Practical Reason and Norms* (n 6) 17–20.

[33] This conception can be subsumed under what has been called value-based theory of reasons, in defence of which see, e.g., EJ Bond, *Reason and Value* (CUP 1983); Parfit (n 28) 17–39. Raz, too, seems generally to support a value-based theory of practical reasons (see, e.g., Joseph Raz, *Engaging Reason: On the Theory of Value and Action* (OUP 1999) 22, 29–31, 63–64; Raz, *From Normativity to Responsibility* (n 29) 70, 75–79), albeit with certain qualifications (see, e.g., Raz, *Engaging Reason* (n 33) 62; Joseph Raz, 'Value and the Weight of Practical Reasons' in Errol Lord and Barry Maguire (eds), *Weighing Reasons* (OUP 2016) 141–56). See other relevant references cited in Barry Maguire, 'The Value-Based Theory of Reasons' (2016) 3 Ergo 233, fn 2. Cf Ruth Chang, 'Can Desires Provide Reasons for Action?' in R Jay Wallace et al (eds), *Reason and Value: Themes from the Moral Philosophy of Joseph Raz* (OUP 2004) 56–90, where Chang advocates a 'hybrid' view, according to which '[s]ome practical reasons are provided by the fact that the agent wants something, while others are provided by the fact that what she wants is of value' (ibid 57).

[34] A notable alternative is Scanlon's 'buck-passing view' of value, according to which reasons have an explanatory priority over value (Thomas M Scanlon, *What We Owe to Each Other* (Harvard University Press 1998) 95–100). But on this view, too, reasons are grounded in properties, or features of the world, external to the agent, and not in the agent's subjective states such as her desires. In this light, it has been suggested by Parfit that the buck-passing view is reconcilable with a value-based theory of reasons, so long as the latter makes no reference to 'value', 'good', or 'bad' save as abbreviations of reason-giving properties, such as safe, effective, painful, etc. (Parfit (n 28) 20).

umbrella.' But part of what one implies when making such a statement is that being soaked by the rain would be a bad thing.[35]

This thumbnail sketch should suffice for my illustrative purposes. But I should add a brief note of caution, which was hinted at above: it is one thing to say that I will operate with this understanding of reasons for action in mind (or will sometimes speak in terms consonant with it), and quite another to say that my arguments will *depend* on this understanding for their cogency. What I mean to say here is only the former. Moreover, it appears to me, prima facie, that the arguments made in this book (if cogent in other respects) may hold good under at least some of the alternative understandings of the concept,[36] though, to avoid lengthening this introductory chapter, I will leave this issue to one side save for brief comment in the footnotes.[37]

1.2.2. The Reasons at Issue are Not Reasons-from-the-Law's-Point-of-View-Only

This inquiry, it should be emphasized, is not focused on reasons in some thin or merely technical sense confined solely to the perspective of the law. It is not primarily concerned, in other words, with that which is regarded as a reason *only* from the point of view of the legal practice (and not from a moral or other extra-legal point of view). Reasons in the above sense (if they can be called reasons at all) are sometimes referred to as *legal* reasons. David Enoch, for example, cites the thesis that '[w]henever … the law requires that you Φ, you thereby have a legal reason to Φ', all the while noting the watered-down

---

[35] See related comments in Raz, *Practical Reason and Norms* (n 6) 22–25; Raz, *From Normativity to Responsibility* (n 29) 14–15.

[36] Thus, for example, I see no reason to suspect that my arguments could not be upheld under Scanlon's 'buck-passing view' (see n 34) or under Broome's understanding of reasons in terms of their relation to 'ought facts' (John Broome, 'Reasons' in R Jay Wallace et al (eds), *Reason and Value: Themes from the Moral Philosophy of Joseph Raz* (Clarendon Press 2004) 28–55).

[37] What about desire-based theories of practical reasons (sometimes referred to as Humean), or Williams's internalist view that a reason for action depends for its existence on there being something in the agent's subjective motivational set that would be served by the action (Bernard Williams, *Moral Luck* (CUP 1981) 101–13)? Such views do not seem to me to fit very smoothly into a discussion of law's normative force. For it is a salient and important feature of law that it seeks to address reasons for action even to those who have no desire or want that corresponds to what it requires. And though the law does not always have the reason-giving power it purports to have, we do not attribute such failures to the absence of this or that desire on the part of a given subject. But a question might be raised here: couldn't desire-based/internalist conceptions fully account for law-given reasons by focusing on more abstract and less immediate human desires whose fulfilment is helped or made possible by the law? Such an exercise, it seems to me, would require considerable strain, but I express no stronger view on whether it might succeed. If and to the extent that it might, I see no other reason why much of what I will argue in this book could not be argued from that theoretical perspective too.

or merely ostensible sense in which reasons are spoken of here.[38] This thesis, Enoch stresses, is *not* about 'moral reasons, or indeed the most general, un-qualified, real, rationality-reasons'.[39] He goes on to clarify this point with the following analogies:

[T]he rules of chess presumably manage to give chess-reasons, the rules of etiquette presumably give etiquette-reasons, the rules of machismo honor presumably give one machismo-honor-reasons, and so on. And in all these cases, it remains an open question whether the practice-qualified reasons are also real, genuine, unqualified reasons ...[40]

If this is what legal reasons mean, they are not what this book is about and are, at best, tangential to my analysis (in much the same way that they oc-cupy a minor place in Enoch's essay cited above). The reasons at the centre of my inquiry are (unlike 'machismo-honor-reasons') genuine reasons. And, at least arguably, they apply to individuals who have not voluntarily entered the relevant practice—which, by contrast, could not tenably be argued about 'chess-reasons'.

Now, a possible qualification for the above understanding of legal reasons runs as follows.[41] While we may say that legal reasons are reasons-from-the-law's-point-of-view-only, from the law's point of view itself—as embodied in the acts and words of legal officials—it is not claimed or implied that legal re-quirements are merely legal reasons which are not morally binding. The claim made by the law through its officials is a claim for *legitimate* authority[42]—'le-gitimate' in a genuine and morally significant sense. It is a claim that legal subjects have genuine, moral reasons to abide by the system's requirements. Of course, the law's claim for legitimacy, and for real reason-giving power, can be, and sometimes is, a false claim, but the fact that it makes such a claim is nonetheless an essential characteristic of law, and is, thus, part of the background presupposed by the talk of legal reasons. Now, what this qualification says about law's normative claim is not free from controversy,[43]

---

[38] Enoch (n 29) 16.

[39] ibid. See related points in Torben Spaak, 'Legal Positivism, Law's Normativity, and the Normative Force of Legal Justification' (2003) 16 Ratio Juris 469, and Frederick Schauer, *The Force of Law* (Harvard University Press 2015) 227, fn 28.

[40] Enoch (n 29) 17.

[41] Some of Enoch's arguments suggest that he accepts the general tenor of what follows in the body text, but he also expresses important reservations in this regard (ibid 22, 33–36).

[42] See, in a similar vein, Raz, *The Authority of Law* (n 19) 30; Raz, *Ethics in the Public Domain* (n 18) 215; Gardner (n 21) 125–48; Scott J Shapiro, *Legality* (Harvard University Press 2011) 186–88.

[43] For relevant criticism, see, e.g., Kenneth E Himma, 'Law's Claim of Legitimate Authority' in Jules Coleman (ed), *Hart's Postscript: Essays on the Postscript to the Concept of Law* (OUP 2001) 271–309; Ronald Dworkin, 'Thirty Years On' (2002) 115 Harvard Law Review 1655, 1666–67. In

but we need not consider it on its merits at this point. For, even if correct, it does not change the primary focus of this inquiry: its primary focus remains genuine reasons, rather than legal ones in the thin, practice-qualified sense described above.[44] And, although I will not ignore the claim law makes about its reason-giving power,[45] most of my efforts will be focused on direct normative arguments about its reason-giving power—arguments about the justificatory grounds and moral implications of different answers to this question.

1.3. The Competing Models Expounded

I have already mentioned the two competing positions that form the foci of Parts I and II, but a more detailed description of them is appropriate before we plunge into critical discussion. The first of these positions is associated with Joseph Raz, whose work in the interface between practical reason, authority, and law has stimulated and set the agenda for much of the subsequent discourse in this context. Most pertinent at this point is a thesis Raz calls the pre-emption thesis, which reads thus:

[T]he fact that an authority requires performance of an action is a reason for its performance which is not to be added to all other relevant reasons when assessing what to do, but should exclude and take the place of some of them.[46]

This thesis, it bears emphasizing, is about the normative force of authority, in the sense of legitimate (not merely de facto) authority.[47] It does not refer to

---

defence of the idea that law claims legitimate authority, see, e.g., Gardner (n 21) 125–48; Bas van der Vossen, 'Assessing Law's Claim to Authority' (2011) 31 Oxford Journal of Legal Studies 481. On whether legal assertions of obligation must be taken to refer to an obligation in the *moral* sense, and whether they must be taken as assertions of a reason for action, see, e.g., Matthew H Kramer, *In Defense of Legal Positivism* (OUP 1999) ch 4.

[44] There are other possible understandings of 'legal reasons', which stand in contrast to the one mentioned above. Thus, for example, according to natural law theories the very idea of law (or at least its central case) inheres moral attributes that give rise to a genuinely moral type of normativity; and, thus, legal reasons (or at least central cases thereof) are an instantiation of moral reasons. The basic point I made in the body text above does not negate (or endorse) such understandings of 'legal reasons'. For my point was this: *if* there is a sense in which we can speak of reasons from the law's point of view which are not moral or otherwise genuine reasons, this sense is not the one I am concerned with.

[45] It will inform parts of my analysis in indirect ways which will be explicated at the relevant points.

[46] Raz, *The Morality of Freedom* (n 9) 46.

[47] A merely de facto authority is, according to Raz, conceptually parasitic on legitimate authority. It necessarily 'either claims to be legitimate or is believed to be so' (Raz, *Ethics in the Public Domain* (n 18) 211; see also Raz, *The Authority of Law* (n 19) 9). Thus, on his view, a merely de facto authority claims, or is believed, to provide the type of reasons described in the pre-emption

law or make a direct claim about its normative force. However, it may give us the answer to the question of how law bears on practical reasons when it satisfies Razian prerequisites of legitimate authority; and this, even if not *entirely* coextensive with the range of instances I set about to explore,[48] seems to comprise at least part of that range.

Turning to the substance of this thesis, a brief illustration of its core idea may be useful to start with. Suppose I have reasons for and against driving at 90 mph. That it is dangerous is a reason against it, and that I am late for work is a reason for it. But now further suppose that driving at that speed would contravene a speed limit rule issued by lawmakers with legitimate authority over me regarding road traffic matters. The latter fact, according to the pre-emption thesis, is not just another reason not to drive at that speed, such that I should weigh it in the ordinary balance of pros and cons. Rather, on this view, it is a 'pre-emptive reason'[49] not to drive at that speed: namely, a reason not to do so which also excludes from the balance some opposing reasons, such as the fact of my being late for work. The fact of my being late should thus drop out of the set of competing factors on which I base my action.[50]

A pre-emptive reason, then, is a combination of two types of reason:[51] (1) a reason for action (i.e. for performing the authority-required act); and (2) a reason that excludes some other reasons. The second of these two types Raz calls an *exclusionary reason*,[52] and he defines it as follows: a reason to refrain from acting for certain other reasons.[53] Exclusionary reasons are characterized by Raz as reasons that belong to a *second order* of reasons.[54] They

thesis, but does not actually provide them. I should add here, as a terminological point, that henceforth when using the term 'authority' I will normally mean legitimate authority (as I will, *mutatis mutandis*, when using derivatives such as 'authoritative'), unless otherwise specified or made clear by the context.

[48] See relevant comment on p 7.

[49] Raz, *The Morality of Freedom* (n 9) 42. In some places Raz uses the term 'protected reason' for the same idea (e.g. Raz, *The Authority of Law* (n 19) 18; Raz, *Practical Reason and Norms* (n 6) 191). I will be using the term 'pre-emptive reason' throughout.

[50] It should be noted that Raz's claim is not that any reflection or thought about that reason (i.e. my being late) is excluded, but only that the reason should not be allowed to influence my action, insofar as the authority has pronounced on it. See Raz, *The Morality of Freedom* (n 9) 39–42; Raz, *The Authority of Law* (n 19) 26, fn 25; Joseph Raz, 'Facing Up: A Reply' (1989) 62 Southern California Law Review 1153, 1156–57, 1159.

[51] Raz, *The Authority of Law* (n 19) 18; Raz, *Practical Reason and Norms* (n 6) 191 (where, as noted in n 50 above, he uses the term 'protected reason').

[52] Raz, *Practical Reason and Norms* (n 6) 35–48; Joseph Raz, 'Reasoning with Rules' (2001) 54 Current Legal Problems 1, 15; Joseph Raz, 'The Problem of Authority: Revisiting the Service Conception' (2006) 90 Minnesota Law Review 1003, 1022.

[53] Raz, *Practical Reason and Norms* (n 6) 39.   [54] ibid.

are second-order reasons because their primary and direct object is not our actions, but some other reasons that, in turn, bear on our actions (first-order reasons, in Razian terminology).[55] Thus, exclusionary reasons do not operate at the normative level of ordinary reasons and do not compete with them in weight. Rather, in the case of a conflict between an exclusionary reason and an ordinary reason that falls within the exclusionary reason's scope of application, the exclusionary reason prevails regardless of the ordinary reason's weight.[56] Instead of outweighing it, the former defeats the latter by removing it from the range of reasons that should figure in the agent's assessment of how to act.

The pre-emption thesis refers to the exclusion of *some* reasons, rather than all—which prompts the question: which reasons fall within the scope of exclusion? Raz's answer, in a nutshell, is that an authoritative directive excludes first-order reasons 'on which the authority had power to pronounce',[57] that is, first-order reasons which it had power to consider in deciding the matter. On various occasions, however, Raz adverts to a narrower scope of excluded reasons, to the effect that not all the first-order reasons in the authority's deliberation power (whether for or against the required act) are said to be excluded by the directive, but rather only those *against* the required act.[58] There is no need at this point to elaborate further on the scope of exclusion. It will be discussed at greater length in Chapter 4.

Now, Raz's pre-emption thesis has garnered considerable scholarly support, but has also met with criticism.[59] Although objections to it vary in form and content, there is at least one feature that most share: an explicit or implicit claim that legal directives, even those issued by someone who meets Razian or

---

[55] ibid 36.

[56] ibid 36, 40, 189, 190; Raz, *The Authority of Law* (n 19) 22–23. Note that, according to Raz, conflicts between two second-order reasons do turn on their relative weight (Raz, *Practical Reason and Norms* (n 6) 40).

[57] Raz, 'Facing Up' (n 50) 1194. See also Raz, *Practical Reason and Norms* (n 6) 192; Joseph Raz, *Between Authority and Interpretation: On the Theory of Law and Practical Reason* (OUP 2009) 7–8 (the body text and fn 7).

[58] Raz, 'The Problem of Authority' (n 52) 1018; Raz, *Practical Reason and Norms* (n 6) 144.

[59] See, e.g., the following treatments of pre-emptive or exclusionary reasons: DS Clarke, 'Exclusionary Reasons' (1977) 86 Mind 252; Richard E Flathman, *The Practice of Political Authority: Authority and the Authoritative* (University of Chicago Press 1980) 109–25; Chaim Gans, 'Mandatory Rules and Exclusionary Reasons' (1986) 15 Philosophia 373; Michael S Moore, 'Authority, Law, and Razian Reasons' (1989) 62 Southern California Law Review 827; Heidi M Hurd, 'Challenging Authority' (1991) 100 Yale Law Journal 1611; Dworkin (n 43) 1671–72; Emran Mian, 'The Curious Case of Exclusionary Reasons' (2002) 15 Canadian Journal of Law and Jurisprudence 99; David Owens, 'Rationalism About Obligation' (2008) 16 European Journal of Philosophy 403, 411–17, 421–28; Margaret Martin, *Judging Positivism* (Hart Publishing 2014) 81–89. For a survey of relevant literature, see Kenneth M Ehrenberg, 'Critical Reception of Raz's Theory of Authority' (2011) 6 Philosophy Compass 777.

other legitimacy prerequisites,[60] cannot exclude otherwise applicable reasons, but can at most provide us with reasons that operate (and, when in conflict with other reasons, compete with them) in terms of their *weight*.[61] Raz himself referred to this or a similar position in his writings as '[t]he common view' and used it as his foil.[62] And I, too, will consider here a position of this type, which I will call the *weighing model*.[63]

According to the weighing model, our action as human agents should be responsive to the reasons that bear (positively or negatively) on its merits even when we are faced with legal requirements issued by a legitimate authority. Since those reasons do not cease to be *relevant* to the merit of our action when the authority pronounces on the matter,[64] the authority cannot exclude them from the set of reasons (for or against the action) that should determine what we do. But this claim comes with the following important caveat. The model

[60] The pre-emption thesis and what I will call the weighing model have different, but partly overlapping, scopes of application: while the weighing model refers to law generally, the pre-emption thesis refers to authority, including, relevantly for this inquiry, authority in its legal instantiations. I will sometimes ascribe to the weighing model claims such as 'law cannot pre-empt/exclude reasons'. The reference to 'law' in such statements is a reflection of the weighing model's scope, and is not meant to imply that the rival view, the pre-emption thesis, claims that 'law pre-empts/excludes reasons'.

[61] Several examples are cited below, some of which are focused on law while others refer to rules, mandatory norms, or authoritative utterances in general, and thus implicitly include legal instantiations thereof. See, e.g., Clarke (n 59); Flathman (n 59); Gans (n 59); Moore (n 59); Tim Dare, 'Raz, Exclusionary Reasons, and Legal Positivism' (1989) 8 Eidos 11, 26; Claus (n 23) 61, 65, 86, 90. See also Gerald J Postema, 'Positivism, I Presume? ... Comments on Schauer's "Rules and the Rule of Law" ' (1991) 14 Harvard Journal of Law & Public Policy 797 (where Postema sides with a similar idea); Philip Soper, *The Ethics of Deference: Learning From Law's Morals* (CUP 2002) 38–48, 176–80 (featuring certain elements of a weighing approach); and Donald H Regan, 'Authority and Value: Reflections on Raz's Morality of Freedom' (1989) 62 Southern California Law Review 995, 1003–33, 1086–95; Donald H Regan, 'Reasons, Authority, and the Meaning of "Obey": Further Thoughts on Raz and Obedience to Law' (1990) 30 Canadian Journal of Law and Jurisprudence 3. Regan stresses that authoritative directives do not themselves constitute reasons for action, but can only be indicative of existing reasons for action or (as coordination facilitators) change or give reasons for action insofar as they affect normatively relevant factual conditions, e.g. the likely behaviour of other actors (Regan, 'Authority and Value' (n 61) 1019–33). But by this understanding, too, conflicts between the relevant reasons should turn on their relative weight.

[62] Raz, *Practical Reason and Norms* (n 6) 191–92. See also Raz, *The Morality of Freedom* (n 9) 40–41, 67–69; Raz, *Between Authority and Interpretation* (n 57) 6–7.

[63] I should clarify that the way I characterize the weighing model is not intended as a detailed representation of the view of any one specific theorist of those cited in n 61. My characterization is kept instead at a relatively high level of generality to provide scope for accommodating a variety of views held by all or most of those theorists.

[64] And Raz, it should be added, may acknowledge that, in some sense, those reasons retain relevance. He notes: 'Exclusionary reasons are reasons for not acting for certain valid reasons. They do not nullify or cancel those reasons ...' (Raz, *Practical Reason and Norms* (n 6) 184); and elsewhere says: '[T]he reasons which are to disregard are not canceled' (Raz, 'Facing Up' (n 50) 1158). The moot point, then, is not their validity, but whether they should drop out of the balance of reasons that influences the agent's action.

readily accepts that when the conduct we consider has been prescribed or pro-
scribed by the law, the balance of relevant reasons may include more than just
the reasons for and against that conduct per se as were applicable prior to the
introduction of a directive (reasons which I will often refer to as *background* or
underlying reasons). The balance may then also incorporate, according to this
model, reasons that enter the normative picture in virtue of certain beneficial
attributes attached to the operation of the relevant legal institutions—but such
reasons alter the balance by means of their weight, not by way of exclusion.
What precisely those reasons are and when exactly they apply are questions
that different proponents of the weighing model may answer somewhat differently. And there is no need here to fix the model to this or that specific answer,
or exhaustively list all the possibilities. But something more concrete should
nonetheless be said in this regard if only for illustrative purposes.

Reasons that may be brought into play through the act of issuing a directive can be conveniently divided, for our purpose, into epistemic and non-
epistemic reasons.[65] The former apply if and insofar as the directive-issuers
enjoy certain epistemic advantages, such as better access than the subject
has to relevant information or expertise regarding the regulated matter, or
better acquaintance with relevant policy considerations. To the extent that
such conditions obtain, according to the weighing model, the subject may
have reasons to regard the case for doing what the directive-issuer requires as
weightier than it would have seemed to her in the absence of a directive.[66] No
less important are the potential non-epistemic inputs of legislative or regulatory action into the applicable array of practical reasons. Take, for example, its
potential contribution to social coordination. In situations where social coordination is desirable and the law (due to its salience or enforcement measures, or both) is comparatively well placed to enable and facilitate it, we have
pro tanto a coordination-based reason to comply with legal requirements.[67]
In such situations, the introduction of a legal requirement brings into the
normative picture a reason for action that was previously not applicable, at
least not in a concrete form that can translate into a specific act.[68] Arguments

---

[65] As will become apparent in the following chapters, there is some overlap between, on the one
hand, the factors mentioned in the body text as possible grounds for the above reasons, and, on the
other hand, the factors that Raz treats as grounds for exclusionary reasons.

[66] See Regan, 'Authority and Value' (n 61) 1004–18, 1086–95; Hurd (n 59) 1667–77. I say
'may' because whether such reasons actually apply depends on some other conditions, e.g. that the
directive-issuer makes actual use of her favourable epistemic resources.

[67] See Regan, 'Authority and Value' (n 61) 1025–31.

[68] I have already mentioned (in n 61) Regan's point about giving reasons merely by changing
relevant factual conditions (e.g. people's behaviour) against the backdrop of a coordinative need.
A largely consistent, but more general, notion has been developed more recently by Enoch under
the label 'triggering reason-giving' (Enoch (n 29) esp 4–5, 26–33). I am unsure, however, whether

along similar lines can be formulated by recourse to other goods and values which are, at least under certain conditions, secured or served by the operation of legal institutions, such as social order in a sense wider than that which is usually intended by the term 'coordination',[69] or considerations of 'fair play' that apply in mutually beneficial cooperative schemes.[70]

These examples will suffice for our purpose. The main point to derive from them is this: according to the weighing model, reasons of the sort mentioned above can and should be factored into our decision-making by (epistemically or otherwise) adding weight to the law-following side of the balance. And when such reasons apply, unless there are significant enough countervailing reasons, their weight will tip the balance in favour of acting as the law requires. This, according to proponents of the weighing model, makes it clear that their model enables law to make a normative difference in the domain of practical reasons, albeit not by way of excluding otherwise applicable reasons. I will say more about both the pre-emption thesis and the weighing model in the following chapters. At this point, however, we are ready to embark on critical discussion. Part I, to which I now turn, will focus on the pre-emption thesis.

Enoch can be considered a weighing model proponent. While he holds that the law, in fairly decent systems, often gives reasons in the triggering sense (ibid 26–29), he is not conclusive about whether and to what extent the law or the state can 'robustly give quasi-protected reasons', a type of reason-giving which he ascribes to legitimate authority, and which is closer (though not identical) to Razian pre-emption (ibid 29–30; David Enoch, 'Authority and Reason-Giving' (2014) 89 Philosophy and Phenomenological Research 296, 330–31). Leaving this to one side, however, I should add a further point about triggering reason-giving. Although the weighing model is not committed to this notion, it is compatible with it, as reflected, e.g., in the terminology I will be using in connection with this model: terms such as 'the law gives/gives rise to/provides/brings into play reasons' are, I think, capacious enough to accommodate the triggering sense, but are not necessarily tied to it.

[69] As the qualifier 'usually' suggests, 'coordination' is sometimes construed as a more comprehensive notion, as is the case, e.g., in John Finnis's work (Finnis (n 3) esp 470; John M Finnis, 'Law as Co-ordination' (1989) 2 Ratio Juris 97).

[70] See on 'fair play', though not specifically in the context of reasons discourse, HLA Hart, 'Are There Any Natural Rights?' (1955) 64 Philosophical Review 175, 185–86; John Rawls, 'Legal Obligation and the Duty of Fair Play' in Sidney Hook (ed), *Law and Philosophy* (New York University Press 1964) 3–18; George Klosko, *The Principle of Fairness and Political Obligation* (Rowman & Littlefield 1992); Richard Dagger, *Civic Virtues: Rights, Citizenship, and Republican Liberalism* (OUP 1997) 68–78; Noam Gur, 'Actions, Attitudes, and the Obligation to Obey the Law' (2013) 25 Journal of Political Philosophy 326, 333–37; Justin Tosi, 'A Fair Play Account of Legitimate Political Authority' (2017) 23 Legal Theory 55.

PART I

A CASE AGAINST THE PRE-EMPTION THESIS

2

The Challenge and Possible Replies

This part of the book places the pre-emption thesis under a critical examination which focuses on the thesis's ability to accommodate situations
of justified disobedience. The logic and structure of this critical exercise can be conveniently introduced through the following hypothetical
exchange.

SMITH: Reasons of type X (hereafter: *Reasons X*) exclude reasons of type Y (hereafter: *Reasons Y*), instead of merely operating as weighing reasons factored into
the balance alongside Reasons Y. Thus, whenever there occurs a conflict between
Reasons X and Reasons Y, the former will defeat the latter regardless of their relative
weight.

JONES: Appealing as it may be, I believe your claim is ultimately false. Reasons X do not
exclude Reasons Y; conflicts between them are resolved by their relative weight. In many
instances, Reasons X and Reasons Y are not in conflict at all. And where they do conflict,
it will often be the case that Reasons Y are inferior in weight, thus yielding to Reasons
X. So, the appearance of many cases, as far as their bottom-line practical resolution is
concerned, is similar to that which an exclusionary model would produce, but what
is really taking place in those cases is that Reasons X are aligned with Reasons Y or
outweigh them.

SMITH: Can you substantiate this claim?

JONES: One way of substantiating it is to show that in some cases of a conflict between
Reasons X and Reasons Y, the latter defeat the former. In fact, even one such case
would suffice. This practical resolution could not be accounted for by your exclusionary model, and would be readily explicable by a weighing model. If you would
agree with me (as I think you would) on what the right practical resolution—the right
thing to do—is in those cases, your remaining lines of defence will be to show that
I have misidentified the reasons involved as Reasons X or Reasons Y. In other words,
your available routes of defence will be to show that, despite our agreement on the
practical resolution, (i) the defeated reasons in those cases are in fact not Reasons X
(thus not the type of reasons alleged to be exclusionary), or (ii) the overriding reasons
in those cases are in fact not Reasons Y (thus not the type of reasons alleged to be excluded). If I manage to show that in some such instances neither (i) nor (ii) can be

Legal Directives and Practical Reasons. Noam Gur. © Noam Gur 2018. Published 2018 by Oxford
University Press.

established, I will have made the case against your account and lent support to the alternative account.

A similar form of argument will be advanced here against the claim that legal authoritative directives are exclusionary reasons. I will begin by drawing attention to two categories of cases in which subjects should disobey a directive of state officials or institutions for moral reasons (Section 2.1). I will subsequently examine two ways in which proponents of the pre-emption thesis may try to account for those cases: namely, (i) by saying that the directives in question fail to qualify as authoritative, and thus the pre-emption thesis does not purport to apply to them (hereafter: 'the no-authority reply', to be discussed in Chapter 3); or (ii) by saying that the exclusionary force of authoritative directives has a limited scope, and that the reasons calling for disobedience in the relevant cases are not within that scope—that they are not, in other words, part of the allegedly excluded reasons (hereafter: 'the scope-of-exclusion reply', to be discussed in Chapter 4). It will be argued that neither of these replies can be established, at least not without resorting to arguments which themselves run counter to the pre-emption thesis. The cases in question will thus turn out to be cases where subjects should act for reasons which, were the pre-emption thesis correct, would be excluded reasons, or reasons indistinguishable from supposedly excluded ones. As such, they will lead me to reject the pre-emption thesis.

2.1. The Challenge Set Out: Situations 1 and 2

I will label the first category of cases for consideration *Situation 1*. In Situation 1, a subject is faced with a directive (issued by a state official or institution)[1] that is *clearly immoral in the extreme*. Assume that the immorality involved is so grave that it decisively requires disobeying the directive, notwithstanding any other consideration for obedience (if any such consideration applies). Thus, for example, a directive to take the life of, or cause serious physical injury to, an innocent person; a directive to launch a manifestly unjustified military campaign with serious destructive effects; or a directive to commit a gravely harmful act of collective retaliation against a group (e.g. a local or ethnic community) due to the wrongdoing of one of its members—all these

---

[1] At this stage, I leave open the question of whether that official or institution exercises *authoritative* power, generally or according to Raz's conditions of authoritativeness. I elaborate on this issue in ch 3.

(when clearly identifiable as such) would fall within the category I have called Situation 1.[2] Labouring our imagination or stretching our memory in the search for other or more specific examples is not necessary, for both human history and contemporary world affairs regrettably furnish many of them. Now, in Situation 1, subjects ought to disobey the directive, and it is right and appropriate for their disobedience, as an act of responsible human agents, to be based on moral grounds.[3] In doing so, they would be acting for what Raz calls first-order reasons which pertain to the conduct they are told to engage in. There are, as was indicated, further pertinent questions to be discussed regarding Situation 1, such as whether we can rule out the directive's authoritative status in a manner coherent with the pre-emption thesis. But the point just made—that when encountering directives such as the above we ought to disobey them because of their gross immorality—is not a point of controversy among legal, political, or moral philosophers,[4] and, I take it, not something on which the reader needs to be persuaded.[5]

   The second category of cases for consideration will be entitled *Situation 2*. Situation 2 involves a legal rule not itself morally objectionable.[6] However, certain circumstances crop up in the situation, which clearly present extremely weighty moral reasons against following the rule. Again, those

---

   [2] Even if someone holds that some such acts might be justified under circumstances where they would bring about an increase of total net utility, he or she is likely to add the important caveat that if this justification ever applies in practice it applies only in very rare and unusual circumstances.

   [3] In such cases, even when some superior positive law that defeats the directive is in force, it seems appropriate and desirable that disobedience would be motivated, at least in part, by moral reasons. At any rate, as will become apparent, in order to place the question in the sharpest possible focus I will examine some situations in which no positive law that can defeat the directive is in force. In such cases, moral considerations are the only available resort.

   [4] There are, as earlier mentioned, thinkers who maintain that a gravely iniquitous directive cannot be a law in the proper (or focal) sense of the word (e.g. St Thomas Aquinas, *Summa Theologica* (Fathers of the English Dominican Province tr, 2nd edn, Burns, Oates & Washbourne 1927) pt I-II, qq 92.1, 95.2, 96.4; see further John M Finnis, *Natural Law and Natural Rights* (2nd edn, Clarendon Press 2011) 363–66) or is, as some have called it, a 'lawless law' (Gustav Radbruch, 'Statutory Lawlessness and Supra-Statutory Law (1946)' (2006) 26 Oxford Journal of Legal Studies 1; Gustav Radbruch, 'Five Minutes of Legal Philosophy (1945)' (2006) 26 Oxford Journal of Legal Studies 13; see further Robert Alexy, *The Argument from Injustice: A Reply to Legal Positivism* (Stanley L Paulson and Bonnie Litschewski Paulson trs, Clarendon Press 2002) 28–81). See contra, e.g., Julie Dickson, 'Is Bad Law Still Law? Is Bad Law Really Law?' in Maksymilian Del Mar and Zenon Bankowski (eds), *Law as Institutional Normative Order* (Ashgate 2009) 161–83. There seems to be a basic discord, however, between the above natural law conceptions of legality and the idea that the law can, *stricto sensu*, pre-empt its background reasons.

   [5] And Raz himself is not likely to disagree—see, e.g., the extract below (text to n 20) featuring a soldier's remark about refusing an order 'to commit an atrocity'.

   [6] And it may well be that, in the ordinary run of cases, subjects conform better to relevant background reasons by following that rule (see p 33).

moral reasons prevail over any other present consideration and compel non-compliance. Take, for example, the case of a driver ('John') who en route notices a critically injured person on the roadside. Suppose that the injury and other relevant circumstances are such that the person is not likely to survive unless John rushes him to hospital in excess of the speed limit. Also suppose that in the relevant jurisdiction there are no potentially overriding positive legal provisions (legislative or case-law) which apply to the case.[7] Situation 2, then, is another type of case where subjects should disobey a rule on moral grounds. And, in so doing, they would be acting on what Raz calls first-order reasons which pertain to their conduct in the situation at hand.

Situation 2 instantiates a familiar normative phenomenon[8] that has been attributed to factors such as the generality and prospective application of rules, including, more pertinently here, legal rules.[9] The degree of generality with which legal rules are typically (and, to some extent, inevitably) cast means that, desirable and essential as they may be, they remain a somewhat blunt instrument in terms of their ability to serve background reasons applicable in particular situations. Intimately connected is the fact that, while legal rules are meant to provide for future events and actions, their formulators cannot (and are not expected to) foresee all possible factual contingencies that might crop up in their future application. Such factors make it clear that particular instances wherein a (good) rule 'misfires', in that it points to a morally objectionable outcome, are inevitable.

It is worth pausing to emphasize that the categories I am calling Situations 1 and 2 are not meant to encompass every case wherein the prescribed act is less than optimal or even morally flawed. Compliance in the face of such deficiencies may (though need not always) be compatible with both the pre-emption thesis and the weighing model. From the weighing model's perspective, the

---

[7] Such as Good Samaritan laws or general defences of necessity or emergency. See further on this on pp 53–54.

[8] See, e.g., Kent Greenawalt, *Conflicts of Law and Morality* (paperback edn, OUP 1989) 191–92; Frederick Schauer, *Playing by the Rules: A Philosophical Examination of Rule-Based Decision-Making in Law and in Life* (Clarendon Press 1991) 25–37, 47–52, 88–93, 118, 128–34; Larry Alexander, 'The Gap' (1991) 14 Harvard Journal of Law & Public Policy 695; William A Edmundson, *Three Anarchical Fallacies: An Essay on Political Authority* (CUP 1998) 9–10.

[9] The generality point may bring to mind Aristotle's words that 'all law is universal but about some things it is not possible to make a universal statement which will be correct' (Aristotle, *Nicomachean Ethics*, 1137b, in *The Complete Works of Aristotle* (Jonathan Barnes ed, Princeton University Press 1984)). See also, on the characteristic generality of law, HLA Hart, *The Concept of Law* (3rd edn with an introduction by Leslie Green, OUP 2012) 21; Lon L Fuller, *The Morality of Law* (2nd edn, Yale University Press 1969) 33–34, 46–49. On generality as an attribute of rules, see Schauer (n 8) 17–37.

explanation may refer to reasons for compliance (independent or relatively independent of the particular content of the directive) such as the benefits of social order or reliance interests of relevant parties, which may tip the balance by outweighing a minor or moderate deficiency attached to the pre-scribed act. Such cases, therefore, are not the most revealing for the present theoretical purpose. Situations 1 and 2, on the other hand, are different: they are situations where it is evident that the moral defectiveness attached to the prescribed act is of very serious gravity, and it becomes justified to dis-obey.[10] Prior to a discussion of possible responses to my emerging critique, I would like to clear out of the way what might mistakenly *appear* to be such responses.

2.2. Clear Choices and Action for Reasons

At one point Raz makes the following statement: 'Establishing that something is clearly wrong does not require going through the underlying reasons'.[11] Let this statement be called Proposition CW. Now, since the immorality of fol-lowing a directive in Situations 1 and 2 is clear, Proposition CW may appear, at first blush, material to the present discussion. Before considering its exact relevance, it should be clarified that Proposition CW is not the only prop-osition found in Raz's relevant text with regard to clearly wrong directives. Another related proposition he mentions (without subscribing to it) contends that 'legitimate authority is limited by the condition that its directives are not binding if clearly wrong'.[12] I will attend to this last proposition in the next chapter, when discussing Raz's conditions of legitimate authority. For the mo-ment, my focus is on Proposition CW.

If Proposition CW is correct, it follows that an agent can recognize that she ought to disobey in Situations 1 and 2 without 'going through the underlying reasons'. Does this mean that her resulting act of disobedience (assuming she consequently disobeys) is, in fact, compatible with the exclusion of those underlying reasons? I will answer this question in the negative. The main ground for my answer is a distinction between deliberating on reasons (or, reflecting on, contemplating, actively thinking about them, etc.) on the one hand, and acting for reasons on the other. The pre-emption thesis makes a

---

[10] This is not to suggest that, generally or from a Razian perspective, disobedience may be war-ranted *only* in these cases. There may be circumstances where a directive-issuer fails to meet the conditions for obtaining authority, and to this extent her directives are not binding, even if some or all of them are not unjust (see Joseph Raz, *The Morality of Freedom* (Clarendon Press 1986) 78).

[11] ibid 62.   [12] ibid.

claim about the latter, not the former,[13] and so does my critique of the pre-emption thesis. I have not suggested that before the actor disobeys in cases such as Situations 1 and 2 she must deliberate on underlying reasons. My only claim was that the actor should act for those reasons.[14] Now, Proposition CW uses the words 'going through the underlying reasons'. Is 'going through reasons' intended to mean acting for those reasons or deliberating on them? It must be intended to mean the latter, because Proposition CW refers to *establishing* that something is clearly wrong. It does not refer to an ensuing action, and to what is or is not included in the reasons for its performance. Proposition CW, therefore, seems to be orthogonal to my claim, rather than running counter to it.[15] Could we not read into Raz's comment, however, a further implied claim about the grounds for an ensuing action? In other words, is Raz not implying here that, when an agent refuses to do that which she recognizes as clearly wrong without deliberation on the underlying reasons, the agent is not acting for those underlying reasons? Let us call this latter claim Proposition CW1. I will argue that Proposition CW1 is, first, a false proposition, and, second, not Raz's position.

Proposition CW1 mistakenly binds together the two notions distin-guished in the previous paragraph: namely, deliberating on reasons and acting for reasons. In fact, the two are not only distinct, but can also come apart in that one can act for reasons without deliberating on them, at least not in a sense that implies active or conscious thought about those reasons.[16] Consider, by way of illustration, the case of a fraternity freshman who is told by the senior fraternity members to perform, as part of a hazing ritual or a loyalty test, an egregiously hazardous act—say, jumping off a high bridge into a shallow river. The act strikes him as clearly foolish and he

---

[13] ibid 39 (where Raz introduces the idea of an exclusionary reason as follows: 'An exclusionary reason is a second-order reason to refrain from acting for some reason'); Joseph Raz, 'Facing Up: A Reply' (1989) 62 Southern California Law Review 1153, 1156–57 (where he explicates this point in response to Michael Moore's critique).

[14] See further in this context Chaim Gans, 'Mandatory Rules and Exclusionary Reasons' (1986) 15 Philosophia 373, 387–90; Donald H Regan, 'Authority and Value: Reflections on Raz's Morality of Freedom' (1989) 62 Southern California Law Review 995, 1113, fn 43 (where the authors com-ment on the distinction between considering reasons and acting for reasons).

[15] Another reason for thinking that Proposition CW is orthogonal to the issue at hand is this: Proposition CW says that going through the underlying reasons is *not required* when one is confronted with a clear error. The normative implication of exclusionary reasons, on the other hand, is that one *should not* act for the first-order reasons excluded by an exclusionary reason. There is a difference, of course, between saying that something is not required and saying that something should not be done.

[16] I set aside here the inverse possibility—deliberating on reasons without acting for them—as it is not material to my argument.

refuses to perform it. Does the clear nature of the situation entail that the freshman's refusal was not motivated by the reason that makes this act so clearly foolish, namely, the fact that jumping would put his life and bodily integrity at peril? Surely not. This reason is likely to have been precisely the basis for his refusal. What does sound like a plausible supposition, instead, is that the freshman did not have to engage in deliberation on that reason to see that he should refuse to jump. But this, once more, does not at all run counter to my argument.

As noted above, I believe Raz does *not* have in mind anything like Proposition CW1. This is not only because imputing this false proposition to him would be an uncharitable interpretation, but also because it stands in opposition to claims and comments he has made both in the context of his theory of authority and in the more general context of his theory of action. These claims and comments (examples of which are given in the following lines) show his acceptance that deliberation on reasons and action for reasons can come apart in the sense that agents can act for reasons—namely, act because they take the action to have some good-making characteristics— without thinking about them.[17] In such instances, as Raz notes in a relatively recent essay, agents 'have the belief that the action has some value' and 'the belief is part of what leads them to take the action', but the belief 'is not present in their mind' (i.e. when opting for the action and performing it).[18] And, similarly, in an earlier text he rejects an assumption of identity between 'acting for a reason' and 'action following conscious rational deliberation', noting that 'people can internalize reasons and act on them automatically and instinctively'.[19] I have rejected Proposition CW1, the only rendering of Proposition CW that actually bears on the issue of acting for reasons, as distinct from deliberating on them. I therefore conclude that Proposition CW does not pose a difficulty for, or offer a response to, the line of argument I am advancing.

---

[17] Joseph Raz, *From Normativity to Responsibility* (OUP 2011) 62. Less pertinently here, he also accepts that agents can engage in thought or reflection on reasons without acting for those reasons (Raz, *The Morality of Freedom* (n 10) 39–42; Joseph Raz, *The Authority of Law: Essays on Law and Morality* (2nd edn, OUP 2009) 26, fn 25; see also Raz, 'Facing Up' (n 13) 1156–57, 1159 and Joseph Raz, *Practical Reason and Norms* (2nd edn, Princeton University Press 1990) 25).

[18] Raz, *From Normativity to Responsibility* (n 17) 62. See also ibid 31–32, where Raz refers to a mode of guidance by reasons which he analogizes with a 'negative feedback mechanism', whereby 'we, automatically and normally without being conscious of the fact, monitor the performance of the intentional action such that if it deviates from the course we implicitly take to lead to its successful completion we correct the performance'.

[19] Raz, 'Facing Up' (n 13) 1180.

2.3. Usual and Unusual Cases

It is readily noticeable that the cases labelled here Situations 1 and 2 are not run-of-the-mill cases. This, in turn, may evoke certain comments of Raz in which he qualifies the claim about exclusionary reasons in respect of some unusual cases. For instance, when discussing a hypothetical example of a soldier who treats his superiors' commands as exclusionary reasons, Raz notes: '[The soldier] admits that if he were ordered to commit an atrocity he should refuse. But his is an ordinary case, he thinks, and the order should prevail'[20] (that is, it should prevail regardless of the balance of first-order reasons). One might get the impression, then, that Raz would respond to Situations 1 and 2 with something like the following assertion: even if subjects should act in those cases on first-order background reasons, those are unusual cases which therefore do not cast doubt on the pre-emption thesis's soundness as an explanation of the ordinary run of cases.

This, however, would be an erroneous impression. Raz's remark above should not be taken to refer to a bare distinction between usual or unusual cases which relies on no further differentiating criteria. Rather, his remark seems to implicitly suggest that there are some relevant criteria that may explain exceptional cases, such as Situations 1 and 2, as belonging to one of two categories: (i) cases where the relevant directive fails to qualify as authoritative and is, thus, not at all a pre-emptive reason; or (ii) cases where the reasons which justify disobedience are not within the scope of reasons supposed to be excluded in the first place. These two categories correspond with the two lines of defence outlined at the outset of this chapter: the no-authority and the scope-of-exclusion replies.

This interpretation of Raz's remark is warranted on two main counts: first, although at some points, such as the above quoted comment, Raz does not explicitly mention the issues of lack of authority or scope of exclusion, at several other points where he distinguishes between ordinary and exceptional cases, he does so expressly on the grounds of authoritativeness conditions or the scope of exclusion.[21] It is likely, then, that the same reasoning is tacitly presupposed by comments such as the above. Second, a different reading of Raz would render his defence plainly inadequate, so much so that it can be ruled out as an implausible reading. It would clearly be insufficient to say, regarding cases wherein subjects should act for background reasons, that these

---

[20] Raz, *Practical Reason and Norms* (n 17) 38. See also ibid 79, 80.
[21] Raz, *The Morality of Freedom* (n 10) 46, 62, 78; Raz, *Practical Reason and Norms* (n 17) 77, 79, 80.

cases are exceptional without further explaining why and in what respects they are exceptional. Surely, one cannot defend a theory merely by asserting that instances incompatible with it are exceptional ones, unless one is able to identify a relevant difference that sets these instances apart from others.

Now, as far as the pre-emption thesis is concerned, the relevant potential basis for an exception lies either in the prerequisites for pre-emptive reasons (namely, the conditions for obtaining legitimate authority) or in some defensible demarcation of their reach (namely, their scope of exclusion). This constraint follows directly from the type of claim made by the pre-emption thesis: the very point of a proposition that a certain kind of reasons excludes another kind of reasons is that the former defeats the latter regardless of their relative weight.[22] In this sense, the idea of exclusion has a conclusive character within its scope of application: whenever the conditions for its application obtain—that is, whenever there is a conflict between an exclusionary reason and the reasons it excludes—the former necessarily wins against the latter.[23] It is this attribute of the thesis under discussion that dictates the way to meet the challenge posed here: if one suspects that in a certain case supposedly exclusionary reasons are defeated by supposedly excluded reasons, and if there is no disagreement over what an agent ought to do in that case, resulting doubts about the pre-emption thesis can only be dispelled by explaining why, in fact, the former reasons are not to be taken as exclusionary reasons or the latter reasons are not to be taken as excluded ones. Any number of instances, however rare or unusual, in which this cannot be established, should hold us back from accepting the pre-emption thesis.[24]

[22] Raz, *Practical Reason and Norms* (n 17) 40, 189, 190; Raz, *The Authority of Law* (n 17) 22–23.

[23] There is a different sense in which it is *not* claimed by Raz that exclusionary reasons must be absolute or conclusive (Raz, *Practical Reason and Norms* (n 17) 27–28), as he accepts that they may be subject to 'cancelling conditions', and that they may be overridden by reasons outside their scope of exclusion or by other second-order reasons. My critique of the pre-emption thesis takes these provisos into account, as it draws attention to situations where none of them apply or can adequately account for the correct practical resolution.

[24] This also means that other arguments pointing at some weaknesses of the weighing model or some appealing features of the pre-emption thesis (e.g. Raz's phenomenological and functional arguments, which will be considered at length in Part II) do not constitute defences against my argument advanced in this part unless they are able to account for the justified disobedience situations discussed here.

3

Lack of Authority

This chapter revolves around the first line of defence mentioned above: the no-authority reply. It will be argued that this reply fails as a defence of the pre-emption thesis because authoritativeness (namely, the possibility that a directive qualifies as authoritative) cannot be ruled out in Situations 1 and 2, at least not on the basis of conditions of authority coherent with the pre-emption thesis itself.

On what basis can the no-authority reply contend that directives in Situations 1 and 2 are not authoritative? To begin with, it should be clear that the no-authority reply cannot establish that a certain directive is not authoritative on the grounds that the directive's content is objectionable, that is, contravening or failing to reflect the relevant background reasons. For it would be self-contradictory and hollow to suggest that a directive, if authoritative, excludes its background reasons, and at the same time to concede that what determines whether a directive is authoritative, and thus excludes its background reasons, is its conformity with these background reasons.[1] To be successful, the no-authority reply must rely on some other conditions of authoritativeness. Such conditions will be my focus throughout this chapter.

3.1. The Service Conception of Authority

Raz's 'service conception of authority' specifies conditions of authority that appear to be distinct and independent from a content-based evaluation of individual directives on their merits, and may thus be suitable to uphold the no-authority reply. On this conception, an ostensible authority (A) must meet the

---

[1] This constraint cannot be overcome by saying that the basis for a no-authority determination is not simply that the directive is wrong, but rather that it is extremely wrong. The difference between wrongness and extreme wrongness, at least in some cases, represents a difference in degree. And whether the wrongness involved is of excessive degree is determined by a balance that includes the background reasons, which are supposed to have been excluded. A relevant illustration can be found on p 46.

Legal Directives and Practical Reasons. Noam Gur. © Noam Gur 2018. Published 2018 by Oxford University Press.

two following conditions for it to have real (legitimate) authority. The first of these conditions, and the one that takes centre stage in Raz's discussion, concerns A's ability to guide an alleged subject (S) to better conformity with applicable reasons (given attributes such as A's knowledge and expertise compared with S's, or A's capacity to facilitate coordination). The condition, encapsulated in a thesis known as *the normal justification thesis*, is that S would be more likely to conform to reasons that apply to her (i.e. reasons other than the directives of A) by following A's directives than by trying to follow those reasons directly.[2] The second condition, which Raz calls *the independence condition*, is that the regulated matter is one regarding which it is more important to act in conformity with reason than to decide for oneself what to do.[3] This condition would not be satisfied in certain areas of life characterized by a special intrinsic desirability that people follow their own light, as is the case, for example, regarding personal decisions such as choosing one's friends and partner.[4] I will assume *arguendo* that authority depends on these two conditions, and will examine whether Situations 1 and 2 must involve a failure to meet at least one of them.[5]

Consider first the independence condition. This condition does not preclude the possible occurrence of Situations 1 and 2. Let us assume with Raz that there exist distinct areas where it is more important to decide for oneself than to conform to reason, and distinct areas where it is more important to conform to reason than to decide for oneself. Situations 1 and 2 cannot be circumscribed within the former category. For instance, an order to take the life of an innocent person (a Situation 1) can be issued in some domains—such as in a military context—which are not characterized by the private nature of decisions such as the choice of one's friends (Raz's example of a context wherein the independence condition is not met). Nor can this private quality be ascribed, for example, to an incident of driving in excess of the speed limit in order to save an injured person's life, which instantiates a Situation 2.[6] In

---

[2] Joseph Raz, *The Morality of Freedom* (Clarendon Press 1986) 53.

[3] Joseph Raz, 'The Problem of Authority: Revisiting the Service Conception' (2006) 90 Minnesota Law Review 1003, 1014.

[4] Raz, *The Morality of Freedom* (n 2) 57.

[5] Raz's 'dependence thesis' (to be distinguished from his 'independence condition' mentioned above) contends that 'all authoritative directives should be based on reasons which already independently apply to the subjects of the directives and are relevant to their action in the circumstances covered by the directive' (ibid 47). As will be explicated on pp 44–45 herein, Raz does not treat compliance with the dependence thesis regarding a given directive as a condition for its authoritativeness (Raz, *The Morality of Freedom* (n 2) 38, 47, 55). Rather, this thesis merely expresses a standard of 'an ideal exercise of authority' (ibid 47) (though, to comply with the normal justification thesis, one would probably need to accomplish at least a fairly good degree of compliance with the dependence thesis in most cases—see ibid 55).

[6] If road traffic is an area of activity in which it is more important to decide for oneself than to act in conformity with reason, what area of activity isn't?

light of this, the analysis in this section will henceforth focus on the first condition of authority mentioned above: the normal justification thesis.

Do Situations 1 and 2 necessarily correlate with failures to meet the normal justification thesis? Or, could they come to pass when the relevant directive emanates from an institution that, or an individual who, meets the normal justification thesis? Let us begin with the easier situation in this regard: Situation 2. In Situation 2, while the rule comes into conflict with weighty reasons presented by the special circumstances at hand, the rule itself is not reprehensible. Indeed, the rule may be such that, by following it in run-of-the-mill cases, subjects better conform to reasons that apply to them. And, so too the rule-issuer's skills may be such that, by usually following her rules, subjects are likely to better conform to reasons that apply to them.[7] Consider once more the example of John, who is rushing a severely injured person to hospital in excess of the speed limit.[8] The rule which he breaks is an innocuous rule, and quite possibly a good rule that yields desirable outcomes overall by contributing to road safety. Thus, it may well be that John does better in run-of-the-mill cases by observing this rule. And, at any rate, it is possible that the rule-issuer's decision-making competence and knowledge of road traffic matters are better than John's, so that the latter is more likely to conform to reason by usually following the former's requirements in the context of road traffic. So the speed limit rule, though rightly contravened in the situation at hand, may well be authoritative according to the service conception of authority.[9]

This observation suffices for present purposes. But it may be added, parenthetically, that even when the normal justification thesis is *not* met in Situation 2, we do not expect this to be the only or the dominant reason for which a conscientious subject defies the rule in such cases. We do not expect, for example, that John's decision to exceed the speed limit in order to bring a severely injured person to hospital would turn exclusively or primarily on calculations of whether, in general, the rule-issuer possesses such skills that her road traffic rules are likely to lead John to better conformity with reason, or even whether the speed limit rule itself is generally desirable. In fact, it would seem odd if

---

[7] I will discuss below three possible understandings of the normal justification condition, and will show that only one of them is endorsed by Raz. But the statement in the body text above holds good under any of these three understandings.

[8] p 24.

[9] Did the legislature consider this situation when crafting the rule? Possibly it did but nonetheless chose not to enact an exception (e.g. in light of slippery-slope concerns). However, even if it did not consider this situation, or if its decision not to enact an exception was a bad decision, the rule does not thereby lose its authoritative status (generally or in the situation at hand) according to Raz's account. Such failures may occur even where the normal justification thesis is satisfied, and, for Raz, the standard of performance requisite for gaining authority consists in the normal justification thesis. I further explicate this point on pp 44–45.

his decision were determined by these factors. Instead, we expect John to defy the speed limit rule primarily because of the compelling importance of saving the injured person's life. This suggests that the distinctive moral ground for disobedience in Situation 2 is not rooted in a failure on the authority's part to comply with the normal justification thesis (even where such a failure coincides with Situation 2). Instead, it is better captured by saying that the special circumstances of the case give rise to a justification for departing from the rule regardless of its general status. A similar point is made by Raz in the following passage:

> The question of the validity of a norm should be clearly distinguished from other questions of justification. A norm may be valid and yet a norm subject may not be justified in performing the norm act in certain circumstances, for there may be present in these circumstances some other conflicting reasons not excluded by the norm which should prevail.[10]

Whether the notion of unexcluded reasons can reconcile Situation 2 with the pre-emption thesis is a question that will be addressed in the next chapter. At this point, our primary observation is that Situation 2 may involve rules that are authoritative according to the service conception of authority.

What about Situation 1? Could this type of situation come to pass when the relevant directive emanates from an institution that, or a person who, meets the normal justification thesis? It will be argued that the answer is positive. Given Raz's characterization of the normal justification thesis, it is possible that a directive-issuer who complies with it would nonetheless produce a Situation 1 directive. As will be explicated shortly, whether a given directive-issuer complies with the normal justification thesis is a matter that turns, inter alia, on the level of generality at which the normal justification thesis is intended to apply. The normal justification thesis refers to the likelihood that, by following an authority, subjects would better conform to the reasons that apply to them. Raz stresses that this should be tested on an individual basis, that is, for each citizen afresh, taking into account individual attributes such as her knowledge, understanding, skills, etc.[11] From this it is clear that the condition Raz proposes is particularistic in respect of the question 'to *whom* authority applies'. But is it equally particularistic in respect of the question 'to *what* authority applies'? In this regard, three possible

---

[10] Joseph Raz, *Practical Reason and Norms* (2nd edn, Princeton University Press 1990) 80.
[11] Raz, *The Morality of Freedom* (n 2) 73–74, 77–78, 104; Joseph Raz, *Ethics in the Public Domain: Essays in the Morality of Law and Politics* (rev paperback edn, Clarendon Press 1995) 341, 347, 350; Raz, 'The Problem of Authority' (n 3) 1029. He agrees, however, that in the case of *some* legal rules the obligation to obey is likely to apply equally to all citizens (Raz, *Ethics in the Public Domain* (n 11) 341, 350).

renderings of the thesis will be set out below, of which the third will emerge as truest to Raz's position. The three renderings are as follows:[12]

Rendering I (hereafter: *the discrete-directives approach*): The test of whether an authority is likely to improve conformity with reasons should be applied separately in respect of each directive. That is, the test refers to the likelihood that an individual would conform better to relevant reasons by following the particular directive in question.

Rendering II (hereafter: *the system-wide approach*): The test should be applied by examining the overall operation of the regulative system in question. In the context of law, the question should thus be whether an individual would, on balance, improve her conformity with reasons by following all the directives of the legal system that apply to her, such that successful conformity with reasons in the case of some directives outweighs failures to conform with reasons in the case of other directives.

Rendering III (hereafter: *the domain-specific approach*): The correct way of applying the test lies between the above two alternatives. While it should not examine each particular directive in isolation, it is flexible enough to take account of variations in the degree of competence possessed by the directive-issuer and the subject in different areas of regulation and activity (say, environmental issues, safety measures in workplaces, financial matters, or national defence). Given variations of competence between different areas, the test refers to the likelihood that an individual would conform better to reasons germane to the area in question by following directives in that area.

It may be useful to illustrate how the difference between these approaches bears on our question regarding Situation 1. I will at this point do so rudimentarily, but will later flesh my argument out. Under the discrete-directives approach, it seems impossible for Situation 1 to occur where the normal justification condition is met: by following an extremely immoral directive, subjects would not better conform to the reasons relevant to their acts in the circumstances covered by that directive. If, on the other hand, the system-wide approach is assumed, compliance with the normal justification condition can no longer rule out the possible occurrence of Situation 1. For a legal system whose *overall* operation helps subjects to better conform to reason may nonetheless produce, *on occasion*, an immoral or even an extremely immoral directive. Finally, under the domain-specific approach, an isolated occurrence of Situation 1 is again possible despite compliance with the normal justification condition by the directive-issuer. This will be the case if, notwithstanding the one flawed directive in question, her directives in the relevant regulative domain are, for the most part, such that they lead subjects to better conformity with the reasons applying to them in that domain. For instance, a directive-issuer who is sufficiently versed in matters of

---

[12] The following are not exhaustive of all possible ways to conceive of the normal justification condition. For a different, but partly overlapping set of possibilities, see Emran Mian, 'The Curious Case of Exclusionary Reasons' (2002) 15 Canadian Journal of Law and Jurisprudence 99, 105. Using Mian's set would not have made a difference to my conclusion.

national defence (as well as generally having the moral judgement required in this context) may nonetheless fail on a specific occasion and issue a wrong directive related to that very context.

Of course, an extremely wrong directive may well be the result of a general or domain-wide incompetence of its issuer. However, occasional instances of an extremely wrong directive that results from an isolated moral failure or misjudgement, a momentary lapse of concentration, situational misinformation, a failure of communication between officials, or other human or technical error, might occur even where the authority is generally, and in the relevant domain, competent. Such occurrences will not be likely or frequent, but—and this is the material point—they are possible. As was noted, I will further substantiate this point below, but not before I identify Raz's approach to the generality of the normal justification thesis. At one juncture, Raz comments directly on this issue as follows:

On the one hand generality is built into the account: the normal justification of authority is that following it will enable its subjects better to conform with reason. One cannot establish that this is the case in one case without establishing that it is the case in all like cases. Authority is based on reason and reasons are general, therefore authority is essentially general.

On the other hand the thesis allows maximum flexibility in determining the scope of authority. It all depends on the person over whom authority is supposed to be exercised: his knowledge, strength of will, his reliability in various aspects of life, and on the government in question.[13]

While noting the generality of the normal justification thesis, Raz stresses here that the thesis depends on factors like the subject's individual knowledge and reliability *in various aspects of life*.[14] This chimes with the domain-specific approach, particularly given that, in reality, individuals' skills do tend to vary from one domain to another. Further textual support for the domain-specific approach can be found in the following comments of Raz:

Of course sometimes I do have additional information showing that the authority is better than me in some areas and not in others. This may be sufficient to show that it lacks authority over me in those other areas.[15]

---

[13] Raz, *The Morality of Freedom* (n 2) 73.

[14] Another method of classifying rules mentioned by Raz is by reference to their function (Raz, *Ethics in the Public Domain* (n 11) 341, 347–50; Raz, *The Morality of Freedom* (n 2) 74). I leave out this classification method for simplicity and because it would not lead to a conclusion different from the one reached here.

[15] Raz, *The Morality of Freedom* (n 2) 68–69. See also Raz, *Ethics in the Public Domain* (n 11) 350 ('the extent of the duty to obey the law in a relatively just country varies from person to person and from one range of cases to another').

Thus, for example:

An expert pharmacologist may not be subject to the authority of the government in matters of the safety of drugs, an inhabitant of a little village by the river may not be subject to its authority in matters of navigation and conservation of the river by the banks of which he has spent all his life.[16]

From these and other comments,[17] it is readily apparent that Raz's understanding of the normal justification thesis accords with the domain-specific approach, rather than the system-wide or discrete-directives approaches.[18] But a further relevant doubt might be raised here. How particularistic, it might be asked, could the classification of domains be under Raz's approach, and, especially, could it be so particularistic that a 'domain', in the relevant sense, becomes as narrow as the scope of a single directive? We can rephrase the question in terms employed by Raz in the following comment:

[A] person or body has authority regarding any domain if that person or body meets the conditions regarding that domain and there is no proper part of the domain regarding which the person or body can be known to fail the conditions.[19]

So we can ask: could a single directive count as 'a proper part of a domain' in the sense used by Raz above? And would that not lead to something effectively similar to the discrete-directives approach? Well, recall Raz's explanation of why 'authority is essentially general': it is because the normal justification for it is its capacity to enable its subjects to better conform with reason, and because '[o]ne cannot establish that this is the case in one case without establishing that it is the case in all like cases'.[20] With this in mind, it does not seem that Raz would consider the fragmentation of domains into discrete directives to be a generally or normally warranted move in applying the normal

---

[16] Raz, *The Morality of Freedom* (n 2) 74. See also ibid 77–78.

[17] For example, his comment that authorities are 'relational both regarding who has to take an authority's word as authoritative, and regarding what matters' (Raz, 'The Problem of Authority' (n 3) 1033–34); and other comments expressive of his piecemeal conception of the scope of legitimate governmental authority, which seems markedly at odds with the system-wide approach (Raz, *The Morality of Freedom* (n 2) 70, 74, 80, 99–100, 104; Raz, *Ethics in the Public Domain* (n 11) 347, 350).

[18] Also pointing away from the system-wide approach is Raz's critical response to Finnis's holistic view of the normative force of law (known as Finnis's 'seamless web' argument)—see Raz, *Ethics in the Public Domain* (n 11) 350–54; John M Finnis, 'The Authority of Law in the Predicament of Contemporary Social Theory' (1984) 1 Notre Dame Journal of Law, Ethics & Public Policy 115, esp 117–21.

[19] Raz, 'The Problem of Authority' (n 3) 1027.

[20] Raz, *The Morality of Freedom* (n 2) 73.

justification thesis. And there are comments of his that expressly confirm this last inference, as when he notes:

An authority is justified, according to the normal justification thesis, if it is more likely than its subjects to act correctly for the right reasons. That is how the subjects' reasons figure in the justification, both when they are correctly reflected in a particular directive and when they are not. If every time a directive is mistaken, i.e. every time it fails to reflect reason correctly, it were open to challenge as mistaken, the advantage gained by accepting the authority as a more reliable and successful guide to right reason would disappear.[21]

[S]ometimes immoral or unjust laws may be authoritatively binding, at least on some people. The existence of the occasional bad law enacted by a just government does not by itself establish much. However just a government may be, it is liable to pass undesirable and morally objectionable laws from time to time.... Even so it may be that regarding each individual, he is less likely successfully to follow right reasons which apply to him anyway if left to himself than if he always obeys the directives of a just government including those which are morally reprehensible.[22]

Raz clearly rejects, then, the discrete-directives approach on the grounds that it would, in essence, forgo the benefits of entrusting a more competent and reliable decision-maker with the power to decide. If this approach were adopted, the normal justification thesis would be robbed of its most essential point, and so would the pre-emption thesis. We can conclude, therefore, that the normal justification thesis is to be understood in accordance with the domain-specific approach.

With this in mind, we may return to the point made earlier about Situation 1: if the domain-specific approach is adopted and the discrete-directives approach is rejected, the possible occurrence of Situation 1 cannot be precluded by compliance with the normal justification thesis. To reiterate, although knowledge and skills possessed by an authority, generally or in the relevant context of regulation, are conducive to its likelihood to decide rightly, they do not entail and cannot guarantee that, in every event, its directives would be right. Even where an authority is sufficiently competent, particular instances of a moral failure, misjudgement, inattention, miscommunication, and other human or technical errors, may occur. This possibility, to put it simply, reflects the difference between competence on the hand and infallibility on the other. A similar point is acknowledged in Raz's comment that '[h]owever just a government may be, it is liable to pass undesirable and morally objectionable laws from time to time'.[23] To which he adds:

---

[21] ibid 61.   [22] ibid 78–79.   [23] ibid.

This need not be due to any moral shortcomings in the government. Even assuming complete good will and unimpeachable moral convictions, inefficiency, ignorance and other ordinary facts of life will lead to objectionable laws being passed.[24]

Conceivably, some such failures may even result in directives that are clearly immoral in the extreme—which is what was entitled here Situation 1. The point can further be fleshed out through some illustrations, to which the rest of this section is devoted.

First, imagine that some members of a minority group in a country are involved in guerrilla fighting against the government. Small teams of insurgents initiate artillery attacks from their local area aimed at military sites in the country. These attacks occasionally result in some casualties: a handful of people have died this way during the few months since the insurgent attacks began, among them soldiers but, unintentionally, also some citizens living near the attacked military sites. When the military locates the sources of insurgents' fire, it launches artillery counterattacks at these locations. Before launched, each of these counterattacks and its targets has to be approved by the president, who holds, in his capacity as such, the supreme command of the armed forces. Assume that the president possesses, and is known to possess, adequate competence, generally and in the context of national defence and military matters like the one at stake, such that he would meet the normal justification condition. He is, moreover, empowered by legislation to issue orders of the above type.

One time the army locates two insurgents taking cover in a civilian apartment block (unlike their fellow insurgents who usually operate at some distance from non-militants), from which they fire with a small-sized artillery piece. It is known to the army that about 200 non-militants live in this block, many of whom would lose their lives if an artillery or aerial counterattack were launched. Other military alternatives, such as an infantry attack, are assessed to be very difficult and risky since the area surrounding the block is thick with insurgents and other obstacles. The president is urgently called upon to decide whether and how to react, and is given the foregoing information. The atmosphere in the headquarters is tense. The president feels he has had enough of these insurgent attacks. Although he considers the likely loss of innocent lives—a loss he deems to be undesirable in itself—he concludes that under the circumstances this is a price worth paying and orders an artillery counterattack.

---

[24] ibid 79. The context makes it clear that the 'inefficiency' and 'ignorance' Raz refers to here are not of a type or extent that entails non-compliance with the normal justification condition. Indeed, the gist of his comment is that the normal justification can be satisfied despite such occasional failures.

Those in the army who are supposed to carry out the order refuse to obey it. They acknowledge the risk to human life engendered by the two insurgents in question. Nevertheless, under the circumstances it is clear that the expected harm associated with these insurgents' activity (i.e. the scale of harm taken together with its probability of occurrence) is much lower than the expected harm to innocent lives associated with an artillery attack on the apartment block. These soldiers acknowledge that the president is aware of the facts described above, that he is generally competent to decide well in this context, and that by and large his decisions are conducive to their conformity with relevant reasons. But this time they clearly observe that a misjudgement has come to pass and the order is egregiously wrong. They contravene the order, although the laws of their jurisdiction include no provision (constitutional or other) capable of defeating such a presidential order.[25] When so doing, they act for pertinent moral reasons, including, particularly, the value of human life, which requires them to curb the use of military force so as to minimize harm to civilians.[26]

Now suppose a similar scenario with certain modifications. The president approves targets for a counterattack. This time the targets are insurgents' bases at a safe distance from civilian population. Michael is one of the soldiers who are supposed to carry out the order. His role is to provide an artillery crew with firing data, such as the firing angles and the amounts of propelling charge to be used. He calculates this data according to target

---

[25] See related comments on p 41–42. Presently existing international humanitarian law could apply to such a case. For present purposes, however, it can be assumed that the case takes place at a time when applicable international laws (conventions or customary law) were not in force. We should not let such laws divert us from the principled issue in question here—i.e. the normative mode of resolution of possible conflicts between laws and practical reasons—by shifting the focus onto a contest between two laws. And the significance of avoiding such diversion is not just theoretical, but also practical, for several reasons: first, international laws may always change (and may themselves go wrong); second, there may be cases of objectionable domestic directives not provided for by international laws; third, there are dissimilarities between the laws of different jurisdictions regarding the interpretation and application of international law within the jurisdiction, as well as differences between the domestic point of view on international law and international law tribunals' point of view; and fourth, which sharpens the practical significance of the previous point, international law itself has at its disposal quite limited means of enforcement. This may mean that international law itself currently lacks the degree of efficacy needed for facilitating coordination sufficiently for acquiring legitimate authority in a Razian sense (see Raz, 'The Problem of Authority' (n 3) 1036–37; Raz, *Practical Reason and Norms* (n 10) 150; Joseph Raz, 'Facing Up: A Reply' (1989) 62 Southern California Law Review 1153, 1194) (though the content of international laws may gain such status in a domestic jurisdiction insofar as they are given effect and enforced by domestic institutions).

[26] It would be surprising if an objector claimed that the order should be obeyed in these circumstances. One possible response to such an objection, however, would be to modify the case description so as to match what is in the objector's view an intolerable immorality. The essential argument would remain intact.

The Service Conception of Authority 41

locations which he receives through his superiors' orders. The orders come in the following form: 'Fire on target ... ', with the target locations communicated in multiple-digit numbers representing latitudinal and longitudinal coordinates. Michael's superiors are professional and highly competent officers who are likely to perform their role successfully, leading their subordinates, including Michael, to better conform to reasons relevant to that context, and this is known to Michael. On the present occasion, however, notwithstanding their general competence, a miscalculation or a slip of the pen results in an error in one digit of the coordinates. Consequently, the location communicated to Michael is in an area densely populated by civilians of the minority in question. As it happens, he notices that the given target is thus located, and consequently refuses to follow the order.[27] Here too, when Michael refuses to follow the order, he acts for relevant moral reasons, such as his concern for the life and physical integrity of other human beings.

In the foregoing scenarios, in view of the (in differing ways) extremely immoral content of the directive, subjects ought to disobey despite the normal justification thesis having been complied with by the authority. Now, while the possible occurrence of such scenarios remains the essential point of the argument, it may be added (similarly to an earlier point about Situation 2) that even when a directive-issuer *fails* to meet the normal justification thesis, we do not expect this in itself to be the sole reason why a conscientious subject would disobey if faced with Situation 1. It would be odd if, when faced with such an egregiously immoral directive, a conscientious subject would nonetheless confine her reasoning merely to the likelihood of her overall conformity with reasons in the relevant domain, rather than treating the specific and immediate deleterious consequences of following that directive as a self-contained consideration. This lends further (if indirect) support to the conclusion drawn above, namely, that the challenge from Situation 1 cannot be met through an appeal to the normal justification thesis.

One further clarification is called for. There is no denying that in some jurisdictions the legal system includes provisions, such as constitutional protection of certain human rights, which allow courts to strike down directives like those discussed above. The first point to note in this connection is that insofar as such judicial rulings are conceived of as changing an existing law or as making new law, rather than merely discovering and declaring the state of the existing law, it follows that if subjects disobey prior to a judicial ruling (and in the cases discussed here they are justified in disobeying even where no judicial

---

[27] Although he does not know whether this is the consequence of a technical error or a different failure.

decision approves), they are acting in defiance of a directive that, at the time of their action, is valid. Second, and quite apart from the preceding point, the fact of a possible override by a superior positive legal provision does not really engage with the issue under consideration. Ours is a question about the interaction between law and practical reasons, a question that calls, inter alia, for an examination of conflicts between the two. To cite in this connection the possibility of an override by a superior positive legal provision—which may or may not be in force, and may or may not apply to the case, depending on the system in question and the case at hand[28]—would merely be to divert the attention to no-conflict situations, or, at least, no conflict of the type we are concerned with, namely those that are not merely intra-legal. To forestall such diversion, the examples given here assume that there is no positive legal provision capable of overriding the relevant presidential directive.[29]

3.2. Jurisdictional and Procedural Limitations

Having considered the legitimacy conditions put forward by the service conception of authority, I turn to some other possible limitations on Razian authority. Legitimate authoritative power, Raz points out, has jurisdictional limits, and may also be subject to restrictions as to the process by which authorities should reach their decisions. Can such limitations be relied upon to successfully uphold the no-authority reply—the claim that the directives flouted in Situations 1 and 2 are not authoritative ones?

Let us start with the more formal of these limitations. First, Raz notes that 'legitimate authority has the right to issue directives within the sphere of its jurisdiction'[30] and that jurisdiction is determined, inter alia, 'by the

---

[28] Two related comments: (1) A non-positivist assumption according to which moral standards are an essential part of the test for legal validity is itself discordant with the notion that law can pre-empt its underlying moral reasons. See p 5. (2) Raz mentions that if a directive 'violates fundamental human rights' it may be open to challenge (Raz, *The Morality of Freedom* (n 2) 46). I understand this basis for challenging authority to be intended to apply only to the extent that the legal system in question includes provisions giving legal effect to the relevant rights (and subject to the provisions of that legal system regarding the appropriate procedure by which directives can be challenged), which is, again, a contingent matter. It is not likely that Raz refers to fundamental human rights in this context as a moral notion independent of positive law, for subjecting the normative force of legal authority to such an open-ended notion would be incompatible with the thought that it excludes underlying moral reasons (see related comment in n 1 herein).

[29] This, once more, is of practical significance partly because positive constitutional laws of many legal systems will fall short of catering for all possible cases in which weighty moral reasons justify disobedience.

[30] Raz, *Practical Reason and Norms* (n 10) 192. See also Raz, *The Morality of Freedom* (n 2) 62.

range of actions the authority can command'.[31] For example, 'the house committee can require paying to a common fund, but not attending church service'.[32] Thus, to the extent that a given authority is restricted to a specific domain of activity (whether the restriction derives from its role definition or from its position in a larger hierarchical structure), that is another criterion of authoritativeness which appears to be distinguishable from an evaluation of its directives' contents on their merits. We know that the residents' committee of an apartment block (to use Raz's example) is in charge of the administration of the block, and possesses no authoritative power to issue directives beyond that domain. And this is so, it may be added, irrespective of the merits of such ultra vires directives, that is, whether the conduct they require is right or wrong, good or bad, and so on. Even if correct, however, this argument fails to meet the challenge of Situations 1 and 2: extremely immoral directives, or normal directives that under certain contingencies lead to a morally unacceptable outcome, may be issued by a person or an institution pertaining to matters that fall within the regulatory domain of which they are in charge. With regard to Situation 1, an illustration of this point can be found in the insurgents' example furnished earlier, where it was supposed that the president of a state, who is, as such, also the commander-in-chief of the armed forces, issues a directive to commit a military action that is extremely immoral. As for Situation 2, the point seems clear enough to render further illustration superfluous.

A second possible type of limitation on the legitimate exercise of authority becomes relevant when some clearly biasing or impairing factors impinge on the authority's decision-making process—as is the case, for example, if the decision-maker was bribed or blackmailed, or if she was intoxicated while making the decision.[33] When such factors are present, it may be suggested, they vitiate the authoritative potential of an ensuing decision. We may accept this suggestion as plausible. However, while this sort of limitation on authority can disqualify *some* cases from serving as counterexamples to the pre-emption thesis, it fails to defuse the problem posed by Situations 1 and 2. For people, including public officials, may occasionally make mistakes, and even bad mistakes that bring about extremely immoral outcomes (Situation 1), when no distinctly exogenous factors, such as bribery or intoxication, are

---

[31] Raz, *Practical Reason and Norms* (n 10) 192.   [32] ibid. See also ibid 46, 79.

[33] Some such factors are mentioned by Raz in the context of an example involving an arbitrator (Raz, *The Morality of Freedom* (n 2) 42). I am not sure whether he attributes their vitiating effect to posited rules in the field of arbitration or to a more general theoretical principle concerning authority.

involved.[34] And, of course, a morally innocuous rule that, under an occasional contingency, widely misfires (as in Situation 2) need not result from or coincide with the presence of any biasing or process-impairing factors.

A third limitation is more substantive in character. When referring to jurisdictional limitations, Raz notes that jurisdiction 'is also determined by the type of reasons the authority may rely upon'.[35] His intention here is not likely to be that when an authority considers a reason that should not be considered, this itself disqualifies the resultant directive from being authoritative. For one thing, such an interpretation seems to be incompatible with his service conception of authority. True, he holds that all authoritative directives should be based on what he calls 'dependent reasons', that is, reasons that 'already independently apply to subjects of the directives and are relevant to their action in the circumstances covered by the directive'[36] (a thesis which he terms *the dependence thesis*). However, compliance with the dependence thesis regarding a given directive is not, according to Raz, a condition for its authoritative status,[37] as can be inferred, for example, from the following passage (and particularly the passage's ending):

The dependence thesis does not claim that authorities always act for dependent reasons, but merely that they should do so. Ours is an attempt to explain the notion of legitimate authority through describing what one might call an ideal exercise of authority. Reality has a way of falling short of the ideal. We saw this regarding *de facto* authorities which are not legitimate. *But naturally not even legitimate authorities always succeed, nor do they always try to live up to the ideal.*[38]

And a few lines later he adds that the normal way to justify authorities is 'not by assuming that they always succeed in acting in the ideal way, but on the ground that they do so often enough to justify their power'.[39] It thus becomes apparent that the dependence thesis does not express an additional prerequisite of authority on top of the normal justification condition. The dependence thesis relates to the normal justification condition, inter alia, in that compliance with the latter is improbable without there being at least a

---

[34] Couldn't one attempt to extend the notion of bias to the point of encompassing any kind of misjudgement? Such an attempt would seem contrived, but, even more problematically, it would render the identification of bias indistinguishable from a content-based assessment of directives on their merits, which we have already ruled out from the pre-emption thesis's armoury of possible defences.

[35] Raz, *Practical Reason and Norms* (n 10) 192. See also Raz, *The Morality of Freedom* (n 2) 47.

[36] Raz, *The Morality of Freedom* (n 2) 47. To be more precise, he maintains that they should rely on dependent reasons for the most part, but may also take into account some bureaucratic considerations that are 'non-dependent reasons' (Raz, *Ethics in the Public Domain* (n 11) 214, fn 6).

[37] Raz, *The Morality of Freedom* (n 2) 38, 47, 55.   [38] ibid 47. Emphasis added.

[39] ibid. See Raz, 'The Problem of Authority' (n 3) 1014, where, listing the conditions for authority applicable under the service conception, he leaves out the dependence thesis.

fairly good degree of overall compliance with the former in the relevant area. But it is the normal justification condition—the condition of being *'more likely* to act successfully on the reasons which apply to its subjects'[40]—that encapsulates the relevant justificatory condition, not the dependence thesis.

Further insight can be gained into this issue by considering the essential point of Raz's service conception of authority. The essential point is that when another decision-maker is better placed than we are in a certain domain, such that she is capable of authoritatively guiding us to better conformity with relevant reasons in that domain, it becomes rational for us (in the sense that it is warranted and required by reason) to entrust her with the normative power to make binding decisions in that domain. One might propose to qualify this idea by saying that if, despite the above condition having been met, subjects happen to discover *direct evidence* regarding the decision-making process in a particular instance, which shows that the decision-maker relied on blatantly irrelevant considerations, it may be rational for them to disregard the ensuing directive. It may be questioned whether the service conception of authority would retain enough of its bite when thus qualified. But even if so, the service conception would not withstand a further qualification to the effect that subjects should disregard an authoritative directive whenever they think the authority took a wrong reason into account, even without direct evidence pertaining to the process of decision-making.[41] For in the absence of direct evidence, subjects can only detect defects in the decision-making process through an exercise of reverse reasoning, inferring from the decision itself what the considerations underlying it are. By this understanding, subjects are expected to examine the authority's decision so as to reconstruct the reasoning behind it. To do so, however, would be tantamount to second-guessing the decisions of those to whom (according to the service conception) they should entrust judgement (and to do so for the practical purpose of deciding how to act)[42]—which would undercut the very essence of Raz's service conception of authority. This, then, further corroborates the textual inference made above: Raz does not suggest that (legitimately) authoritative directives are only those issued on the basis of right reasons.[43]

---

[40] Raz, *The Morality of Freedom* (n 2) 55. Emphasis added.

[41] See related comments in Donald H Regan, 'Authority and Value: Reflections on Raz's Morality of Freedom' (1989) 62 Southern California Law Review 995, 1016.

[42] I add the parenthetical proviso because, as was noted, exclusionary reasons are reasons against *acting* for certain other reasons. They are not reasons against *thinking* about other reasons. See n 50 in ch 1.

[43] For similar reasons, when Raz notes that 'if an authority acted arbitrarily' its directives may be open to challenge (Raz, *The Morality of Freedom* (n 2) 46), it is not likely that he intends this to include every case where the authority's decision-making is affected by some wrong reasons.

But even if the opposite is assumed—namely, that authoritative directives are only those issued on the basis of right reasons—the possibility of authoritative Situation 1 or Situation 2 directives cannot be precluded. This point is straightforward as regards Situation 2, where the rule itself is not objectionable, and its situational failure is not (or at least need not be) attributable to an error on the part of the rule-maker. But it is also true of Situation 1. The insurgents' scenario depicted earlier is, at least arguably, one such example. The scenario, to reiterate, involves an order to carry out an attack on insurgents which is also likely to have the unwished-for effect of civilian casualties.[44] In this example, despite the presence in the apartment block of the two insurgents, who may be a legitimate target, given the expected harm to civilians, the order is a gravely wrong one.[45] However, it cannot be said that the order was necessarily based on a kind of reasons that the directive-issuer has no power to consider. The president, in our example, does consider the relevant reasons: the threat posed by the insurgents on the one hand, and the harm to innocent lives endangered by a military counterattack on the other. His mistake, however bad, consists in a failure to reach the correct resolution of the conflict between these reasons, which is, given (or especially given) the magnitude of expected harm to civilians, to forbear from a counterattack in this instance.[46]

3.3. Clearly Wrong Directives and the Binding Force of Authority

I have already attended to Raz's statement that '[e]stablishing that something is clearly wrong does not require going through the underlying reasons'.[47] But I also noted in this connection another proposition, which Raz mentions without accepting or denying. Having called the former Proposition CW, let this second proposition be called Proposition CW'. Proposition CW' says this: '[L]egitimate authority is limited by the condition that its directives are

---

[44] See pp 39–40.

[45] It is clearly wrong *morally* speaking, and is arguably, given its possible divisive effect which may fan the flames of the conflict even further, also an ill-advised measure from the perspective of an endeavour to inhibit the insurgents' campaign.

[46] Some may even propose that, grave as it is, the wrongness of the order should be viewed as an issue of degree. They may seek to illustrate this through a modification of the numbers of militants and civilians in the example. Thus, for instance, it might be argued that if there were 200 risk-posing militants and one civilian in the apartment block (with all other aspects of the example remaining the same) a counterattack would no longer be wrong in the extreme or would even be justifiable.

[47] Raz, *The Morality of Freedom* (n 2) 62. See my comments in Section 2.2.

not binding if clearly wrong'.[48] Proposition CW' is material here because in both types of situation I have discussed—Situations 1 and 2—the moral justifiability of non-compliance is *clear*. However, as will shortly become apparent, Raz offers in a later text further insight into his position on CW', which dispels the impression of neutrality and shows a marked disinclination of his to accept it. Moreover, it will be argued that acceptance of Proposition CW', by Raz or his proponents, would essentially collapse their model of exclusionary reasons into a substantively different conceptual model.

When initially commenting on the status of clear errors, Raz cautiously notes that he 'wish[es] to express no opinion'[49] on whether legitimate authority is subject to the limitation cited in Proposition CW'. In a later published symposium on Raz's work, however, this question is brought up by one of the contributors, Donald Regan.[50] At one point, Regan considers whether his preferred approach to rules and authority ('the indicator-rule conception', as he calls it), which includes something similar in effect to Proposition CW',[51] could be assimilated into Raz's notion of pre-emption.[52] He flirts with this possibility for a moment,[53] but appears to come down on the side of scepticism.[54] Regan observes that pre-emption, in the sense which Raz champions and considers to be the mark of authority, is importantly stronger than the normative input he (Regan) ascribes to rules and other directives,[55] even if some different sense of 'pre-emption' could be spoken of in connection with Regan's conception (e.g. the sense in which one is 'pre-empted' from simply ignoring the directive's indicative input).[56] He suspects that Raz would insist on the stronger sense of pre-emption.[57]

---

[48] Raz, *The Morality of Freedom* (n 2) 62.   [49] ibid.

[50] Regan (n 41) 1010–18, 1030–31. See also Stephen R Perry, 'Second-order Reasons, Uncertainty and Legal Theory' (1989) 62 Southern California Law Review 913, 933–45, where Perry discusses, under what he frames as 'epistemic limitations' on the deference one should show to authority, considerations for not deferring to the authority's judgement if clearly wrong.

[51] Regan (n 41) 1010 ('[O]ne should ignore an indicator-rule in a particular case if one just happens to be able to see clearly that in that case it leads to a wrong result ... '). See further, ibid 1010–13, 1030–31.

[52] ibid 1015–18 and fn 43. Proposition CW' does not mark the only difference between their approaches, but Raz's response, as will be seen shortly, bears directly on that proposition, thus making their exchange especially pertinent here.

[53] ibid 1015.   [54] ibid 1015–18 and fn 43.

[55] ibid. Perry too seems to conclude that his (comparable) conception of epistemic limitations on authority is at variance with the essence of exclusionary reasons, but for different reasons: 'Epistemically-bounded reasons as a class ... call for a familiarity with the underlying first-order reasoning which, because it can be quite extensive, is fundamentally at odds with what Raz views as the purpose of exclusionary reasons' (Perry (n 50) 944).

[56] Regan (n 41) 1015.

[57] ibid 1015–16 ('Raz may mean, or want to mean, something more when he says authoritative utterances "exclude" other reasons than I mean when I say the same thing about indicator-rules');

Raz's reply confirms this suspicion.[58] Of particular relevance is his response to a suggestion of Regan (tantamount to Proposition CW') that it would be reasonable for subjects of a legitimate authority to adopt the following strategy: 'following their own judgment when they feel that the case is clear and following the authority when they are less clear, or when they feel that the case is close'.[59] In this suggestion, Raz says, lies '[t]he one substantive difference of opinion'[60] between him and Regan. And he goes on to express doubts about Regan's assumption as to how well people generally would fare by this decision-making strategy.[61] I should note, en route to the main point, that I do not think Raz's remarks in this exchange could effectively undermine the premise I am proceeding on as to how ordinary people—people of sound mind and a basic (at least) understanding of the world in which they live—should approach and react to cases of the kind I have called Situations 1 and 2 (e.g. a directive to fire at what one clearly identifies as innocent individuals, a critically injured person who must be rushed to hospital in excess of the speed limit lest it becomes too late, or the like).[62] But the more pertinent point here is that Raz's comments in this exchange show that, far from being neutral on the status of clearly wrong directives, he is markedly disinclined to accept the limitation on authority cited in Proposition CW'.

But could we, despite Raz's disinclination to do so, incorporate Proposition CW' in the pre-emption thesis in a manner coherent with the thesis's core tenets? I think the answer is negative. To see why, recall initially that exclusionary reasons, the idea lying at the very heart of this thesis, are reasons to refrain from acting for some other *reasons*. It is thus reasons themselves that

---

ibid fn 43 ('[Indicator-rules] are *not* reasons for not *acting* on other reasons which we know about, and can evaluate, without active inquiry. At least, they are not reasons-for-not-acting-on-other-reasons in a strong Razian sense'; 'I think there is nothing here that is exactly what Raz has in mind. He wants a stronger sort of preemptive force'). Regan does not, however, entirely rule out the possibility that Raz would opt for a weaker claim (ibid 1017).

[58] Raz, 'Facing Up' (n 25) 1194–96.

[59] Namely, that it would be reasonable for them to do so, even if they have no information showing that those clear cases happen to fall within a subclass of cases where their judgement is generally better than the directive-issuer's and thus the normal justification condition is not met (ibid 1195).

[60] ibid.

[61] That is, the assumption that 'for the most part, people make more mistakes in the latter type of case than in the former' (ibid). 'I doubt this assumption in this general form', Raz writes, and cites some examples where he sees no reason to believe that it holds: 'as when they have a wrong belief about the relations between inflation and the value of shares, or where they hold some astrological theory about the success of wars' (ibid).

[62] And I am not sure his remarks are intended to undermine such a premise. But even if they are, I remain confident about its truth. If moral agency does not mean that one should disobey in such cases, I do not know what it *does* mean.

are said to be excluded,[63] not merely some (uncertain or misguided) perceptions about reasons.[64] This much is evident from the way Raz defines and speaks of exclusionary reasons, and it has also been directly made clear by Raz in his response to critics.[65] Also note that, by thus characterizing exclusionary reasons, Raz does not deny that our perceptions or beliefs necessarily mediate between reasons and our actions.[66] But to acknowledge this much is not to say that exclusionary reasons exclude *only* perceptions about reasons, or only certain (misguided or uncertain) perceptions.[67]

Now consider, by way of comparison, the type of decision-making model that would result from incorporating Proposition CW' into an otherwise Razian outlook (a model which, owing to its Razian affinities, would presumably seek to hold on to at least *some* sort of exclusion). Under such a model, when you are *sure* that the authority-required act is wrong you should depart from its directive—which is to say that, insofar as you identify the correct balance of reasons for action with a high level of certainty, you should act in accordance with it. But, precisely because of this rider, it would be most natural to understand the sort of exclusion involved in such a model as exclusion not of *real reasons*, but merely of some perceptions about reasons,[68] namely perceptions regarding which you have some doubts. Or, at any rate, the exclusion involved in such a model is readily reducible to this slimmer, uncertain-perceptions-limited sort of exclusion, with considerations of parsimony favouring such an interpretation.[69] But this sort of exclusion is, for

---

[63] 'Excluded' in the sense that you have reasons not to act for them—reasons not to let them influence your action.

[64] Raz distinguishes in this context between 'compliance' and 'conformity' (Raz, *Practical Reason and Norms* (n 10) 189–90. See also Raz, 'Facing Up' (n 25) 1158–61). When I refrain from acting for a reason because it was excluded by an exclusionary reason, I comply with the exclusionary reason, rather than the excluded one. But I may nonetheless *conform* to the excluded reason. For example, suppose I have a reason not to let my self-interest influence my advice to you on some career issue of yours, and suppose the advice I give you is free from such influence. The content of my advice may still, inadvertently, be beneficial to my self-interest. Now, what is at issue in this and the next paragraph is compliance with reasons, not conformity with them.

[65] See his response to Perry in ibid 1162–64.

[66] And, thus, that a reason not to act for a reason (*r*) is, in a secondary sense, also a reason not to act for one's perception that *r* is a valid reason (ibid 1163).

[67] See Raz's explanation of why he prefers not to characterize exclusionary reasons as reasons not to rely on one's belief in a reason (ibid 1162–64).

[68] Whether about their validity or their relative weight.

[69] I am conscious of Raz's 'normative/explanatory nexus' thesis (Joseph Raz, *From Normativity to Responsibility* (OUP 2011) 26–35), but, even if granted, I see no reason to think that this thesis militates against the statement in the body text. The 'normative/explanatory nexus' thesis does not deny, of course, that people can mistakenly perceive reasons or their weight, and does not say anything about the likelihood or unlikelihood of such mistaken perceptions. So the thesis, as far as I can see, does not go to show that any conceptual misunderstanding about reasons is involved in saying something like: 'These lawmakers cannot exclude your reasons, but since you are more likely than

reasons explained in the preceding paragraph, a substantially different notion than 'exclusionary reasons'—it is another kind of conceptual beast—which is to say that the model we are presently imagining is not a lightly or moderately qualified pre-emption thesis, but is, in essence, another theoretical model.[70] Now, am I to take on the task of developing and defending such a model? That would be a natural path if I myself was inclined to speak in terms of exclusion, or to think that there is no better alternative to such a model. But, since I am not thus inclined, I will leave this undertaking to those who are. As has already been indicated, my own preferred solution to the conundrum of this book will be put forward and advocated in Part III.

To bring this chapter to a close, let me briefly state my conclusion about the no-authority reply. The various authority prerequisites that can coherently be used in defence of the pre-emption thesis are incapable of ruling out the possible occurrence of Situations 1 and 2 under a legitimate authority. As for Situation 1, I should stress that no contention was made to the effect that the directives in question are authoritative. It is arguable—and was not denied here—that such extremely immoral directives can never be authoritative. What was denied, instead, is the possibility of defending this position without recourse to conditions of authority involving a content-based assessment of the directives' conformity with background reasons—which are conditions themselves inconsistent with the claim that authoritative directives exclude their background reasons. The no-authority reply, therefore, fails to reconcile Situations 1 and 2 with the pre-emption thesis.

---

they are to misperceive the reasons in the area of activity x, their directives in this area are reasons for you not to act on your perceptions (or uncertain perceptions) of primary reasons for action.'

[70] One might say here (echoing Regan (n 41) 1013–14) that the imagined model is Razian in the sense that, similarly to the normal justification thesis, it is underpinned by, and is meant to reflect, the desideratum of enhancing conformity with reason (notwithstanding Raz's own doubts about how well that model would actually satisfy this desideratum). My point, however, refers to a different issue: namely, that the imagined model represents a substantial break from the *pre-emption thesis*. It is not a point about the *justificatory grounds* of exclusionary reasons (which, according to Raz, in some cases do involve, or partly involve, the fallibility of one's perception or judgement), but a point about what exclusionary reasons are. This last distinction plays, I think, an important role in Raz's thinking (see, e.g., Raz, *Practical Reason and Norms* (n 10) 48).

4

Scope of Exclusion

4.1. The Scope Limitation Explained

My focus in this chapter will be another possible Razian defence, which was labelled earlier 'the scope-of-exclusion reply'. According to this defence, the reasons in virtue of which disobedience is justified in Situations 1 and 2 are outside the purview of the exclusionary force exercised by the directive in question. Before considering the defence itself, a brief explanation of the scope limitation on exclusionary reasons is called for.

Exclusionary reasons, according to Raz, vary in the scope of their exclusionary effect. They may exclude all or only a certain subclass of the applicable first-order reasons.[1] To this general statement Raz adds some more specific ones about *which* first-order reasons are within the scope of exclusion of an authoritative directive and which are not. One principle of demarcation that can be derived from different writings of Raz is this: (1) excluded reasons are 'all the reasons both for and against [the prescribed conduct] which were within the jurisdiction of the authority',[2] that is, 'reasons on which the authority had power to pronounce';[3] (2) the foregoing reasons consist primarily of what Raz terms the dependent reasons:[4] namely, reasons that 'already independently apply to subjects of the directives and are relevant to their action in the circumstances covered by the directive'.[5] As was previously noted, in some places Raz refers to a more limited scope of exclusion, which encompasses not all the reasons the

---

[1] Joseph Raz, *Practical Reason and Norms* (2nd edn, Princeton University Press 1990) 40.

[2] ibid 192.

[3] Joseph Raz, 'Facing Up: A Reply' (1989) 62 Southern California Law Review 1153, 1194. See also Joseph Raz, *Between Authority and Interpretation: On the Theory of Law and Practical Reason* (OUP 2009) 7–8 (the body text and fn 7).

[4] I say 'primarily' because, as was already noted, he acknowledges that authorities may also take into account some bureaucratic considerations which are 'non-dependent reasons' (Joseph Raz, *Ethics in the Public Domain: Essays in the Morality of Law and Politics* (rev paperback edn, Clarendon Press 1995) 214, fn 6).

[5] Joseph Raz, *The Morality of Freedom* (Clarendon Press 1986) 47.

Legal Directives and Practical Reasons. Noam Gur. © Noam Gur 2018. Published 2018 by Oxford University Press.

authority was meant to consider for and against the prescribed act, but only those *against* it. Thus, for example, he states that 'authoritative directives preempt those reasons against the conduct they require that the authority was meant to take into account'[6] and that 'the pre-emption excludes only reasons that conflict with the authority's directive'.[7]

How, according to Raz, should we resolve a conflict between a norm (e.g. an authoritative directive) and a first-order reason *outside* its scope of exclusion? When such a conflict occurs, Raz suggests, reasons for compliance with the norm operate in their first-order force, and the method of resolving the conflict should be the method ordinarily employed in first-order conflicts.[8] In other words, one should act in those situations 'on the balance of reasons, comparing the weight of the norm as a first-order reason with the weight of the competing reason'.[9] And when the latter is the weightier of the two, it would be justified to defy the norm. Now, Situations 1 and 2 might be viewed by the Razian as situations of this kind, and if this view can be borne out then Situations 1 and 2 would prove to be consistent with the pre-emption thesis. Whether it *can* be borne out, however, is what I now turn to consider.

4.2. The Scope-of-Exclusion Reply Considered

For reasons of expositional convenience, I begin with Situation 2. If the scope-of-exclusion reply is going to do any work at reconciling the pre-emption thesis with Situation 2, it must (as indicated above) not simply be asserted, but must also be substantiated. That is, given an instance of Situation 2 we should be able to say that the reasons justifying disobedience in the case are not within the scope of exclusion of the relevant rule, and we should be able to explain why they are not within that scope. Let us attempt to do so with

---

[6] Joseph Raz, 'The Problem of Authority: Revisiting the Service Conception' (2006) 90 Minnesota Law Review 1003, 1018.

[7] ibid 1022. See also ibid 1021–23; Raz, *Practical Reason and Norms* (n 1) 144. See further in this connection Christopher Essert, 'A Dilemma for Protected Reasons' (2012) 31 Law and Philosophy 49 (where Essert identifies and discusses a dilemma for Raz concerning the choice between the above two renderings).

[8] Raz, *Practical Reason and Norms* (n 1) 77, 79, 192.

[9] ibid 77. See also ibid 192; Joseph Raz, *The Authority of Law: Essays on Law and Morality* (2nd edn, OUP 2009) 22. According to Raz, '[t]he first-order strength of a norm depends on the values it serves; it depends on the strength of the reasons for the norm which are reasons for doing what is required by the norm', and also 'on the likelihood that deviating from it in a case where this is otherwise justified will increase the risk that it will be disregarded in cases in which it should be followed' (Raz, *Practical Reason and Norms* (n 1) 77).

the following example.[10] In a certain jurisdiction a proposal for new regulations concerning the postal services is put forward by the governmental department in charge of such matters. Due to concerns of the relevant officials over the punctuality and promptness of mail delivery, the following provision is included in the bill: 'No person shall knowingly obstruct or delay the delivery of mail, or knowingly act in a way that brings about obstruction or delay of mail delivery.' The bill is duly passed in the supreme legislative body of the jurisdiction and is then signed by the head of state in accordance with the required legislative process. The new law, including the foregoing provision, proves to be a beneficial measure that improves postal services in the country.

Now, assume the following scenario. A mail carrier on duty (call her Jane) is driving a van loaded with mail on a road with very little traffic. She notices an injured person lying on the roadside in the aftermath of a car accident. His condition is evidently critical. She realizes that the most effective—and in all likelihood the only—way to save him is to rush him immediately to a hospital, and she does just that. This involves a digression from her normal route, which results in a delay to mail delivery. There is no legal provision (including judicial precedent) in the relevant jurisdiction that requires or permits Jane to defy the rule in order to assist another person in jeopardy, such as a legally recognized Good Samaritan obligation. When taking this course of action, Jane acts on moral reasons.

An attempt might be made to nip this example in the bud. There *must* be some law, one might insist, on the grounds of which Jane's act could be justified: if not provisions requiring one to assist people in danger, then, at least, general legal defences pertaining to situations of necessity or emergency. On this view, our premise that such legal defences are not available in the case is an impossibility, for any legal system would either explicitly incorporate generally applicable defences of this type or at least must be seen as tacitly containing them, irrespective of its enacted provisions and of whether there is anything in previous courts' decisions to support this conclusion.[11] While the

---

[10] There are certain similarities, but also differences, between the example assumed here and the case of *United States v Kirby* 74 US 482 (1869). The latter case is discussed in Michael S Moore, 'Authority, Law, and Razian Reasons' (1989) 62 *Southern California Law Review* 827, 869, as part of Moore's objection to the view that judges treat statutory enactments as reasons that exclude background moral reasons (ibid 864–65). Raz, in reply, suggests that this case is not a counter-example to the thesis that legal provisions exclude moral (non-legal) reasons since it 'turn[s] on judicial discretion to weigh various *legal* considerations against each other ... ' (Raz, 'Facing Up' (n 3) 1169). Questions about the grounds for the judgement in *U.S. v Kirby* cannot and need not be discussed here.

[11] I doubt that Raz would endorse such a claim, inter alia, in view of the following remark, with an emphasis on its ending sentence: 'There are many legal doctrines specifically designed to allow

initial purpose of this argument was to fend off a potential counterexample to the pre-emption thesis, its effect seems to be to reinforce my challenge to the pre-emption thesis. For, if the aforementioned defences are applicable regardless of the law's positive provisions, this must be accounted for by moral considerations. It must be accounted for by the fact that reasons for compliance with authoritative directives are amenable to be overridden by compelling moral reasons that may militate against compliance.[12] But such overridability represents the very intuition at the heart of my objection to the pre-emption thesis. At this point, the objector might want to reconcile the pre-emption thesis with the overridability of authoritative directives by saying that they can be overridden only by moral reasons outside their scope of exclusion. This, however, brings us back to the starting point of this chapter: the scope-of-exclusion reply. No work is done by the foregoing objection.

Let us proceed with the analysis, then, by reference to the above-described scenario. The crucial difficulty with the assertion that Jane has acted on reasons outside the scope of exclusion arises when we ask questions such as: Why are these reasons not within the scope of exclusion? What makes them reasons not within that scope? And how do we know that they are such reasons? As Chaim Gans noted in his own critique of the idea of exclusionary reasons, we do not have, for every rule, a list of reasons excluded by the rule and a list of reasons not excluded by it.[13] Rules do not come with such lists and to prepare them would be unfeasible, for there are too many possible contingencies and varied scenarios that would have to be foreseen, considered, and specified in advance for that task to be carried out even for a single rule.[14] And even if

---

exceptions to legal requirements, doctrines such as self-defence, necessity, public policy ... The point is that the law demands the right to define the permissible exceptions' (Raz, *The Morality of Freedom* (n 5) 77).

[12] As Kent Greenawalt notes, even where legal rules are drafted as well as they can be they remain susceptible to such override (Kent Greenawalt, *Conflicts of Law and Morality* (paperback edn, OUP 1989) 191–92). See further, Frederick Schauer, *Playing by the Rules: A Philosophical Examination of Rule-Based Decision-Making in Law and in Life* (Clarendon Press 1991) esp 118, but also 25–37, 47–52, 88–93, 128–34; Larry Alexander, 'The Gap' (1991) 14 Harvard Journal of Law & Public Policy 695; William A Edmundson, *Three Anarchical Fallacies: An Essay on Political Authority* (CUP 1998) 9–10; Richard HS Tur, 'Defeasibilism' (2001) 21 Oxford Journal of Legal Studies 355.

[13] Chaim Gans, 'Mandatory Rules and Exclusionary Reasons' (1986) 15 Philosophia 373, 385.

[14] ibid. In a different but related context, Raz makes the following relevant remark: 'Nor can one maintain that universal ought-propositions are abbreviations of very detailed propositions which include a complete list of exceptions, all the circumstances in which one does not have a conclusive reason to act as the proposition indicates. It is plausible to think that ... no one can know all the exceptions (i.e. that no one can know either a list of them or a generalization stating them ...). Hence the propositions normally expressed by universal ought-propositions are what they appear to be. They are not (identical with) detailed propositions listing all the cases, or circumstances, in which one need not do what the proposition states that one ought to do' (Joseph Raz, *From Normativity to Responsibility* (OUP 2011) 24).

we could and were to produce such lists, how would we demarcate the line between excluded and unexcluded reasons? Wouldn't the demarcation depend on the *weight* of reasons for and against compliance with the rule? Raz's answer could not be 'yes, it would'.[15] For, as noted by Gans,[16] it would be self-undermining for the pre-emption thesis to claim that some reasons are excluded from competing with others by their weight, but that the question of which reasons are thus excluded is determined by their weight. The weight of reasons is the one thing that the scope of exclusion cannot depend on.

We must search, then, for scope-determining factors other than the weight of reasons. Raz does point out some such factors. Let us consider whether they pick out the reason for Jane's act as an unexcluded reason. To start with, he refers to auxiliary reasons such as the directive-issuer's rank and role, which affect the scope of her jurisdiction and, as a result, the scope of exclusionary force attached to her directives.[17] So, for example, a directive issued by high-ranking officials may have a scope of exclusion broader than that of a directive issued by low-ranking officials. As regards the directive-issuer's role, by way of example, a chess club administration committee can only issue valid directives related to the club's administration, and thus cannot exclude reasons by issuing directives on other matters. Such factors, however, do not hold the key to a solution of our case. Our example supposes a rule issued by an empowered authority that is in charge of the subject regulated and is of the highest echelon; these factors seem to assign to the authority the broadest scope they can possibly assign. If, in view of this, it is conceded that the scope can cover Jane's reasons for defying the rule, we are facing a counterexample for which the scope-of-exclusion reply fails to account. Alternatively, it must be shown what other criterion establishes that these reasons are not within the scope of exclusion.

As was noted, the reasons excluded by an authoritative directive are, according to Raz, reasons on which the authority had power to pronounce.[18] And these, in turn, consist primarily of what he calls the 'dependent reasons'. Perhaps, then, if we found that the reasons for Jane's action do not form part of the dependent reasons, we would have a certain indication for their being outside the scope of exclusion. Are the reasons for Jane's action not part of

[15] And he explicitly notes regarding the reasons excluded by a norm: '[T]heir exclusion is not a matter of weight. It is determined by the fact that the norm is a second-order reason' (Raz, *Practical Reason and Norms* (n 1) 79).

[16] Gans (n 13) 385, 389–90. See also relevant comments in William A Edmundson, 'Rethinking Exclusionary Reasons: A Second Edition of Joseph Raz's "Practical Reason and Norms" ' (1993) 12 Law and Philosophy 329, 336–37.

[17] Raz, *Practical Reason and Norms* (n 1) 46–47, 79, 192.

[18] Raz, 'Facing Up' (n 3) 1194. See also Raz, *Between Authority and Interpretation* (n 3) 7–8 (the body text and fn 7).

the dependent reasons in respect of the mail-delay prohibition? The definition of dependent reasons does not seem to provide any basis for drawing this conclusion. To reiterate, the definition refers us to 'reasons which already independently apply to subjects of the directives and are relevant to their action in the circumstances covered by the directive'.[19] The words 'action in the circumstances covered by the directive' may, on one possible understanding, encompass every action to which the directive has direct practical relevance. Circumstances *not* 'covered' by the mail-delay prohibition are, on this understanding, circumstances where the action performed is not one that might obstruct or delay mail delivery. Thus, for example, Jane's partaking in recreational activity in her free time is most likely action in circumstances not 'covered' by the mail-delay prohibition. But, on this reading, Jane's rushing the injured person to hospital in the scenario assumed *is* action in circumstances 'covered' by the mail-delay prohibition, because her doing so has the direct consequence of delaying the mail; and, thus, her reasons for doing so are part of the 'dependent reasons'.[20] On this understanding of 'dependent reasons', then, the example presents us with a case where subjects should violate a rule for its dependent reasons—reasons that would be excluded from affecting their action if the pre-emption thesis were correct.

So maybe Raz's notion of dependent reasons is narrower. But, once more, it is hard to find any basis for that in the definition of dependent reasons.[21] On the basis of what criterion can we establish that Jane's reasons for changing her route are *not* reasons that 'independently apply to subjects of the

---

[19] Raz, *The Morality of Freedom* (n 5) 47.

[20] The pre-emption thesis's formulation suggests that Raz's intention is different: '[T]he fact that an authority requires performance of an action is a reason ... which is not to be added to all other relevant reasons ... but should exclude ... *some* of them' (ibid 46). Emphasis omitted, save the word 'some'.

[21] Similar questions arise regarding the following remark by Raz: 'Usually each rule is based on a number of reasons, and they reflect a judgement that those reasons defeat, within the scope of the rule, various, though not necessarily all, conflicting reasons. Rules are, metaphorically speaking, expressions of compromises, of judgements about the outcome of conflicts.... Characteristically, cases are "simply" outside the scope of the rule if the main reasons which support the rule do not apply to such cases. Cases fall under an exception to the rule when some of the main reasons for the rule apply to them, but the "compromise reflected in the rule" deems other, conflicting reasons to prevail' (Raz, *Practical Reason and Norms* (n 1) 187). Jane's case does not come under the first type of case Raz mentions. Does this mean that she acts for reasons within the scope of exclusion? The answer must be 'yes', unless we understand Raz's words 'the scope of the rule' to mean a scope wider than the rule's scope of exclusion. If we thus understand Raz, the question remains: how do we know whether or not Jane's reasons for action fall under the (narrower) scope of exclusion? For Raz to reply by reference to the second type of case in the quoted passage would be problematic, for the distinction relied upon—a distinction between conflicting reasons that the 'compromise reflected in the rule' deems to be defeated and some 'other, conflicting reasons' that the 'compromise reflected in the rule' deems to prevail—seems to implicate recourse to the weight of these reasons.

directives [i.e. the mail-delay prohibition] and are relevant to their action in the circumstances covered by the directive'?[22] An assertion that *special* circumstances where subjects come upon a critically injured person are not included in 'the circumstances covered by the directive' would not do. For how and on what grounds (apart from the compelling weight of the reason to save a person's life) do we know that these circumstances are special circumstances that are not covered by the rule? No exception was specified to this effect, and, just as the rule was not issued with a list of reasons earmarked as excluded or unexcluded, so too no list was appended to it which enumerates circumstances where delaying the mail is covered or not covered by the rule. It is not clear, then, how the question faced by Jane—whether a moral reason for assisting a dying person justifies disobedience of the mail-delay prohibition—can depend on whether this reason is outside an undefined scope of exclusion, rather than on its compelling weight.

A further reply runs as follows. True, rules do not normally come with appended catalogues of specific circumstances delineating their exact scope. But there are situations where we know that a rule is not meant to apply even if its plain meaning indicates otherwise, just as there are situations where we know that a rule *is* meant to apply. Contrast, for example, the scenario under consideration, where Jane brings a dying person to hospital, with a different scenario in which she digresses from her normal route in order to visit a friend she has not seen for a while and who happens to live nearby. Undoubtedly the prohibition is meant to apply to the latter scenario, and is not meant to apply to the former.[23]

This reply would be of no avail if it simply reflects an intuition that the statute *should* not be set aside for the purpose of visiting a friend, but *should* be set aside when necessary in order to save lives. For this intuition, however sensible, stems directly from a judgement of the comparative weight of the reasons involved. In order to learn whether this reply successfully resolves our puzzle, we must unpack the term 'meant' as featuring in the reply. We must search for some tools of legal interpretation, not themselves subversive to the pre-emption thesis, which indicate that the mail-delay prohibition is not meant to cover Jane's circumstances. I should clarify, however, that my following arguments are not intended as an endorsement of this or that method of legal interpretation. Nor is it my purpose here to suggest or deny

---

[22] Raz, *The Morality of Freedom* (n 5) 47.
[23] Cf Raz's comment that '[i]f the addressee [of an order] did not perform the prescribed act because of the presence of an overriding reason not meant to be excluded by the order he is not regarded as having disobeyed the order ... since he did not act contradictory to the intention of the prescriber' (Raz, *Practical Reason and Norms* (n 1) 84).

that legal interpretation must always have recourse to moral reasoning. The limited question I wish to consider is which tool of legal interpretation, if any, could uphold the scope-of-exclusion reply in the case under consideration. Thus, objections to the method of interpretation employed here, or arguments pointing in the abstract to other theories or tools of interpretation, would hardly engage with the material issue at hand. What must be demonstrated, instead, is how such interpretation methods affirm, in a manner itself consistent with the pre-emption thesis, that the mail-delay prohibition is not meant to cover the circumstances of our example.

There are methods of interpretation which could perhaps ground the conclusion that the mail-delay prohibition is not meant to cover our example, but which are not available for the pre-emption thesis's defender because they involve recourse to background moral reasoning. Whether the interpreter frames her arguments in terms of the moral purpose underlying the rule, its *raison d'être*, principles that provide the best justification of the relevant practice,[24] or similar terms that implicate background moral reasoning, she is thereby invoking (at least in part) what the pre-emption thesis alleges to be excluded. We must consider, then, other possible modes of interpretation.

Might the word 'meant' in the preceding reply refer to an intention of the lawmaker in the sense of a subjective, existing state of mind regarding the circumstances in question? This line of response, it should be noted, does not represent Raz's position. He denies that the intentions or thoughts that members of the legislature actually had in mind when enacting a statute are determinative of its meaning.[25] And, at any rate, searching for a subjective legislative intention regarding the example in question does not seem to be a promising route. The enacting legislators did not make any provision or reservation for a case of this type, and it is anything but implausible that they simply had not thought about such a situation.[26] If that is so, intention in the sense of an actual state of mind of the lawmaker as to the relevant circumstances did not really exist at the time of the incident.[27] Could we say that

---

[24] Ronald Dworkin, *Law's Empire* (Fontana 1986) 14–130.

[25] Joseph Raz, 'Why Interpret?' (1996) 9 Ratio Juris 349, 355; Raz, *Ethics in the Public Domain* (n 4) 229, 232; Joseph Raz, 'Intention in Interpretation' in Robert P George (ed), *The Autonomy of Law* (Clarendon Press 1996) 249–86, esp 263. See further, Joseph Raz, 'Intention Without Retrieval' in Andrei Marmor (ed), *Law and Interpretation* (Clarendon Press 1995) 155–76.

[26] Cf Donald H Regan, 'Authority and Value: Reflections on Raz's Morality of Freedom' (1989) 62 Southern California Law Review 995, 1010, where Regan makes a similar comment regarding an analogous example.

[27] It might be the case that some government officials or members of the legislative body who passed the mail-delay prohibition had in mind a more general notion such as an 'emergency' or 'necessity' exception, but then again, it might be the case that they had no such thought in mind (and there isn't any factual indication that they had). Surely, Jane's disobedience should not depend

the very fact that the lawmaker did not envisage the situation means that it is not covered by the rule? This, too, would be at variance with Raz's position. He expressly rejects the idea that 'the law is determined only regarding cases which the law-maker actually contemplated and had in mind when making the law'.[28] And it is easy to appreciate why such an idea would be problematic. The expectation that an authority would envision all possible scenarios that might come under its rules is unrealistic. Moreover, to require that this be done as a condition for the application of rules is quite incongruous with their nature and function. Rules are practical solutions that involve generalization;[29] and their character as such would be heavily watered down if every set of circumstances not actually contemplated by the authority were to be regarded as not covered by its rules.

If intention in the sense of an actual state of mind of legislators regarding the scenario in question may have never existed, and if its absence does not preclude the scenario from the rule's ambit, the solution probably lies elsewhere. Perhaps it can be found in Raz's own approach to the interpretation of authoritative intention. According to Raz:

While the theory of authority shows that the legitimacy of legislated—that is, authority-based—law depends on it being interpreted in accordance to its authors' intentions, the guide to interpretation which the theory of authority indicates is reliance on the conventions for interpreting legislative texts of the kind in question prevailing in the legal culture when the legislation in question was promulgated.[30]

The thesis [i.e. what Raz calls the authoritative intention thesis] requires one to understand the legislation as meaning what the legislator said. What the legislator said is what his words mean, given the circumstances of the promulgation of the legislation, and the conventions of interpretation prevailing at the time.[31]

The latter passage refers to a combination of three factors: (1) the words of the legislature, given (2) the circumstances of legislation, and (3) prevailing conventions of legal interpretation. Before we come to the second and third of these factors, we may want to consider the common usage meaning of the

on such a contingent factual question. She ought to contravene the rule regardless of the legislators' subjective state of mind. An objector might say that, regardless of their subjective state of mind, the legislators should be presumed to have reasonable intentions, and therefore should be presumed to have no intention that the prohibition would apply in circumstances such as ours. I will discuss this type of reply on pp 61–63.

[28] Raz, *Ethics in the Public Domain* (n 4) 232.　　[29] See citations on p 24, n 9.
[30] Raz, 'Intention in Interpretation' (n 25) 280.

[31] ibid 271. Two clarifications by Raz should be mentioned: (1) The above thesis 'is not itself a method of interpretation. Rather it refers courts to the conventions of interpretation prevailing at the time of legislation' (ibid); (2) '[T]he doctrine of authority cannot provide a complete and exhaustive basis for all ways in which interpretive arguments feature in adjudication' (ibid 280).

statutory language. But we already know that it offers no indication that the mail-delay prohibition does not cover our case. The statute refers to persons who 'knowingly act in a way that brings about obstruction or delay of mail delivery'. Jane's action clearly falls within the meaning of these words in ordinary usage.[32] The problem in our case is not a problem of linguistic ambiguity (as, for example, when we ask whether the words 'cost of production of a good' refer to the marginal cost of producing each unit thereof or to their average). Nor does our case instantiate a problem of linguistic vagueness (as, for example, when we ask whether an activity emitting 65-decibel sound is 'noisy').

What about the second factor mentioned by Raz, the circumstances of legislation? The legislation in question, we have assumed, has stemmed from an initiative to regulate post services in the jurisdiction. The considerations leading to this regulatory measure involved officials' concern to ensure prompt and punctual mail delivery. Let us suppose that this much can be learnt from records of pre-legislative consultations and from a preamble to the statute. Securing the promptness and punctuality of mail delivery appears, therefore, to be part of the 'authoritative intention' behind the rule. However, as Raz points out, a rule typically reflects a 'compromise' between competing considerations.[33] And there is nothing in the aforementioned legislative circumstances (and statutory language) to denote that Jane's reasons for changing her route are not part of the 'compromise' reflected in the prohibition, namely, that her action falls outside the scope of the prohibition. True, the legislative backdrop might involve additional circumstances, which might be available to the interpreter, and which might be indicative of an intention to preclude a scenario such as Jane's from the scope of the prohibition. But, then again, all this might *not* be the case; and it is against the background of *this* assumption that we must test the pre-emption thesis. To focus instead on cases where we happen to find legislative circumstances that support our desired outcome is to skirt around the real question—the question of whether our reasons can really be excluded.

The third determinant of authoritative intention, according to Raz, is the prevailing conventions of legal interpretation. These, however, cannot be the solution to our problem. The primary reason (which bears similarity to the point made in the previous paragraph) is that conventions of legal interpretation are contingent on their being adopted by legal officials (most likely judges) in the relevant jurisdiction. In contrast, that the mail carrier in our assumed scenario should save the injured person in defiance of the mail-delay

---

[32] Cf the analysis of *U.S. v Kirby* in Moore (n 10) 869.
[33] Raz, *Practical Reason and Norms* (n 1) 187.

prohibition is surely not contingent on the practices of legal officials. She should not leave him to die, whether or not legal officials in her jurisdiction have embraced a convention of legal interpretation to that effect. Having said that, it is worth making a brief excursus in order to consider what type of convention of interpretation could be resorted to in the case in question.

Given that there is no positive law (including case law) that conflicts with the mail-delay prohibition, and that the case unambiguously comes under the statutory wording, what convention of interpretation could bring us to the conclusion that the case is not covered by the statute? It is hard to think of any, except for one doctrine of interpretation, which might be viewed as a doctrine grounded in a convention (a view I shall not contest here). What I am referring to is a general presumption of interpretation according to which the legislature never means statutory language to lead to injustice or an absurd consequence, or the like.[34] As the US Supreme Court put it in *U.S. v Kirby*, '[i]t will always … be presumed that the legislature intended exceptions to its language, which would avoid results of this character [i.e. injustice, oppression, or an absurd consequence]'.[35] 'The reason of the law in such cases', added the Court, 'should prevail over its letter'.[36] And, as clarified by the Court in *Crooks v Harrelson*, 'to justify a departure from the letter of the law upon that ground, the absurdity must be so gross as to shock the general moral or common sense'.[37] I am not certain whether Raz would subsume the recourse to this (or a similar) doctrine under his authoritative intention thesis or would instead regard it as an example of 'innovative' interpretation (a possibility he acknowledges).[38] The second possibility will be discussed at a later point. Let us begin with the first.

An initial question is who the intended addressees of the above doctrine are. We are assuming that an interpretative presumption against injustice or absurd consequences has been conventionally accepted by judges in the relevant jurisdiction and that it serves them as a guide in judicial decisions. We must recall, however, the distinction highlighted by Jeremy Bentham between conduct rules

---

[34] I am indebted to Moore's discussion of this presumption in Moore (n 10) 869–71.

[35] *U.S. v Kirby* (n 10) 486–87. See Moore (n 10) 869.

[36] *U.S. v Kirby* (n 10) 486–87.

[37] *Crooks v Harrelson* 282 US 55 (1930) 60. The court, however, makes the further qualification that '[t]here must be something to make plain the intent of Congress that the letter of the statute is not to prevail' (ibid). In view of this, I am not sure that the interpretive presumption discussed by the court is the same one we are discussing. But I put this doubt to one side. If the presumption were dependent for its application on the manifestation of legislative intent against the letter of the law (rather than merely on the gross absurdity or injustice generated by a literal interpretation), it would not be available for use in our example.

[38] Raz, 'Intention in Interpretation' (n 25) 274–77.

and judicial decision rules.[39] If Bentham was right to note that the two are not the same (as I, for one, think he was), then the fact that judges use the above interpretive presumption does not entail that it has become a legal instruction addressed to *non-judicial actors* and intended to *guide their conduct*. If this interpretive presumption is addressed only to judges, when discussing the reasons for action of non-judicial actors, as we now do, it must be ruled out as a possible basis for the scope-of-exclusion reply.

Suppose, however, that the presumption against injustice or absurdity is an interpretive tool addressed also to non-judicial actors. Even if so, it cannot lend real support to the scope-of-exclusion reply. The presumption makes reference to evaluative terms of a noticeably high degree of generality, such as 'injustice' or 'absurd consequence'. It thus raises questions that by now will have a familiar ring: what specific factors determine whether or not a given action falls within the compass of those terms? And how do we know whether the injustice or absurdity is significant enough to warrant departure from the ordinary meaning of the statute? The answer is that these factors necessarily include the reasons for and against that action, and their relative weight—which, in turn, precludes the above interpretive presumption from the pre-emption thesis's armoury of defence.[40] As Michael Moore put the point in his critique of Raz's exclusionary reasons account, if '[j]udges may consider as an unexcluded reason for overruling the moral absurdity to which a plain meaning interpretation would lead if the absurdity is large', then the rule 'seems to exclude nothing, for any type of moral absurdity can count, if its weight as a reason is great enough'.[41] Moore, it should be clarified, is not denying here that the rule changes what ought to be done by its addressees. He accepts that it does so in a range of cases, including cases where the rule-prescribed action is suboptimal, so long as it does not amount to gross injustice or moral absurdity of considerable weight.[42] Moore's point, however,

---

[39] Jeremy Bentham, *A Fragment on Government and An Introduction to The Principles of Morals and Legislation* (first published 1776, Wilfrid Harrison ed, Basil Blackwell 1948) 430. See also Meir Dan-Cohen, 'Decision Rules and Conduct Rules: On Acoustic Separation in Criminal Law' (1984) 97 Harvard Law Review 625. At least at one point, Raz seems to acknowledge some version of this distinction: Joseph Raz, 'Postema on Law's Autonomy and Public Practical Reasons: A Critical Comment' (1998) 4 Legal Theory 1, 18.

[40] From a Dworkinian perspective of 'law as integrity' (Dworkin (n 24) 147–275), the matter would be framed somewhat differently (at least as far as judicial decisions are concerned). It would be framed not simply as a matter of competition between reasons to endorse the rule's 'plain meaning' and reasons to set it aside, but rather as an interpretive effort to identify what propositions follow from a set of principles which figure in the most appealing account of the community's practice. As noted earlier, however, this conception of law is itself incompatible with the pre-emption thesis.

[41] Moore (n 10) 870–71.

[42] ibid 871 (where Moore notes: '[W]hat the Court says in *Crooks* is this: overrule whenever, on the balance of all reasons, you ought to—with the caveat that, since there are usually good

is that the rule's capacity to do so depends on, and is mediated by, the weight of reasons, rather than their exclusion.

The comments made in the last three paragraphs remain a mere digression from what I consider to be the main difficulty with resting the scope-of-exclusion reply upon conventions of legal interpretation: namely, the fact that such conventions are contingent on whether officials of the legal system in question have adopted them. We have assumed *arguendo* that an interpretive presumption against injustice has been conventionally adopted in the relevant legal system. But what if it has *not* been adopted? This alternative appears to leave no basis for the argument that the mail-delay prohibition is not *meant* to cover Jane's case. If the argument is retained after all, it loses the appearance of an argument about what Raz terms 'authoritative intention'. It now presents itself not as an attempt to trace an implicit legislative intention, but simply as a judgement about the compelling weight of the reasons at hand, which it cannot be if it is going to ground a defence of exclusionary reasons. If, on the other hand, given such a legal system the argument from statutory meaning is abandoned, are we to think that now Jane should avoid saving the injured person so as to comply with the mail-delay prohibition? Surely not.[43]

The question of what would be the judgement and its grounds if, after the fact, Jane's case were brought before a court is not our primary concern here. It is worth noting, however, that Raz does not deny the possibility of judicial resort to moral reasoning in such cases. As an exclusive positivist, he maintains that the law's existence and content can be identified without recourse to evaluative arguments.[44] But 'legal reasoning'—the reasoning courts are engaged in—includes, according to Raz, more than the identification of the law's existence and content. It includes 'any reasoning to conclusions which entail that, according to the law, if a matter were before a court the court should decide thus and so'.[45] And, once the law's existence and content are identified, the rest of legal reasoning can and (at least sometimes) does, in Raz's view, involve recourse to evaluative arguments. In this vein, he notes:

In legal reasoning, legal rules and standards appear among the reasons inclining the argument towards one conclusion or another. But they compete with other reasons.[46]

reasons (of predictability, legislative supremacy, etc.) not to overrule the seemingly obvious import of statutory language, it will require weighty reasons in favor of overruling in order to tip the balance that way').

[43] This might also suggest that the motivation for invoking an interpretive presumption against injustice in cases such as ours is rooted, first and foremost, in the moral reasons for avoiding a result of this kind, and has little to do with conventions of interpretation.

[44] Raz, *Ethics in the Public Domain* (n 4) 210–37.

[45] Raz, 'Postema on Law's Autonomy' (n 39) 4.

[46] ibid 5–6. See also ibid 4; Raz, *Ethics in the Public Domain* (n 4) 230, 233–35.

In the case assumed here, this type of competition between reasons may well lead to a judicial decision to overrule the prohibition. Does this mean that, in Raz's view, the pre-emptive force of legal authority does not apply to courts? No. According to Raz, 'courts are only bound by the laws that apply to them'[47] and, therefore, 'the question is: What does the law [of a given legal system] require the courts to do regarding laws which apply not to them but to the litigants in front of them?'[48] Thus, it is possible that the legal system under consideration empowers courts to change, or depart from, laws in cases such as Jane's, and that the court would exercise this power.[49] We need not inquire further into these aspects of Raz's outlook. Our focus remains reasons applicable to a private actor in her practical settings, rather than judicial reasoning exercised after the fact. What is worth noting, however, is that the above analysis of judicial response to the case, if assumed *arguendo* to be correct, has problematic implications for the Razian claim we *are* examining: if a judicial decision not to apply the mail-delay prohibition in Jane's case is seen as changing, or departing from, an existing law, it follows that at the actual time of the event we could not say that the prohibition does not cover the case. This, once more, entails that Jane was acting (as she should) on moral reasons that, at least at the time of her action, could not be said to be unexcluded ones. It would not do to assert here that the law was indeterminate in this case. For our case, as was already noted, is a case where there is nothing in the legislative language, circumstances of legislation, and other features of the law, to prompt doubts about the prohibition's applicability. What seems to prompt such doubts, instead, is the (out-of-bounds-to-Raz's-defender) fact that the rule leads to an outcome sharply inconsistent with the balance of reasons.

One further clarification is called for. Raz criticizes 'the unimaginative assumption that either the law is determined by the thoughts actually entertained by the lawmaker when making the law or it must include all the implications of those thoughts'.[50] 'The dichotomy', Raz explains, 'is a false one',[51] for there is a spectrum of possibilities between these two extremes. He further notes that

in fact we often rely on our ideas of what is reasonable in reconstructing other people's thought. But if we are any good at the task, we do so only when we have reason to think those others share our view of what is a reasonable opinion, or a plausible argument.[52]

---

[47] Raz, 'Postema on Law's Autonomy' (n 39) 18.   [48] ibid.   [49] ibid.
[50] Raz, *Ethics in the Public Domain* (n 4) 232.   [51] ibid.
[52] Raz, 'Postema on Law's Autonomy' (n 39) 15.

Raz, therefore, does not think that any interpretation reaching beyond the actual thoughts or explicit pronouncements of legislators must amount to what is simply the interpreter's conviction about the balance of reasons.[53] Do my foregoing arguments rest on any of the assumptions Raz rejects here? No. I have not denied that successful communication (within or outside the legal domain) depends in part on inference of implied meaning, and that the part played by such inference may vary in extent or degree from one communication to another. I have merely contended that, in cases such as Jane's, neither the thoughts actually entertained by legislators, nor any kind of implication of their thoughts or words, indicates that the prohibition does not cover the case, unless we presume that legislators never intend statutory language to lead to injustice or absurd outcomes. Nor have I insisted that utilizing such a presumption amounts to nothing more than a conviction about the balance of reasons, as opposed to an appeal to the balance of reasons made on the basis of a convention of interpretation as part of a genuine attempt to identify the legislature's intention. But if we accept the latter view of the presumption, we must, once more, confront questions about its applicability, such as: what if it was intended to operate merely as a tool of *judicial* interpretation? And, at any rate, even recourse to the balance of reasons in order to infer an intention is recourse to the balance of reasons, which, as such, renders the question of whether a given reason is excluded dependent on an ineligible criterion: its weight.

I now wish to consider briefly the scope-of-exclusion reply as a possible response to what I have called Situation 1.[54] 'Briefly' because this should suffice, I believe, to show that this reply is ill suited in the context of Situation 1. Situation 1, to remind ourselves, differs from Situation 2 in the following respect: while Situation 2 involves a particular contingency where a (usually innocuous) directive points to an objectionable outcome, in Situation 1 the directive itself has morally objectionable content. Initially it should be recalled that Situation 1 will often be the result of negative attributes of the directive-issuer, such as his or her moral depravity, injudiciousness, adherence to an intolerant extremist ideology, or the like.[55] Under such circumstances it is most likely that the directive-issuer fails to meet Raz's conditions of authority, and, if that is the case, the question of the scope of exclusion does not even arise. But these are not the only kind of circumstances under which

---

[53] Raz, *Ethics in the Public Domain* (n 4) 229, 231, 233, 234; Raz, 'Intention in Interpretation' (n 25) 256; Raz, 'Why Interpret?' (n 25) 355.

[54] pp 22–23.

[55] Or the result of obvious defects in the decision-making process, such as the influence of bribery or intoxication.

Situation 1 may occur. As was noted in the previous chapter, it may come to pass, due to the occasional occurrence of an isolated failure, even where Raz's normal justification condition is met and the relevant prerequisites of procedure are satisfied. In such cases, the question might be asked whether the scope-of-exclusion reply could provide a defence for the pre-emption thesis.

Due consideration of this question, however, should make it apparent that the scope-of-exclusion reply is misplaced here. Disobedience in Situation 1 is warranted on account of a flagrant failure of the directive to correctly reflect the moral reasons relevant to the issue it regulates. It is plain, therefore, that the appropriate ground for defying such a directive lies in a conviction about the main moral reasons germane to the regulated issue. And such reasons will come under what Raz calls dependent reasons, which are alleged to be excluded. This may be illustrated by the insurgents' example described in the previous chapter.[56] I supposed there a Situation 1 featuring an order to carry out an artillery attack on two insurgents operating from a civilian apartment block, with the likely outcome of many non-combatant casualties. The order is flouted, as it should be, on the basis of moral reasons connected with the value of human life—reasons to curb the use of military force so as to avoid (or, at least, minimize) harm to civilians. Being among the main moral reasons relevant to operational orders regarding the use of military force, these reasons are surely what Raz calls dependent reasons in respect of such orders, and are thus supposed to fall within the scope of exclusion.

A possible objection: true, it may be said, disobedience in the insurgents' example should be based on reasons not to take the lives of innocent civilians, but my analysis of this example is mistaken in another respect. Even if the order-issuer possesses authority over the relevant domain (national defence, internal security affairs, or the like) and over the subjects in question, this authority encompasses no power to exclude reasons not to take the lives of innocent civilians. Thus, the objection proceeds, when subjects in my example contravene the order, they act for reasons not within the order's scope of exclusion. This objection, however, has an anomalous implication given Raz's demarcation principle for the scope of exclusion. According to Raz, excluded reasons are the reasons that the authority was meant to consider[57] (or, at least, the reasons *against* the prescribed action which the authority was meant to consider).[58] Thus, to submit that reasons not to take the lives of innocent civilians are unexcluded reasons would entail that the order-issuer was

---

[56] pp 39–40.
[57] Raz, 'Facing Up' (n 3) 1194. See also Raz, *Between Authority and Interpretation* (n 3) 7–8 (the body text and fn 7).
[58] Raz, 'The Problem of Authority' (n 6) 1018.

not meant to consider these reasons before issuing an order. This implication is, needless to explain, unacceptable. And its unacceptability is yet another sign that the scope-of-exclusion reply is not a suitable route for reconciling Situation 1 with the pre-emption thesis. If there is a suitable route for this purpose it lies not with the notion that exclusionary reasons have a limited scope, but with the notion that legitimate authority is subject to certain justifying conditions and constraints. The latter notion, however, has been the focus of my analysis in the previous chapter, where it was ultimately found to be incapable of grounding an adequate defence of the pre-emption thesis.

Before bringing this chapter to a close, I wish to consider another attempt to uphold the scope-of-exclusion reply. There is a way to mark out Situations 1 and 2 as cases of action on unexcluded reasons, it might be said, which does not require recourse to the weight of the reasons involved. Instead of recourse to their weight, the argument continues, the scope-demarcating criterion to be relied upon is the distinction between moral and non-moral reasons. On this position, authorities (in a sense that implies legitimacy) generate reasons that exclude *non-moral* reasons—e.g. reasons of self-interest[59]—in conflict with their directives. Authority-given reasons do not, however, exclude moral reasons on this view. When moral reasons come into conflict with authority-given reasons, the conflict should be resolved on the basis of an assessment of their comparative weights. For ease of reference, I will call the above argument the non-moral-scope response. Since Situations 1 and 2 present us with *moral* reasons for disobedience—e.g. reasons not to harm non-combatants through military action or reasons to assist a person in jeopardy—they are, according to the non-moral-scope response, reconcilable with the pre-emption thesis. Now, I will not inquire into possible explanations of why, according to the non-moral-scope response, moral reasons are outside the scope of exclusion. I leave the explanation unspecified, first, because there is more than one explanation that might conceivably be invoked, and, second, because I wish to debunk the non-moral-scope response directly, irrespective of its underlying explanation.

It should first be noted that Raz himself has never used the non-moral-scope response or made a similar claim. In fact, this line of response is incompatible with central tenets of his theory of value and action, and, as such, would be rejected by him. Raz has criticized at length the view that moral considerations form a special subclass or 'a distinct body of considerations which differs from that involved in other areas of practical thought'.[60] There is

---

[59] See comment in n 66.

[60] Joseph Raz, *Engaging Reason: On the Theory of Value and Action* (OUP 1999) 274. See his arguments to this effect in ibid chs 11–12.

no theoretically significant distinction, Raz has argued,[61] between moral and non-moral considerations, no 'divide—epistemological or metaphysical—between moral considerations and values and non-moral ones'.[62] And more recently, in a discussion relating directly to his conception of authority, Raz expressed a similar position, citing for support his previous arguments 'for the theoretical unimportance of the classification of reasons into moral and others'.[63]

But let us, for the sake of the discussion, momentarily ignore Raz's scepticism about the distinction between moral and non-moral reasons. Even so, it remains doubtful that Raz or his followers would resort to the non-moral-scope response. To curtail the scope of exclusion to only non-moral reasons would introduce a significant inroad into that scope—one that is unlikely to be conceded by the Razian. The extent of this inroad may be illustrated by a couple of examples involving reasons for non-compliance that, if the non-moral-scope response were assumed, would fall outside the scope of exclusion. Consider, for example, the case of Rachel, who wishes to evade taxes in order to be able to donate a greater share of her income to needy people in the Third World. Or take the case of Steve, who intends to coercively silence Jack so as to prevent him from making offensive statements he is about to make—statements that, although liable to have adverse consequences which morally ought to be prevented, enjoy legal protection under free speech laws. In such cases the reasons for non-compliance are moral reasons, which, therefore, according to the response under consideration, fall outside the purview of authority and its exclusionary force. Now consider another example: Cynthia, a keen animal rights activist morally committed to preventing the killing of animals for purposes such as meat consumption, decides to disrupt the operation of butchers in her town, which can only be effectively achieved by recourse to unlawful means (e.g. sabotaging their shops). While the moral character of reasons to prevent meat consumption might be subject to disagreement, cases such as this help to uncover the significant potential extent of the limitation we are considering for the scope of exclusion, thus casting further doubt on the thought that Razians would concede such a limitation.

I will offer one further ground for rejecting the non-moral-scope response. The non-moral-scope response, to repeat, contends that (legitimate) authorities generate reasons that exclude non-moral reasons against the prescribed action. A straightforward way of refuting this claim is to find an example where, in a conflict between an authority-given reason and a *non*-moral

---

[61] ibid chs 11–12.   [62] ibid 295.
[63] Joseph Raz, 'On Respect, Authority, and Neutrality: A Response' (2010) 120 Ethics 279, 289.

reason, the latter wins. The scenario depicted in the immediately following text is, I suggest, a case in point. An eccentric billionaire approaches you and offers the following deal. He will pay you one million pounds if you do what he requests,[64] which is that you violate a parking restriction (which, let us assume, was issued by an authority that meets Raz's prerequisites of legitimacy).[65] Any infraction would do, even, say, leaving your car for a few minutes in a manner and place where it poses no physical risk to others. The fact that you would be paid one million pounds for parking in a prohibited place is a reason to do so, but not a *moral* reason (and, let us further assume, nor are your underlying reasons for wanting the money: you want to use it for self-interested purposes that have no positive or negative moral value).[66] And yet it wins the conflict with an authority-given reason, namely the parking restriction. When I say it wins I do not mean that it wins merely as a motivational force that would impel you to park in a prohibited place. I mean that it wins as a reason in a sense that favours and supports the action.[67] To forgo the prize offered by the billionaire in order not to infringe a parking restriction would be plainly irrational and sharply at odds with reason. You would be mad to do so.[68] We seem, then, to be facing a counterexample to the non-moral-scope response.

---

[64] The description thus far might evoke Gregory Kavka's example known as 'the toxin puzzle', but the rest of the scenario bears no resemblance or relation to the toxin puzzle.

[65] Why is he making such an offer? For reasons immaterial to our purpose. Maybe he has a keen interest in law and psychology, and wishes to empirically verify the limits of law-abiding attitudes. Or maybe he just has an inexplicable urge to do so. None of this bears on the point and significance of the example.

[66] It is true that on some moral theories, such as act-utilitarianism, your self-interested use of the money may have moral value due to its contribution to happiness (in this case your own). But it would be odd if proponents of the non-moral-scope response would adopt such a moral theory, because their position would then imply that authority does not exclude self-interested reasons—and if authority does not exclude even self-interested reasons, it is not clear which reasons it does exclude.

[67] I put aside the question of whether an authority-given reason such as the parking restriction is a moral reason. This question is immaterial to my point. If my opponent considers it to be a moral reason, he or she will have to acknowledge, on pain of absurdity, that it is a moral reason which loses in the conflict against an offer of one million pounds. Of course, such a position would imply that moral reasons (or at least some moral reasons) do not always win against non-moral reasons in determining what we most reason to do—which is not an implausible proposition, though a contested one. For a relevant and relatively recent edited collection, see Sebastian Schleidgen (ed), *Should We Always Act Morally? Essays on Overridingness* (Tectum 2012). See also, e.g., Philippa Foot, 'Are Moral Considerations Overriding?' in her *Virtues and Vices* (Clarendon Press 2002) ch XIII; Sarah Stroud, 'Moral Overridingness and Moral Theory' (1998) 79 Pacific Philosophical Quarterly 170; Douglas W Portmore, 'Are Moral Reasons Morally Overriding?' (2008) 11 Ethical Theory and Moral Practice 369; Alfred Archer, 'Moral Rationalism without Overridingness' (2014) 27 Ratio 100. I do not and need not adopt here any position on this issue.

[68] Unless, perhaps, your particular circumstances, goals, projects, needs, or ultimate desires are such that (contrary to what I assumed above) additional funds would be of no use for you. Even so, however, the example would apply to the many individuals for whom that is not the case.

My adversary could not respond to this example by saying that even non-moral reasons sometimes fall outside the scope of exclusion, and that this is the case with the reason given by an offer of a million pounds for infringing a parking restriction. For the difference between this reason and, say, the reason given by an offer of *five pounds* (which the adversary would surely regard as an excluded reason) is merely a difference in degree, or, in the terminology we have been using, a difference of weight. Nor could my adversary fend off the example by proposing to adopt a narrow definition of 'reasons' which encompasses only moral considerations, while asserting that non-moral considerations—such as the monetary incentive in question—are mere motivational forces, not reasons. Apart from being an unwarrantedly and unconventionally narrow conception of 'reasons', it is a conception unavailable to my adversary since the very claim he or she is trying to defend— the non-moral-scope response—presupposes a distinction between moral and non-moral reasons.

My primary observations in this chapter can be summed up as follows: in at least some of the cases labelled here Situations 1 and 2, the reasons that justify disobedience are either reasons that would fall within the scope of exclusion if the pre-emption thesis were correct, or reasons that cannot be marked out as unexcluded reasons without relying on demarcation criteria inconsistent with the pre-emption thesis itself. At this point, not only this chapter but also the larger critical exercise that comprises this part of the book can be brought to a close. If I am right to make the observations I have made in this part of the book, neither the no-authority reply nor the scope-of-exclusion reply adequately reconciles the pre-emption thesis with the justified disobedience situations discussed here.[69] And since no other route of reconciliation is available for the pre-emption thesis, my analysis calls for its rejection.

---

[69] Nor does the combined effect of the no-authority and scope-of-exclusion replies square those situations with the pre-emption thesis, for, as can be seen from the analysis in this part, there are Situations 1 and 2 in which neither of these replies affords a defence to the thesis (either because they are inapplicable or because they cannot be adequately upheld).

PART II

A CRITICAL EXAMINATION OF THE WEIGHING MODEL

Introduction to Part II

The situations considered in Part I do not merely show the pre-emption thesis to be inadequate. They also lend some credence to the antithetical model, the weighing model, which seems well suited to account for them. But those situations do not exhaust the range of phenomena that a theoretical model should be able to explain in our context; nor do they reveal the full array of considerations that such a model should successfully reflect. The question remains, then, whether the weighing model adequately explains law's potential bearing on our practical reasons. This is the focal question of this part of the book.

The discussion in this part will proceed by reference to two principal Razian arguments against the weighing model which, I believe, can beneficially inform this inquiry: an argument about the phenomenology associated with authority (hereafter: *the phenomenological argument*) and an argument about the function of authority (hereafter: *the functional argument*). It should be clarified immediately that these two arguments do not merely oppose the weighing model but also endorse the pre-emption thesis—and, to this extent, the pre-emption thesis will continue to feature in this part of the book. By discussing these arguments, however, I do not intend to detract or withdraw from my earlier criticism of the pre-emption thesis. There need not be a contradiction between my earlier criticism and the potential benefits of discussing the aforementioned pair of arguments. For a theoretical model that suffers from certain flaws, and even critical ones, may nonetheless capture or highlight some elements of truth about its explanandum. It is primarily this possibility that warrants consideration of a *variety* of arguments for and against the competing models in question. Also noteworthy here is the possibility that this variety of arguments will show that *both* models ought to be rejected. Such a conclusion would not be anomalous. It would only imply that the answer to our conundrum should be sought in the form of an alternative model.

But since it is nonetheless the weighing model that will constitute my main subject of inquiry in this part, it may be useful briefly to restate its core principles at this point.[1] According to this model, law's modus operandi in the domain of practical reasons is best understood in terms of normative weight. The model does *not* suggest that the reasons for or against compliance with a legal requirement necessarily or normally boil down to the balance of reasons that pre-existed the enactment. The enactment of a legal requirement—at least when certain moral and other prerequisites of competence are met by the enacting institution or individuals—may change the normative picture in virtue of some beneficial attributes attached to the operation of the relevant institution or individual lawmakers.[2] These may include, for example, epistemic advantages gained through reliance on expert advice or through close acquaintance with relevant policy considerations, or other advantages such as the capacity to help solve problems of social coordination, if and insofar as these attributes are actually possessed by the relevant institution or individuals. But, once more, the normative significance of such attributes is explained by this model in terms of comparative weight, not in exclusionary terms. Take, for example, a lawmaker in possession of more information than a subject has about the matter regulated. This, according to the weighing model, is not a reason for the subject to take no account whatsoever of information she has about the applicable background reasons. Rather, it only provides the subject with a reason to regard the case for doing what the law requires as weightier than it would have seemed to her in the absence of a legal requirement.[3] Or, to take another example, when social coordination is desirable and the law is comparatively well placed to facilitate it, this is a reason for us to comply with the law.[4] However, the value of our actions normally does not lie exclusively in whether or not they are well coordinated with the actions of

---

[1] See pp 15–17 for a fuller description of this model.

[2] Attributes whose normative significance enjoys some (relative) independence of the content of the particular requirement at hand, in a sense that I have elsewhere called 'weak content-independence' (Noam Gur, 'Are Legal Rules Content-Independent Reasons?' (2011) 5 Problema 175, 178–83). See more generally on content-independent reasons: Paul Markwick, 'Law and Content-Independent Reasons' (2000) 20 Oxford Journal of Legal Studies 579; Paul Markwick, 'Independent of Content' (2003) 9 Legal Theory 43; Stefan Sciaraffa, 'On Content-Independent Reasons: It's Not in the Name' (2009) 28 Law and Philosophy 233; NP Adams, 'In Defence of Content-Independence' (2017) 23 Legal Theory 143.

[3] See Donald H Regan, 'Authority and Value: Reflections on Raz's Morality of Freedom' (1989) 62 Southern California Law Review 995, 1004–18, 1086–95; Heidi M Hurd, 'Challenging Authority' (1991) 100 Yale Law Journal 1611, 1667–77.

[4] See Regan (n 3) 1025–31.

others—coordination reasons may conflict with other reasons. What is more, laws that are generally conducive to coordination may, on occasion, fail to serve, or even contravene, that very goal. Thus, the weighing model contends that reasons associated with the coordinative role of law should be considered along with, and at times compete against, all other relevant reasons for action. It may be true, according to the weighing model, that reasons to comply with the law—whether epistemic, coordinative, or other—are reasons of substantial weight. But 'substantial weight' is one thing and 'power to exclude other reasons' is another—and the weighing model categorically rejects the latter.[5]

---

[5] See, e.g., Richard E Flathman, *The Practice of Political Authority: Authority and the Authoritative* (University of Chicago Press 1980) 111–12, 191; Laurence Claus, *Law's Evolution and Human Understanding* (OUP 2012) 65.

5

The Phenomenological Argument

Phenomenological arguments focus on the way things—e.g. objects, events, or abstract notions—feature (appear, manifest themselves, or the like) in human experience.[1] Such arguments will be employed here in a specific manner instrumental to the purposes of this inquiry. Their invocation should not be taken to express a commitment to the philosophical movement known as phenomenology; nor is it meant to confine the outlook of this inquiry to phenomenological arguments alone. What exactly is the role of phenomenological arguments in the context of this inquiry, then? We may start with the way Raz uses this type of argument. He describes his phenomenological argument as 'an argument about features of our concepts, based on the way they function in our discourse and thought'.[2] When Raz discusses the way authoritative directives typically figure in people's experience, therefore, his purpose is to elucidate the *concepts* of authority and authoritative directives.[3] In particular, he seeks to illustrate in this way that the concepts of authority and authoritative directives are bound up with the type of reasons he calls pre-emptive reasons, as distinct from first-order reasons that merely compete in weight with others.[4]

Now, my own objectives are somewhat different from Raz's. I do not take the explanation of concepts to be one of my primary objectives in this inquiry. My primary concern here lies in the normative question of what kind of practical reasons the law can provide us with (when it meets certain justificatory prerequisites).[5] Can phenomenological arguments contribute to a discussion of this normative question? I think they can, even if indirectly and

---

[1] Michael Hammond, Jane Howarth, and Russell Keat, *Understanding Phenomenology* (Basil Blackwell 1991) 1; Dermot Moran, *Introduction to Phenomenology* (Routledge 2000) 4; Robert Sokolowski, *Introduction to Phenomenology* (CUP 2000) 2.

[2] Joseph Raz, 'Facing Up: A Reply' (1989) 62 Southern California Law Review 1153, 1165.

[3] See ibid.

[4] But note again: by claiming that authoritative directives are pre-emptive reasons, Raz means to say that they are both first-order reasons and exclusionary, second-order reasons (see, e.g., Joseph Raz, *Practical Reason and Norms* (2nd edn, Princeton University Press 1990) 42).

[5] This is not to suggest that all of Raz's arguments about authority are concerned with the explanation of its concept. Some of his arguments regarding authority are normatively evaluative. These

Legal Directives and Practical Reasons. Noam Gur. © Noam Gur 2018. Published 2018 by Oxford University Press.

only provisionally. The authority-related 'features of our concepts' highlighted by the phenomenological argument are some foundational and long-standing elements of our relevant system of concepts that seem to have gained currency in a variety of cultures and social contexts. As such, they are not likely to be the mere product of chance or the personal whim of this or that individual. Indeed, it would not be implausible to conjecture that their development has occurred in a manner that is at least partly sensitive to common human needs; and that, insofar as they are the product of such a process, those elements of our conceptual apparatus are likely to be such that they enable and facilitate the performance of essential functions of authorities in social life (whether or not they also have certain negative by-products that should be taken into account in our final analysis). At any rate, those conceptual elements, as reflected in our phenomenology, can give us some cue regarding relevant candidate solutions to the normative question at hand. Their cue is merely provisional because they cannot ultimately resolve the normative question at hand and should not be regarded as a substitute for evaluative arguments. But, insofar as we can identify widespread phenomenological patterns in relation to authoritative institutions which have endured through the practical test of real life in society, it would seem ill-advised simply to disregard the indicative help they can offer, certainly in a field of inquiry as difficult and uncertain as the present one.[6]

5.1. The Phenomenological Argument Presented

Raz's phenomenological argument centres on people's characteristic experience when confronted with (what they take to be) an authoritative directive which fails to comport with relevant reasons for action. Raz advances this argument by reference to an example, which I will now briefly describe. The example features a soldier, Jeremy, whose superiors in the army order him to appropriate a van owned by a tradesman and to use it for some military purpose.[7] Jeremy believes that the balance of reasons favours non-compliance with the order.[8] The van is in fact not essential to the successful performance of the relevant task, and appropriating it would cause undue loss to the tradesman.[9] No one would discover that Jeremy made no use of the van, so

aspects of his account have been more focally relevant to Part I, and will be discussed from another angle—i.e. with a focus on the beneficial function of authorities—in ch 6.

[6] Raz notes that his phenomenological argument is not 'an argument that the common experience of people is evidence of the structure of real moral reasons' (Raz, 'Facing Up' (n 2) 1165). But this does not in any way prevent one from using the phenomenological argument in the way it is used here.

[7] Raz, *Practical Reason and Norms* (n 4) 38, 41.   [8] ibid 41.   [9] ibid 41–42.

there is no danger that his disobedience would undermine the authority of his commanders in the eyes of other soldiers.[10] Nevertheless, he thinks that, as a soldier, he generally ought to obey the orders of his commanders, including this one. Raz describes this line of reasoning as follows:

[Jeremy's] friend urges him to disobey the order pointing to weighty reasons for doing so. Jeremy does not deny that his friend may have a case. But, he claims, it does not matter whether he is right or not. Orders are orders and should be obeyed even if wrong, even if no harm will come from disobeying them. That is what it means to be a subordinate. It means that it is not for you to decide what is best. You may see that on the balance of reasons one course of action is right and yet be justified in not following it. The order is a reason for doing what you were ordered regardless of the balance of reasons. He admits that if he were told to commit an atrocity he should refuse. But his is an ordinary case, he thinks, and the order should prevail. It may be that Jeremy is wrong in accepting the authority of his commanders in this case. But is he not right on the nature of authority?[11]

The best way to explain Jeremy's argument is by saying that he regards his commander's order as both a first-order and an exclusionary reason. It is for him a reason for appropriating the van and for not acting on certain first-order reasons which apply to the case and which but for the exclusionary reason would have entailed that he ought not to appropriate the van.[12]

Immediately after this passage, Raz contrasts the weighing model with the way Jeremy understands his situation: we cannot say that Jeremy regards the order 'solely as a (first-order) reason to which he assigns a weight sufficient to override the other conflicting reasons'.[13] The fact that he was commanded to appropriate the van does not in his view mean simply that yet another reason is added to the balance. His understanding (which, Raz stresses, is not an untypical one) is that it is no longer for him to act on a complete assessment of the reasons for and against the action. His personal view on the case, he believes, should no longer influence his action, because, given that an order was issued, all or most of the other reasons are to be excluded from the set of factors that determine his action.[14]

Another relevant phenomenological feature comes into view when Raz introduces the following modification to Jeremy's example. Jeremy delegates the task to one of his subordinates, Dick. He instructs Dick to appropriate the van. Dick comes to the conclusion that doing so would be incompatible with the balance of reasons, and disobeys.[15] When Jeremy learns that his order was disobeyed he finds himself torn between two

---

[10] ibid 42.   [11] ibid 38.   [12] ibid 42.
[13] ibid.   [14] ibid.   [15] ibid 43.

feelings. On the one hand, he wants to blame Dick for failing to comply with the order. On the other hand, he recognizes that what Dick did was right on its merits, and for this he seems to be worthy of praise. In some form and degree, such mixed feelings may have been part of Jeremy's experience when he himself followed the order to appropriate the van (whether by assigning the task to his subordinate or, in the original scenario, by performing it on his own).[16]

The ambivalence felt in these situations, says Raz, suggests that there exist two different ways of assessing the matter, and that although only one of them should be followed, there is a sense in which both retain their autonomous existence.[17] This ambivalence can hardly be accounted for by the thesis that all relevant reasons should be weighed on one level of assessment. When a person fails to act on the weightier of two competing reasons we may criticize her or, perhaps, identify some extenuating circumstances, but we do not feel torn in the same way.[18] What is needed in order to capture the complexity of our experience in conflicts between authoritative directives and other reasons, according to Raz, is a two-level model of reasons, whereby reasons of one level have the power to exclude reasons of the other from determining our actions, without invalidating those reasons. This way we can both accept that one assessment is subordinate to the other and still treat it as having a certain autonomy such that it is not simply cancelled by the other.[19] The distinction between first-order reasons for action and second-order exclusionary reasons constitutes precisely such a model.[20]

So much for introducing the phenomenological argument. My discussion of this argument will consist of two parts correlating to the two phenomenological features described above. I will start with the latter, that is, with the way in which Jeremy feels drawn by the forces of two conflicting assessments at the same time, and will then turn to the former, namely, the way in which he takes himself to be bound by the order only because it emanates from an authority and despite his contrary judgement of the action on its merits.[21]

---

[16] See ibid 41, 45.   [17] ibid 43, 45.   [18] ibid 43.   [19] ibid.

[20] ibid 44. See also ibid 74–75. As will be seen on pp 81–82, Raz makes a later concession that can be understood as a withdrawal from the claim described in the last paragraph. But I will nonetheless consider this claim, partly because I am uncertain whether his later concession amounts to a complete withdrawal from it or a mere acknowledgment that the phenomenology of 'conflicting assessments' carries limited probative significance.

[21] In one place Raz points out that his phenomenological argument includes, in addition to the feeling of ambivalence, two other phenomenological features (Raz, 'Facing Up' (n 2) 1165). Both additional features he mentions are, I think, encompassed by what will be referred to here as a belief or sense that one is bound by the authority's directives.

5.2. The Phenomenological Argument Considered

5.2.1. The Experience of Conflicting Assessments

The argument from the experience of conflicting assessments has been questioned by a number of Raz's critics.[22] Chaim Gans and Michael Moore, for example, have both argued that the phenomenon of ambivalence generated by conflicts of reasons is not coextensive with conflicts of reasons that (according to Raz) involve an exclusionary reason, such as conflicts involving mandatory rules, promises, or decisions.[23] Thus, they suggest, there is a lack of correlation between the evidence invoked (i.e. the phenomenon of ambivalence arising from conflicts between reasons) and that which it is meant to be evidence for (i.e. the notion of exclusionary reasons). From this they conclude that the phenomenology of conflicting assessments lacks the probative force Raz seems to ascribe to it in his arguments cited above: it does not show that one of the conflicting reasons involved is treated as an exclusionary reason.[24]

The alleged miscorrelations are two. First, according to Gans, there exist conflicts between rules and reasons where people are not likely to feel torn about their choice.[25] This, if true, means that the phenomenon of ambivalence is under-inclusive evidence for Raz's purpose. Two types of conflict are mentioned as cases in point. The first arises when the course of action prescribed by a rule fails to comport with background reasons, but the stakes, one way or another, are very low, in the sense that our choice whether to comply with the rule or not would hardly have any significant and tangible consequences.[26] I have doubts as to whether this example of Gans's successfully bears out his argument. It may be true that when the stakes are very low we are not likely to find people pondering for long over the choice of whether or not to comply, or feeling seriously torn about it. But either compliance or non-compliance in such circumstances may involve a certain degree of uneasiness. On the one

---

[22] Chaim Gans, 'Mandatory Rules and Exclusionary Reasons' (1986) 15 Philosophia 373, 387–90; Michael S Moore, 'Authority, Law, and Razian Reasons' (1989) 62 Southern California Law Review 827, 860–63. See also William A Edmundson, 'Rethinking Exclusionary Reasons: A Second Edition of Joseph Raz's "Practical Reason and Norms"' (1993) 12 Law and Philosophy 329, 334–35; Christian Piller, 'Kinds of Practical Reasons: Attitude-Related Reasons and Exclusionary Reasons' in Sofia Miguens, João Alberto Pinto, and Carlos E Mauro (eds), *Analyses* (Porto University 2006) 98–105, at 103–04.

[23] Gans (n 22) 387–90; Moore (n 22) 860–63.

[24] Gans goes on to argue that the phenomenology of feeling torn and uneasy about certain practical conflicts is explicable, instead, by facts such as the importance of the issue at stake, the strength of reasons for each of the alternatives in conflict, and their incommensurability (Gans (n 22) 389–90). A similar observation is made by Moore (Moore (n 22) 860–63).

[25] Gans (n 22) 388–89.   [26] ibid 388.

hand, one may feel slightly awkward when performing an act of compliance that serves no tangible rationale. On the other hand, some people are generally inclined to follow rules of conduct and required procedures which they recognize as applicable, and may therefore feel a certain (if small and short-lasting) unease or embarrassment about the fact of breaking such a rule or departing from such a procedure, even when there is little or no substantive reason to follow it in the case.

The second type of conflict mentioned by Gans involves cases where there is a marked disparity of strength between the opposing reasons, namely the reason provided by a rule and the reason against following the rule.[27] An example furnished is of a conflict between a rule of etiquette and the saving of a life:[28] Smith omits to tip his hat when passing two ladies of his acquaintance (a courtesy required by an etiquette rule he accepts and regularly follows) as he dashes to rescue another person in jeopardy. We would think something was wrong with Smith if he felt awkward after this omission. Yet, the conflict Smith faces is a conflict between a reason in its first-order force (i.e. saving life) and a rule of etiquette which he accepts, that is, according to Raz, an exclusionary reason.[29]

As Gans notes, a likely response of the Razian is that the exclusionary force of the rule is not at work in the above example, since the reasons for the actor's rush are not within the rule's scope of exclusion. Given the phenomenological focus of this discussion, an initial question relevant for assessing this Razian response is: do actors in scenarios such as the above characteristically *experience* their action as one that comes under an exception to the rule and is thus not within its scope (rather than as an action that, at the time of its performance, justifiably contravenes the rule)? If the answer is positive, a second question ensues: can actors determine that their action falls outside the scope of the rule on grounds that are themselves compatible with the pre-emption thesis (i.e. without recourse to the weight of reasons underlying the rule)? A negative answer to this (or the previous) question would be detrimental to the foregoing Razian defence. The first question will not be discussed here, partly because the second has already been answered negatively in Chapter 4, where I have rejected the scope-of-exclusion reply.[30] Those who find the scope-of-exclusion reply persuasive, however, may insist that Raz's account sustains no damage from Gans's hat-tipping example.

But there is, as noted earlier, a second claimed miscorrelation, and it is one that, I think, Razians would find harder to deny. The phenomenology of

---

[27] ibid.   [28] ibid 389.   [29] ibid 389.   [30] Consistently with Gans's view (ibid).

ambivalence, it is argued, is also *over*-inclusive evidence for Raz's purpose: we sometimes feel torn between alternative courses of action which pit against each other reasons that Raz considers to be first-order reasons. When a first-order reason is outweighed by another it may continue to exert some force upon us even after we have opted for doing what is indicated by another, stronger reason, and, if both reasons are important enough and not easily commensurable, we may feel uneasy whenever we look back at the choice we had to make.[31] Gans and Moore illustrate this point by an example originating with Jean-Paul Sartre.[32] Sartre tells us about a student who, at some time during World War II, sought his advice on the following dilemma. The student is keen to join the Free French Forces and fight the Germans. However, this would mean leaving behind his mother who, estranged from his father and bereaved of her older son (who has died in the war), finds her only consolation in him. The young Frenchman is torn between the pulling forces of, on the one hand, his reasons for wishing to join the fighting forces and, on the other hand, his concern for his mother.[33] Each type of reason retains a certain autonomy in the sense that it is not simply cancelled by the other type. And each of them may continue to make its weight felt whichever way he will eventually choose to go. Yet neither would be considered by Raz to be a second-order reason.[34]

Following the above critiques, Raz reviews (or clarifies) his argument. Referring to Moore's observation that the experience of conflicting assessments can be accounted for without recourse to the notion of exclusionary reasons, Raz states:

Moore's criticism concentrates on my invocation of perceptions of conflicting assessments of what we ought to do. He rightly points out that there could be other explanations of such conflicting assessments. However, he largely disregards two other features of our self-understanding which I relied on. These features are not explicable as the expression of perceived conflicts of reasons. As I mentioned, they are characteristic of certain situations only and are entirely absent from ordinary conflicts of reasons.[35]

He adds:

I wrongly said that the presence of conflicting assessments alone can be decisive proof of the belief in reasons which should be understood as exclusionary ones.[36]

---

[31] See Piller (n 22) 103–04.
[32] Gans (n 22) 387–88; Moore (n 22) 861. See Jean-Paul Sartre, *Essays in Existentialism* (The Citadel Press 1965) 42–43. For other examples, see Tim Dare, 'Raz, Exclusionary Reasons, and Legal Positivism' (1989) 8 Eidos 11, 28.
[33] Sartre (n 32) 42–43.   [34] Gans (n 22) 387–88; Moore (n 22) 861.
[35] Raz, 'Facing Up' (n 2) 1165.   [36] ibid fn 21.

I am less than certain whether this concession means that Raz no longer relies on the phenomenology of conflicting assessments or merely that he accords it limited probative significance. Even if the former alternative is assumed, however, the concession does not signify a general retreat from his phenomenological argument. For the argument, as the former quotation reminds us, includes other phenomenological features, to which I now turn.[37]

5.2.2. Bound by Authority

According to the weighing model, when faced with the requirements of a legal authority,[38] subjects should decide how to act by recourse to the balance of reasons for action as applicable in the situation at hand. Raz is right to argue that this idea is at odds with some dominant features of our phenomenology with regard to authority and its requirements. The weighing model depicts situations of action under authoritative requirements as situations in which it is open to us to act on our own assessment of the balance of reasons applicable in the case (including reasons for action which may have entered the balance as a result of the issuance of a requirement). In fact, however, when we recognize that an authoritative requirement applies to us, there is, characteristically, a sense in which we think that it is no longer for us to decide what the best course of action is. The acknowledgement that someone has authority over us, in other words, characteristically involves the thought or implicit belief that we are, in some sense, bound by his or her directives.[39] The sense of bindingness involved in such situations is implicit in the very idea of *authority* and is manifest in the vocabulary often employed in connection with it:[40] it would make little or no sense to use in this context words with hierarchical or mandatory connotations such as subject, superior, subordinate, preside over,

---

[37] See clarification made in n 21.

[38] It should be noted that some weighing-model proponents believe that the law can never have *legitimate* authority. They are philosophical anarchists of the a priori type (but I will call them, for brevity, philosophical anarchists). Should philosophical anarchists have any interest in arguments about the phenomenology of authority? I believe they should have at least *some* interest in these arguments, for the following two-step consideration: first, even philosophical anarchists should find it hard to deny that authority is *phenomenologically* relevant to law, in that it is closely intertwined with ordinary experience and conceptions of the law; and, second, if phenomenology has the indicative (if weakly indicative) relevance I claimed it has for this inquiry (pp 75–76), it seems that even philosophical anarchists would be advised to at least take notice of it.

[39] This normative sense of bindingness often coincides with the fear of sanction for disobedience, but the two are conceptually distinguishable and need not, practically speaking, appear in tandem.

[40] To be more precise, I refer here specifically to authority in the practical sense, as distinct from the merely theoretical sense which we invoke when describing someone as an authority on, say, early medieval history or quantum mechanics.

govern, orders, commands, and punishment if our conceptions of authority were truly compatible with the weighing model.

This, I think, is part of what Raz seeks to illustrate through his example of Jeremy, the soldier. Consider the way Jeremy responds to his friend's suggestion to contravene the relevant order. He does not reply by enumerating the reasons for and against performance of the prescribed act as they apply to the case at hand, comparing their weight and deriving from this weight comparison a practical conclusion. In fact, he believes that such an assessment would not support following the order. So why does he not accept his friend's suggestion to contravene it? His reply is quite simple: he refers to the binding effect of the order qua (a valid) order. And even if his first-order assessment were different than it is—say, if he did fear that disobedience on his part would be discovered and cause disorder in the unit—his reply could well be the same reply, which, instead of entering a discussion of those first-order factors, simply invokes the binding nature of the order. Note that it is not suggested here (nor does Raz suggest) that people always respond in the way Jeremy does. Rather, the argument is that Jeremy's line of reasoning is fairly typical among people in his position and that many of us are well acquainted with it.

These features of the experience of acting under authorities have been given, I believe, insufficient attention, qua phenomenological features, by Raz's critics. And some critics who have engaged with them have not, to my mind, done so satisfactorily. Consider, for instance, the following comment by Richard Flathman:

Raz ... [gives the example of] an order, validly issued by a commanding officer, requiring a soldier (Jeremy) to perform an action that Jeremy judges unjustified by the balance of 'primary' reasons ... Jeremy nevertheless decides that he ought to obey the order.

Raz rightly says that Jeremy's resolution of his problem is quite typical. But does that resolution reflect an (at least implicit) recognition of the distinction between primary and exclusionary rules [*sic*]? Clearly Jeremy makes the command the decisive factor in reaching his decision. But does this show that the commander's order is something other than a primary reason which Jeremy judges to outweigh the primary reasons against the action? Raz's first move is simply to assert that interpreting the order as a primary reason to which decisive weight has been accorded would be to disregard 'Jeremy's own conception of the situation [Flathman continues to quote Raz here].' Needless to say, this assertion (concerning an example of Raz's own construction) does nothing to establish the distinction for which Raz is contending. Thus far, decisions such as Jeremy's could perfectly well be explained as resting on the view that the orders of commanding officers should be obeyed because the primary reasons for maintaining authority are so strong that they are virtually always decisive or because the commander is a recognised *an* authority [i.e. in the sense of being an expert] on the subject matter of the action and hence his judgements can be counted on to give a correct assessment of the balance of primary reasons.[41]

Flathman's criticism seems to be unwarranted for a number of reasons. To start with, he appears to place an emphasis on 'Jeremy's resolution'—that is, the bottom line of his thought process, his eventual answer to the question, 'how should I act?'—rather than Jeremy's conception of *why* he acts the way he does. Raz's claim regarding Jeremy is, by contrast, focused more on the latter aspect, as one expects of a phenomenological claim. When Flathman does refer to Jeremy's reasoning process he says that Jeremy 'decides that he ought to obey the order'. But in what sense does Jeremy see himself as *deciding* this? In a very specific sense: he *regards himself as being under a duty* to obey—this is an inference he derives directly from the fact of his being a soldier in his position (in Raz's words: 'He interprets his position in the army as entailing that he has to obey';[42] 'That is what it means to be a subordinate'[43]). By overlooking these features of Jeremy's reasoning, Flathman's description of the situation does little to bring out the particular mode of reasoning Jeremy is engaged in.

   In the rest of the quoted passage it becomes clear that the issue is not merely one of semantics. Flathman seems to believe that the notion of having a duty to obey the commander is reconcilable with the notion that 'the commander's order is ... a primary reason which Jeremy judges to out-weigh the primary reasons against the action'.[44] These two notions can be reconciled, he supposes, once allowance is made for another assumption: that the primary reasons for following the commander 'are so strong that they are virtually always decisive'.[45] However, the difference between a belief that one has a strong primary reason for action and a belief that one has a duty to obey is a *qualitative* difference, and, as such, cannot be smoothed over through a quantitative assumption as to how strong a given reason is. If having a duty to obey were to imply that one ought to follow an order only if the reasons for doing so outweigh reasons to the contrary, it would be qualitatively similar to notions such as following a piece of advice or complying with a request.[46] When we act in accordance with a piece of

---

[41] Richard E Flathman, *The Practice of Political Authority: Authority and the Authoritative* (University of Chicago Press 1980) 111–12.
[42] Raz, *Practical Reason and Norms* (n 4) 42.   [43] ibid 38.
[44] Flathman (n 41) 111.   [45] ibid.
[46] See related comments in Raz, *Practical Reason and Norms* (n 4) 82–84 and Joseph Raz, *The Authority of Law: Essays on Law and Morality* (2nd edn, OUP 2009) 13–15. See contra: Gans (n 22) 377–79, 381. But there is arguably also a conceptual feature shared by authoritative directives and requests, and absent in the case of advice. The utterer of an authoritative directive or a request

advice or a request, we typically understand our action as being conditional on how we judge the pros and cons of what is advised or requested.[47] When referring to these modes of action, however, we do not normally make use of terms such as 'duty' or 'to obey'. We do not normally make statements such as 'Richard is under a duty to obey his neighbour's advice/requests' or 'Claire obeyed her friend's advice/request'.[48] This is precisely because the notions of advice and request—and the mode of action associated with them, namely action on the balance of reasons—do not partake of the mandatory and binding nature of authoritative requirements.

One may, of course, point at some *moral* difficulties that the notion of a duty to obey authority arguably involves.[49] However, the moral difficulties involved in this notion, real as they may be, do not change its existing meaning in common discourse and thought. Another theorist whose arguments can be seen partly as a reaction to the difficulties surrounding the notion of obedience is Donald Regan.[50] Regan, unlike Flathman, correctly construes the meaning of obedience, but his way around the problem is to suggest (if tentatively) that we should 'dispense with the language of "obedience" … '.[51] However, removing the terminology of obedience from our academic texts would not lessen the theoretical significance of the facts that this terminology exists in common language, appears in our dictionaries, and is ordinarily utilized in connection with the experience of action under authority. One of the working premises adopted and explained at the outset of this chapter is that phenomenological findings have some indicative value for the purpose of our inquiry. If I was right to adopt that premise, we have no warrant simply to

---

typically intends her utterance to be taken as a reason for action in itself, whereas an adviser, it may be argued, typically only intends his advice to be regarded 'as a reason to believe that what he says is true, correct or justified' (Raz, *The Authority of Law* (n 46) 14).

[47] Which is not to say that we take no account of the adviser's expertise and wisdom, or that we accord no weight to the very fact that a request has been made.

[48] To say that authoritative directives are intended to be (or are perceived as) weightier reasons than requests would not only fail to capture the qualitative difference between them, but would also seem untrue in at least some instances (see Raz, *The Authority of Law* (n 46) 15). Compare, for example, a request such as the last wish of a close relative with an authoritative directive such as a parking restriction. A similar point could be made, *mutatis mutandis*, as to the relation between authoritative directives and advice.

[49] Such as the difficulty to reconcile it with our moral autonomy and responsibility as individual agents. And Flathman is concerned to show that his understandings of authority and agency offer a solution to such difficulties (see, e.g., Flathman (n 41) 8–9, 124–25, 177–91).

[50] Donald H Regan, 'Authority and Value: Reflections on Raz's Morality of Freedom' (1989) 62 Southern California Law Review 995, 1020, 1029–31; Donald H Regan, 'Reasons, Authority, and the Meaning of "Obey": Further Thoughts on Raz and Obedience to Law' (1990) 30 Canadian Journal of Law and Jurisprudence 3, 14–22.

[51] Regan, 'Authority and Value' (n 50) 1020. See further: ibid 1029–31; Regan, 'Reasons' (n 50) 14–22.

disregard the fact that the notion of obedience figures widely in people's experience vis-à-vis authority.

Do these observations hold good for the context of law? Do they apply, in other words, to *legal* authority? From the fact that authorities are characteristically experienced by their subjects as a source of binding requirements, it does not necessarily follow that this experience shows itself in an equally salient, frequent, or clear fashion with regard to legal authorities. But it is plausible that *some* manifestations of this experience will be found in the context of law, and, since the operation of law is closely intertwined with the idea of authority, those manifestations are not likely to be insignificant. Before looking at such manifestations, however, a note of caution is called for to forestall confusion between our current, phenomenological focus and another avenue of inquiry not pursued at this point: namely, an empirical inquiry into the causes of people's behaviour. Our current concern is not with the empirical question of whether and to what extent citizens obey the law qua law or authority, as distinct from merely acting in conformity with the law for other, moral or prudential reasons. The latter question is subject to a debate that will be discussed at a later point in this book.[52] Our current focus remains phenomenological: people's conscious experience and self-perception.

The first thing to note is that weighing up reasons for action does not seem to be a salient feature of the common experience associated with our response to rules of law in the ordinary run of cases. Think about the various actions you performed in compliance with legal rules in the last few days. They are likely to be multiple. Some you would probably have performed even if they were not legally required—such as paying the supermarket cashier for your groceries—and others you would possibly have not performed in the absence of a legal requirement—such as driving on the left side of the road, stopping your car when faced with a red traffic light, parking only in certain designated zones, refraining from smoking in pubs, restaurants, or public buildings, complying with workplace safety standards required by the law, and so on. In how many of these situations do you remember yourself weighing up reasons for action prior to your act of compliance? If in any, they are probably very few. Compliance in such situations is normally a matter of course—it is habitual.[53] Even if it is preceded by some cursory evaluation of the prescribed

[52] See pp 184–92, where I will discuss, inter alia, the notable study reported in Tom R Tyler, *Why People Obey the Law* (with a new afterword by the author, Princeton University Press 2006), as well as counter-arguments recently made in Laurence Claus, *Law's Evolution and Human Understanding* (OUP 2012) 65–70 and Frederick Schauer, *The Force of Law* (Harvard University Press 2015) 57–67, 73–74.

[53] In ch 2, it was stressed that the merits of an action may be part of the reasons for which an agent performs it even where they are not consciously deliberated or thoroughly contemplated.

action, this is an evaluation that hardly leaves a trace in our conscious experience, and therefore lacks phenomenological salience.

To speak of compliance as habitual, however, is not to reduce it to a *mere* habit, similar to, say, a routine of going for walks every evening or inviting friends over for dinner every second week.[54] Normally at least some members of society—who form more than a negligible or insignificant segment thereof—regard themselves as doing something more than following a mere habit when complying with its laws.[55] They see themselves as engaged in a practice of following rules that they accept as valid and binding.[56] Consider, for example, the case of Caroline, who, upon stopping her car at a red traffic light, is asked by another driver why she has just stopped. Her (surprised) response is simply to point at the red light or to say that this is what the law requires without further attempt to justify her action by reference to the balance of ordinary reasons as applicable to the case. Of course, not everyone would react this way. Some, for example, would choose to go beyond the mere invocation of the rule and cite the reasons behind the rule. But Caroline's response is one that would be widely regarded as a perfectly intelligible response and one that represents a familiar way of perceiving legal rules. Might, however, the mere gesturing to the red light or the mere mentioning of the rule be intended as a shorthand way of saying that the balance of ordinary reasons for action points to stopping? It might, but it is perfectly conceivable and by no

Nothing I say at this point is meant to imply the opposite. As phenomenological claims, the claims made at this point are not about the way legal authority shapes our conduct, but about the way we experience or perceive its impact on our conduct.

[54] For Hart's famous discussion of the distinction between mere habits and a practice of rules, see HLA Hart, *The Concept of Law* (3rd edn with an introduction by Leslie Green, OUP 2012) 55–61. Cf Sylvie Delacroix, 'Law and Habits' (2017) 37 Oxford Journal of Legal Studies 660.

[55] I do not rely on an assumption that *all or most* people view their action under the law in this way. But it is interesting to note some studies which suggest that the bulk of people believe they are under an obligation to obey the law: GR Boynton, Samuel C Patterson, and Ronald D Hedlund, 'The Structure of Public Support for Legislative Institutions' (1968) 12 Midwest Journal of Political Science 163, 165–67; Harrell R Rodgers and George Taylor, 'Preadult Orientations Toward Legal Compliance: Notes Toward a Theory' (1970) 51 Social Science Quarterly 359, 542; Harrell R Rodgers and Edward B Lewis, 'Political Support and Compliance Attitudes: A Study of Adolescents' (1974) 2 American Politics Research 61, 66–67; Austin Sarat, 'Support for the Legal System: An Analysis of Knowledge, Attitudes, and Behavior' (1975) 3 American Politics Quarterly 3, 7–10; Tyler (n 52) 45. For example, in one anonymous survey conducted by Tyler, 82% of the participants agreed with the statement: 'People should obey the law even if it goes against what they think is right' (ibid). For some critical comments on Tyler's surveys, see Leslie Green, 'Who Believes in Political Obligation?' in Jan Narveson and John T Sanders (eds), *For and Against the State* (Rowman & Littlefield 1996) 301–17, at 311–15; Schauer (n 52) 60–61; Claus (n 52) 73–74. See discussion on pp 189–90 herein.

[56] This way of perceiving legal rules will be reminiscent, of course, of Hart's 'internal point of view' (Hart (n 54) 89–90).

means implausible that it is not. To gain a clear view of this, we can further suppose that Caroline recognizes that in the case at hand the overall balance of primary reasons happens to moderately tip against stopping (having taken into account her and the authority's epistemic attributes). She may still respond to the query by pointing at the red light or citing the rule—and her response would remain a perfectly intelligible and familiar one even with the latter assumption in mind.

Caroline's reply to her fellow driver, like Jeremy's reply to his friend discussed earlier, represents a type of phenomenology that coheres better with the preemption thesis than with the weighing model. As will be argued in the next section, however, this is not the only relevant and significant type of phenomenology found among actors such as Caroline and Jeremy.

5.2.3. The Phenomenology of Principled Disobedience

There exists another relevant part of the phenomenological picture that, I will argue, stands in opposition to the one Raz emphasized in his phenomenological argument. Although he does not focus on it or analyse it at length,[57] there are comments of his that might evoke it, as, for example, when he notes:

> [Jeremy] admits that if he were told to commit an atrocity he should refuse. But his is an ordinary case, he thinks, and the order should prevail.[58]

Now, I put to one side Raz's exact intention here—my claims in this section are not made within the framework of *his* phenomenological argument. It is possible, however, to understand a rider of the type just quoted as enfolding the following two ideas. (1) Jeremy implies that he would not follow orders that fail to comport with some minimal level of moral appropriateness. The kind of disobedient acts he refers to do not typically ensue from calculations of personal convenience or selfish motivations. Instead, such acts are typically embedded in a principled approach—'principled' not in any narrow or stringent sense (e.g. in the sense that the agent must rely on a systematic and coherent set of ideas about moral rights and duties which he or she can fully articulate), but in a broader and looser sense which signifies that the agent acts out of a conviction that he or she is doing the right thing.[59] We may call such acts, in this broad sense, acts of

---

[57] That is, not from a phenomenological perspective. He does devote considerable discussion to it from other perspectives (see, e.g., Raz, *The Authority of Law* (n 46) chs 14–15).

[58] Raz, *Practical Reason and Norms* (n 4) 38.

[59] One indicator of whether an act of disobedience is principled (in the sense used here) consists in asking whether the relevant agent would still support such an act if she were to make the decision from the standpoint of an uninvolved observer, rather than someone with a vested personal interest in the act. A positive answer indicates that the act is a principled one.

principled disobedience.[60] (2) Jeremy seems to imply that not every deficiency of an order would or should lead him to disobey. The deficiency involved has to be a serious one to prompt his resistance.

This twofold proviso seems to express an idea to which many people would subscribe,[61] even if fewer would live up to it in practice in all or most cases where they should. And, to the extent that it resonates with people's view of their moral responsibility, it should be treated as one part of the phenomenology of attitudes related to authority (whether people conceive of the relevant instances of immorality as cases that mark out the ambit of legitimate authority or as cases where disobedience is justified regardless of whether the directive originates from a legitimate authority). It is worth noting, however, that in the normal course of events the principled-disobedience proviso stated above is likely to remain a latent rather than manifest element of our practical deliberation. In the ordinary run of everyday innocuous activity, we are not likely to preoccupy ourselves, for purposes of *practical deliberation*, with hypothetical scenarios of atrocities, torture, or the like. There are specific contexts in which the proviso associated with such extremities is more likely to surface and gain salience in our consciousness. For instance, when we are confronted with questions such as: What would you do if the authority were to order you to commit such morally unacceptable acts? Would you still obey? Or, when exposed to information (whether through history books, news reports, or other sources) about past or current events involving serious injustice perpetrated under the orders of officials, which prompts us to reflect on the moral implications of obedience in those scenarios. Or, finally, as a result of real-life experience: when or after people are actually faced with a law or command requiring them to commit morally deplorable acts.

While history and present world affairs abound with examples of wrongful acts committed under the orders of higher-ups, they also offer myriad examples of principled disobedience. The Boston Tea Party, Gandhi's Satyagraha campaigns, civil resistance to Jim Crow laws, and Mandela's battle against apartheid are but a few iconic examples among countless other prominent and less prominent instances. Exploring these examples, however interesting and important, is not part of the purpose of this inquiry. But a brief illustration of the type of reasoning that may lead to an act of principled disobedience is

[60] I borrow the term from Herbert C Kelman and V Lee Hamilton, *Crimes of Obedience: Toward A Social Psychology of Authority and Responsibility* (Yale University Press 1989) 56. See also ibid 53–76, where the authors explore the historical and cultural origins of what they label 'the duty to disobey'.

[61] See, e.g., June L Tapp and Lawrence Kohlberg, 'Developing Senses of Law and Legal Justice' (1971) 27 Journal of Social Issues 65, 83, where the authors report, inter alia, the results of a survey among US college students whose responses seem largely consistent with the above statement.

nonetheless called for. Consider the celebrated example of Rosa Parks, who on 1 December 1955 refused to give up her seat to a white passenger on a segregated bus in Montgomery, Alabama. She recounts the event as follows:

I was riding the bus home from work. A white man got on, and the driver looked our way and said, 'Let me have those seats.' It did not seem proper, particularly for a woman to give her seat to a man. All the passengers paid ten cents, just as he did.... Bus drivers then had police powers, under both municipal and state laws, to enforce racial segregation....

'Y'all better make it light on yourselves and let me have those seats,' Blake [the driver] said.

... I stayed in my seat and slid closer to the window. I do not remember being frightened. But I sure did not believe I would 'make it light' on myself by standing up. Our mistreatment was just not right, and I was tired of it. The more we gave in, the worse they treated us....

I knew someone had to take the first step. So I made up my mind not to move. Blake asked me if I was going to stand up.

'No. I am not,' I answered.

Blake said that he would have to call the police. I said, 'Go ahead.' In less than five minutes, two policemen came, and the driver pointed me out. He said that he wanted the seat and that I would not stand up.

'Why do you push us around?' I said to one of the policemen.

'I don't know,' he answered, 'but the law is the law and you're under arrest.' I did not get on the bus to get arrested; I got on the bus to go home. Getting arrested was one of the worst days in my life. It was not a happy experience....

I had no idea that history was being made. I was just tired of giving in.[62]

Parks's reasoning, as reflected in this passage, is not focused on institutional or personal attributes of the relevant lawgiver, but on the iniquitous content of the law ('It did not seem proper'; 'Our mistreatment was just not right'). One might try to read into her comment some indirect assumptions about the (deficient) moral character or sensibility of the lawgiver, but the focus of her comment—and what seems to be the decisive consideration in her reasoning—remains the morally objectionable content of the law in question. This type of reasoning seems consonant with the weighing model, while, as argued at length in Part I, possible attempts at reconciling it with the pre-emption thesis do not stand up to close scrutiny.

However, the example of Parks (or similarly iconic figures) may prompt something like the following question: is the way Parks conceived of her

---

[62] Rosa Parks and Gregory J Reed, *Quiet Strength: The Faith, the Hope, and the Heart of a Woman Who Changed a Nation* (Zondervan Publishing House 1994) 21–23. See also Rosa Parks and James Haskins, *Rosa Parks: My Story* (Penguin 1992) 108–24; Douglas Brinkley, *Rosa Parks: A Life* (Penguin 2000) 104–09.

moral responsibility as a citizen faced with an unjust law indicative of *ordinary* people's conceptions? The question may seem warranted because there are some respects in which Parks was not exactly what we might call the ordinary person: at the time of the incident, alongside her work as a seamstress, she was an active member of the National Association for the Advancement of Colored People (NAACP).[63] Moreover, her act of defiance was not a common behaviour among African American passengers on segregated buses.[64] However, we ought to distinguish between two different issues here. First, the fact that Parks's action in that situation was uncommon and heroic. Second, the question of whether the basic set of concepts and terms that made Parks's action a conceivable and intelligible option in her eyes is one that many of us share. It is a fairly conspicuous fact that different people show different levels of deference (or resistance) to unjust or oppressive orders.[65] This issue, however, need not detain us here. For it is not the aim of this inquiry to define by reference to specific circumstances the conditions in which most or many people cease to comply. Rather, the material issue here is that many people possess the conceptual apparatus that makes disobedience in *some* circumstances of extremely immoral or oppressive orders—whatever those circumstances are—a conceivable and intelligible way of proceeding. The point is that many of us, irrespective of whether we would find the courage to act as Parks did if we were in her position, are familiar with the basic notions she invokes in the above passage, particularly the very possibility of justified disobedience in the face of an oppressive or unjust order. Indeed, we become familiar with those notions partly *through* the educational and cultural resonance of stories such as Parks's.

A well-known experiment that might give rise to further doubts about the foregoing claim is the Milgram experiment. Milgram tested whether participants would obey instructions to inflict (what were presented to them as real) electric shocks on another person in what was described to them as an experiment concerning the effect of punishment on learning. A large number of the participants, ordinary American citizens, had followed the experimenters' instructions to deliver high-voltage shocks to the learner.[66] Does

---

[63] Parks and Haskins (n 62) 80–89; Brinkley (n 62) 67–77.

[64] Though Parks was also not the first African American to refuse to surrender a seat on a segregated bus. For some other examples, see Parks and Haskins (n 62) 111–12; Brinkley (n 62) 87–90, 103–04.

[65] See in this connection Kelman and Hamilton (n 60) 236–306. One clear illustration of this fact can be seen in Milgram's experiment, which I discuss below. See further Thomas Blass, 'Understanding Behavior in the Milgram Obedience Experiment: The Role of Personality, Situations, and Their Interactions' (1991) 60 Journal of Personality and Social Psychology 398.

[66] See Stanley Milgram, *Obedience to Authority: An Experimental View* (Pinter & Martin 2005) xi.

this not discredit the thought that principled disobedience forms part of the mental horizon of ordinary people? Note preliminarily that questions can be raised about the extent to which participants in Milgram's experiment understood themselves to be obeying orders, rather than, for example, acting out of identification with the experimenter and his goals, and a wish to assist his scientific enterprise.[67] These questions, however, can be left to one side. For even on the assumption that participants understood their actions in terms of obedience/disobedience, the results of the experiment are not inconsistent with the modest claim made here: namely, that the possibility of principled disobedience has enough manifestation in human consciousness and deliberation to be considered phenomenologically significant. Before taking a closer look at the experiment, a further parenthetical comment worth making is that the Milgram experiment is not the only obedience experiment consistent with this modest claim.[68] But it is singled out for consideration here because, as a classical reference for excessive obedience, it might be thought at first to be in tension with my claim.

None of what is said below about the experiment should be understood as questioning the common observation that participants generally showed a disturbing level of compliance with the experimenter's instructions. However, if we are to correctly understand the experiment's bearing on our inquiry, some qualifications and clarifications should be made. (1) The electrocution procedure used in the experiment was graduated. Participants were instructed to increase the intensity of shocks from one trial to another, on a scale ranging from 15 to 450 volts.[69] Many participants who followed the instructions a considerable way up that scale nonetheless disobeyed when the intensity of shocks further increased. As the shocks intensified (and with them the learner's expressions of agony and protest) the possibility of disobedience became more overt and less latent in the practical deliberation of such subjects, as manifested verbally, through their body language, and eventually in actual disobedience.[70] (2) 'The Milgram experiment', as it is often called, is in fact a series of experiments. Milgram tested obedience in several experimental settings, differing on dimensions such as the physical proximity between the

---

[67] See Stephen D Reicher, S Alexander Haslam, and Joanne R Smith, 'Working Toward the Experimenter: Reconceptualizing Obedience Within the Milgram Paradigm as Identification-Based Followership' (2012) 7 Perspectives on Psychological Science 315 (though the authors focus on the participants' motivations, rather than their self-perception).

[68] See, e.g., William A Gamson, Bruce Fireman, and Steven Rytina, *Encounters with Unjust Authority* (Dorsey Press 1982); Wesley Kilham and Leon Mann, 'Level of Destructive Obedience as a Function of Transmitter and Executant Roles in the Milgram Obedience Paradigm' (1974) 29 Journal of Personality and Social Psychology 696.

[69] Milgram (n 66) 20–23.   [70] See Milgram's description of this process in ibid 155–65.

victim and the electrocuting participant,[71] the physical proximity between the experimenter and the electrocuting participant,[72] and so on. Although in some of those variants most of the participants were fully obedient, in other variants most of the participants disobeyed at one stage or another.[73] (3) In nearly all the variants in which most participants were fully obedient, the portion of participants who disobeyed was nevertheless significant.[74] These comments should suffice to allay possible doubts as to the compatibility of my moderate claim with the experiment's results.

Assuming that participants in Milgram's experiment understood their actions in terms of obedience/disobedience, it is worth taking brief notice of how disobedient participants explain and justify their acts of disobedience. They do so primarily by reference to the content of the relevant instruction and its deleterious implications.

I think he's trying to communicate, he's knocking .... Well it's not fair to shock the guy ... these are terrific volts. I don't think this is very humane ... Oh, I can't go on with this; no, this isn't right. It's a hell of an experiment. The guy is suffering in there. No, I don't want to go on. This is crazy.
[Subject refuses to administer more shocks.][75]

He's banging in there. I'm gonna chicken out. I'd like to continue, but I can't do that to a man.... I'm sorry I can't do that to a man. I'll hurt his heart. You take your cheque.... No really, I couldn't do it.[76]

These and other comments of defiant participants focus mainly on what we call here background moral reasons—in this case, the value of human life, concerns about the physical and mental integrity of the supposedly electrocuted person, and concerns about the pain and suffering caused to him. Such recourse to background reasons, once more, seems to accord with a weighing paradigm better than with a pre-emption paradigm.

The following objection might be raised by the Razian. It is doubtful that the directive-issuers in examples such as the foregoing (Rosa Parks's case or the Milgram experiment) have actually complied with Raz's conditions of legitimacy, and particularly with his normal justification thesis. While these directive-issuers claimed to have authority, the objection runs, they did not really have it. Thus, phenomenological manifestations of principled disobedience in these examples do not cut against Raz's claim, which attributes

---

[71] ibid 33–44.   [72] ibid 62–63.   [73] ibid 36–37, 60–61, 96–97, 121.
[74] ibid. It is also worth mentioning that in a group of respondents who, instead of taking an active part in the electrocution exercise were asked hypothetical questions about it, all the respondents said that they would disobey at a certain point in the sequence of orders (ibid 28–29).
[75] ibid 33.   [76] ibid.

exclusionary force to real authorities, that is, ones that meet his conditions of legitimacy. The reply to this objection need not rely exclusively on the discussion in Chapter 3, where it was observed that Raz's conditions of legitimacy are incapable of ruling out the possibility of authoritativeness in cases of justified disobedience (at least not in a manner consistent with the very notion of exclusionary reasons). Quite apart from that observation, the objection should be rejected as misplaced. This chapter is concerned with arguments of a specific type, namely phenomenological arguments. As such, it focuses on the way things *appear* in *people's experience*. When it comes to phenomenological arguments about the pre-emption thesis, it is irrelevant whether a directive-issuer really has authority. What matters is how people consciously experience their reactions to what *they take to be* an authority.

Can the above objection be reframed as a claim about actors' *belief*, namely as a claim that defiant actors believed that the directive-issuer had no authority? It was already noted that comments of defiant actors in the foregoing examples were focused not on attributes of the directive-issuer, but primarily on the immoral content of the directive involved, its harmful consequences, and its failure to adequately reflect the relevant background reasons. It might be said that we ought to *infer* from these comments a belief about lack of authority. However, such an assertion would run into problems. For one thing, it would prompt questions such as: Why should we make that inference? On what grounds should we attribute to the actor the above belief? The thought that it would lend support to this or that theoretical model is, needless to explain, not itself a valid basis for inferring the above belief. Another difficulty for the Razian objector is that, insofar as actors' reasoning in those settings was directive-specific, to make the above suggested inference would effectively presuppose that legitimate authority is validated through a content-based assessment of individual directives. Such a test of legitimate authority is, as seen in Chapter 3, at odds with Raz's service conception of authority.

5.3. Conclusion

The phenomenological picture emerging from this discussion is composite. On the one hand, the recognition that someone has authority over us is typically accompanied by a sense that we are bound by his or her directives.[77] When the authority decides and issues a directive that we recognize as applicable to us, we characteristically think that it is no longer for us to decide what

---

[77] Section 5.2.2.

the best course of action is. This type of phenomenology is compatible with the pre-emption thesis. On the other hand, if faced with a directive that fails to accord with a minimum standard of moral appropriateness (or if presented with a hypothetical scenario of this sort), we may come to view the situation in terms very different from bindingness, obedience, or the like.[78] In these situations, we may refuse to follow the relevant directive and justify our refusal by reference to what we believe to be compelling moral reasons against the required act. We may then add something along the lines of: people are morally accountable for their actions, and this is above the law, rules, or authority. By way of clarification, the word 'may' in these statements is meant to capture the fact that, although many of us fail to stand up against authority in many of the cases we ought to, there are circumstances in which an appreciable segment of us would, and, at any rate, the set of concepts and beliefs many of us possess recognizes the *possibility* of such action as an intelligible and conceivable one. This type of phenomenology accords well with the weighing model.

To the extent that our phenomenology is consistent with the pre-emption thesis, it is inconsistent with the weighing model. To the extent that our phenomenology is consistent with the weighing model, it is inconsistent with the pre-emption thesis. How can we account for this mixed phenomenology, then? We cannot account for it by saying that the pre-emption thesis applies only in those cases where the sense of bindingness manifests itself, whereas the weighing model applies only in those cases where the possibility of principled disobedience emerges. This type of theoretical 'division of labour' cannot be an adequate answer to our puzzle. For both the pre-emption thesis and the weighing model purport to apply to a range of cases wider than the ones just mentioned. The pre-emption thesis does not claim to apply solely to 'good' directives, and not even solely to morally acceptable ones, and could not do so on pain of eviscerating the idea of exclusion. (Recall here Raz's comments that the service conception of authority and the pre-emption thesis are consistent with the fact that an authoritative directive may on occasion 'fail to reflect correctly the underlying reasons which it is meant to reflect',[79] and that 'sometimes immoral or unjust laws may be authoritatively binding'.[80]) And the weighing model, on the other hand, does not claim to apply solely to bad or morally unacceptable directives.

Moreover, the phenomenological features identified here have implications broader than their scope of visible manifestation. The fact that John would

---

[78] Section 5.2.3.   [79] Raz, 'Facing Up' (n 2) 1161.
[80] Joseph Raz, *The Morality of Freedom* (Clarendon Press 1986) 78.

flout applicable directives if and when these directives grossly contravene pertinent moral reasons (and would do so *because* of their moral deficiency) tells us something general about the antecedents of his action: it tells us that compliance on his part is conditional on there being a certain degree of conformity between what he is instructed to do and what he has reasons to do.[81] That is, the moral reasons for action that Raz terms first-order reasons are part of what determines whether or not John follows directives in any given case. In this sense, first-order reasons play a normative role for John, not merely on those exceptional occasions when he would conscientiously flout a directive, but also when he complies with directives.

If the phenomenological picture identified here cannot be accounted for by the pre-emption thesis, by the weighing model,[82] or by both, and if we are to stand by our working premise that phenomenological cues have some indicative use for our purpose, how are we to proceed? One possible way is to search for a third model—that is, a model that can accommodate and adequately explain both the regularly experienced sense of being bound by authority and the less frequent experiences associated with principled disobedience. If it exists, such a model would be phenomenologically superior to the contenders we have been discussing. At the same time, the fact that both the weighing model and the pre-emption thesis find *partial* support in a phenomenological analysis may help orientate our search for such an alternative. It points in the direction of a model that would not be entirely divorced and removed from either the pre-emption thesis or the weighing model, but would bear a close relation with both and possibly even integrate qualified elements thereof. Proposing and developing such a model is a task that will be taken up in the final part of this book. Prior to this, however, it will be useful to consider another argument of Raz that may throw light on our subject matter. This will be done in the next chapter.

---

[81] Note that this argument differs from Flathman's (see extract on pp 83–84) in two important respects. (1) For Flathman, the idea that compliance is conditional on moral reasons is compatible with the phenomenology of authority, whereas I refer to it as an idea that, although entailed by some aspects of the relevant phenomenology, fails to correspond with other, central aspects of it. (2) It is one thing to say that someone acts *on the balance of reasons*—as Flathman does in his argument discussed above—and quite another to say that compliance on one's part is conditional on there being *a certain degree of* conformity between what one is instructed to do and what one has reasons to do—which is the statement I made above.

[82] Arguably, the weighing model's phenomenological deficiency is more noticeable than that of the pre-emption thesis. If that is so, the reason may be that cases dominated by the experienced bindingness of authority tend to be more common than cases dominated by the experience of principled disobedience.

6

The Functional Argument

The Razian argument discussed in this chapter focuses on the function authorities are meant to fulfil in human affairs. Put in its most general form, the argument suggests that authorities would not be able to fulfil their intended function if their directives operated through the modus operandi of reasons for action that compete with opposing ones in weight (what I have referred to as the weighing model). To perform their function, contends the argument, authorities must operate as a source of pre-emptive reasons, that is, reasons that both require an action and exclude some opposing reasons from the range of factors that influence the decision how to act.[1]

The first question that may be prompted by this initial and merely skeletal description of the argument is: what function of authorities does the argument refer to? That is, what is the function that, according to the argument, they cannot fulfil unless their directives operate as pre-emptive reasons? For one thing, it is plain that the function referred to *cannot* be simply *to exclude* or *pre-empt reasons* or anything synonymous with these terms, for the argument collapses into circularity when thus construed; it turns into a statement that is trivially true but proves nothing. For the functional argument to succeed in bearing out the pre-emption thesis, there must be some other function of authorities that they cannot perform unless their directives operate as pre-emptive reasons.

As will become apparent shortly, Raz does mention such other functions, which render the argument under consideration tenable, and which

---

[1] A similar argument is discussed in Chaim Gans, 'Mandatory Rules and Exclusionary Reasons' (1986) 15 Philosophia 373, 377, 381–82 (who refers to it as 'the argument from justification'); William A Edmundson, 'Rethinking Exclusionary Reasons: A Second Edition of Joseph Raz's "Practical Reason and Norms"' (1993) 12 Law and Philosophy 329, 340–43 (who calls it the 'teleological argument'); and Roger A Shiner, 'Exclusionary Reasons and the Explanation of Behaviour' (1992) 5 Ratio Juris 1, 10–14. The functional argument should be understood to refer to the function authorities perform through *their normative force*. The argument does not (and need not) deny that there is an extent to which authorities can effectively employ coercive measures to bring their subjects to comply even if those subjects do not regard authoritative directives as exclusionary reasons.

Legal Directives and Practical Reasons. Noam Gur. © Noam Gur 2018. Published 2018 by Oxford University Press.

correspond with his own statement that he has 'tried to give ... functional reasons'[2] in support of his notion of exclusionary reasons. But the previous paragraph's caveat retains its relevance because there are some points at which Raz seems to refer to pre-emption (or similar terms) as part of the function of authority.[3] These latter statements are (and, on pain of circularity, must be understood as) *conceptual* claims about authority[4]—namely, claims to the effect that the concept of authority implies the idea of pre-emptive reasons— and, as such, they are perfectly tenable. But such conceptual claims cannot be the argument which ultimately establishes that pre-emptive reasons (in the normative sense of 'reasons') actually exist.[5] The fact that a certain concept implies this or that does not by itself answer questions about the way we ought to act. There exist many different concepts, and only some of them entail actions which are compatible with the demands of morality and rationality. One may, of course, use conceptual claims as a type of argumentative starting point that leads on to the moral issue, or that serves as a preliminary indication for that purpose: one may say, for example, that if the idea of pre-emptive reasons is implicit in the very concept of authority, then it is probably worth asking whether there is any justificatory argument which confirms that such reasons actually exist, or that it is likely that there is such an argument. This may be so. But we should not end the inquiry at that and assume that such reasons exist without directly examining their moral foundation— and that is the type of examination I will focus on in this chapter.

6.1. The Functional Argument Expounded

Rules are usually adopted for a *purpose*, and it is their ability to serve the purposes for which they are adopted that the functional argument focuses on.

---

[2] Joseph Raz, 'Facing Up: A Reply' (1989) 62 Southern California Law Review 1153, 1164. As Raz notes at this point, functional arguments are not the only type of argument he has invoked in support of his exclusionary reasons conception.

[3] For example, when Raz refers to authorities as *mediating* between people and primary reasons for action, the term 'mediating' can be understood to contain the idea of pre-emption or exclusion, though there are also some textual cues against this interpretation (Joseph Raz, *Ethics in the Public Domain: Essays in the Morality of Law and Politics* (rev paperback edn, Clarendon Press 1995) 214–15).

[4] Or a phenomenological claim to the effect that exclusionary reasons feature in people's common experience of authority. This argument was the focus of the previous chapter.

[5] It might be thought that if, on the one hand, Raz is correct to say that the idea of pre-emption is implicit in the concept of authority, and, on the other hand, no justificatory argument successfully shows that governments can ever have the capacity to generate such reasons, this would point to the outcome that governments can never be legitimate authorities (at least not in the full or strict sense

In *Practical Reason and Norms*, where Raz calls this argument '[a]n argument from the justification of norms',[6] he thus states:

> In trying to explain the nature of mandatory norms, I have suggested that they are to be understood as being exclusionary reasons. This can be seen by examining possible justifications of norms, because the nature of the justification shows that the justified norm will fail to achieve its purpose if it were not regarded as an exclusionary reason.... The argument has been that these rules would not serve their purpose unless they were treated as exclusionary reasons.... [T]he same is true of the instructions of authorities....

> To show that this is indeed so, we must once more examine the ways in which authority can be justified.[7]

As the passage's ending makes clear, a similar argument is made regarding authorities and their directives. The basic point of having authorities lies in their capacity to serve the governed by guiding them to better conform to reasons for action that apply to them. And that is also the normal way in which they can be justified: an authority is legitimate if it is likely to direct its subjects to better conform to reasons that apply to them.[8] For this to be the case, it must be in possession of certain attributes that render it likelier than its subjects to successfully track relevant reasons for action. Institutions or persons who claim authority but lack those attributes have no legitimate authority,[9] and should not be obeyed.[10] Not so with a legitimate authority: the ability of such an authority to track relevant reasons for action better than its subjects do can translate into practical benefit only if those subjects follow its directives, rather than their own convictions as to the best action in the case at hand.[11]

---

of the term). Some would perhaps feel uneasy about such an outcome, but their unease would not by itself prove that governments can have the capacity to generate pre-emptive reasons.

[6] Joseph Raz, *Practical Reason and Norms* (2nd edn, Princeton University Press 1990) 74. He clarifies that such an argument cannot establish that *all* norms are exclusionary reasons. When using this type of argument, he focuses on rules of thumb and norms issued by an authority (ibid 59–65).

[7] ibid 62–63.

[8] See Joseph Raz, *The Morality of Freedom* (Clarendon Press 1986) 47–57, 61. For purposes of this analysis, I will assume with Raz that the justification of authority is the instrumental justification of improving conformity with reason.

[9] Raz, *Ethics in the Public Domain* (n 3) 215.

[10] He notes that the existence of such directives in itself is not a reason for action, though the fact that other people are influenced by them may provide such reasons (Joseph Raz, *Between Authority and Interpretation: On the Theory of Law and Practical Reason* (OUP 2009) 6).

[11] Raz, *Practical Reason and Norms* (n 6) 62–64, 195; Joseph Raz, *The Authority of Law: Essays on Law and Morality* (2nd edn, OUP 2009) 25; Raz, *The Morality of Freedom* (n 8) 61; Joseph Raz (ed), *Authority* (New York University Press 1990) 10–11; Joseph Raz, 'The Problem of Authority: Revisiting the Service Conception' (2006) 90 Minnesota Law Review 1003, 1019.

Of course, there is a certain extent to which legal authority can effectively induce compliance even among subjects who do not treat its directives as exclusionary reasons: it can do so by using, or threatening to use, its coercive force in the event of non-compliance. Invoking this fact and ending the discussion at that, however, would not engage with Raz's functional argument, which refers to the *normative* force of authority—namely, the way in which one *should* regard authoritative directives in order to better conform to background reasons, rather than the measures taken when one refuses or fails to do so. Moreover, to engage with Raz's argument and, thus, to consider the function of legal authorities through a normative lens remains a practically important task due, inter alia, to the impracticality and unattractiveness of a system of governance that would depend for its efficacy *solely* on the use of coercive measures and on the fear of punishment. Reverting to the argument itself, then, from a Razian perspective, precisely because the justification of the binding force of authority rests on its ability to reach decisions that better reflect background reasons, these reasons are supplanted by the authority's directives.[12] This explains why, according to Raz, subjects who factor into their decision both an applicable authoritative directive and their own views on the merits of the action are 'guilty of double counting'[13] the merits, and are essentially defeating the point of having authoritative institutions.[14] I will designate the proposition arising from the preceding discussion (as applicable in the legal context)[15] F1:

> [F1] A legal authority can fulfil (by means of its normative force)[16] the function of leading subjects to better conformity with reason only if it is taken to provide exclusionary reasons.

Now, Raz highlights some more specific benefits obtainable through the operation of legitimate authorities. Thus, for instance, some of the potential benefits of authoritative rules lie, according to Raz, in their ability to provide a common framework for social life in the face of fundamental disagreements and differences between members of society:

> [T]he practice [whereby 'rules mediate between deeper-level considerations and concrete decisions'] allows the creation of a pluralistic culture. For it enables people to unite in support of some 'low or medium level' generalizations despite profound disagreements concerning their ultimate foundations … The point is that an orderly

---

[12] Raz, *The Morality of Freedom* (n 8) 59.

[13] Raz, *Ethics in the Public Domain* (n 3) 215; Raz, *The Morality of Freedom* (n 8) 58–59.

[14] See references in n 11.

[15] Raz's functional argument refers to authorities in general, not only legal authorities. F1 focuses on the argument's application in the legal context.

[16] Once more, the argument does not refer to coercive measures and the threat to use them.

community can exist only if it shares many practices, and that in all modern plural-istic societies a great measure of toleration of vastly differing outlooks is made pos-sible by the fact that many of them enable the vast majority of the population to accept common standards of conduct.[17]

Also focal to Raz's ideas about the beneficial functions of authorities are epi-stemic advantages gained through reliance on expertise and the ability to se-cure schemes of social coordination:

The two basic arguments for authority depend on its ability, through concentrating expertise on various issues, to overcome common ignorance and on its ability to help solve common difficulties in securing coordination. Overcoming both problems requires adopting an indirect approach to conformity to reasons, that is, it requires securing conformity [to reasons] not through an attempt to comply [with them dir-ectly]. In the case of failure to conform due to ignorance ... the cure is in deferring to the judgement of the expert rather than trying to rely on one's own judgement of the balance of reasons.[18]

A similar line of reasoning will apply to authority based on the need to co-ordinate the action of several people.... Authority can secure co-ordination only if the indi-viduals concerned defer to its judgement and do not act on the balance of reasons, but on the authority's instructions. This guarantees that all will participate in one plan of action, that action will be co-ordinated. But it requires that people should regard authoritative utterances as exclusionary reasons ... To accept an authority on these grounds is not to act irrationally or arbitrarily. The need for an authority may be well founded in reason. But the reasons are of a special kind. They establish the need to regard authoritative utterances as exclusionary reasons.[19]

---

[17] Raz, *The Morality of Freedom* (n 8) 58.

[18] Raz, *Practical Reason and Norms* (n 6) 195. See also ibid 63–64; Raz, *Authority* (n 11) 5–6.

[19] Raz, *Practical Reason and Norms* (n 6) 64. For further comments on coordination and ex-clusionary reasons, see ibid 195; Raz, 'Facing Up' (n 2) 1191–93; Raz, *Authority* (n 11) 10–11. Elsewhere Raz makes a similar point by reference to an example: '[T]he reason for the validity of the rule is that it is best if club affairs are regulated by the committee which made the rule. That is presumably because, on the whole, if members follow the judgement of the committee their ac-tions will track reason better than if they act on their best judgement without taking account of the judgement of the committee. Usually when this is the case it is so through a combination of two fac-tors. First, the good judgement of the committee. And, second, the fact that it can secure desirable co-ordination among people, which, left to their own devices, the members are less likely to secure. These factors are ... a reason for not second-guessing the decision of the committee. So if the com-mittee, having had the opportunity to weigh the pros and cons of imposing the no-more-than-three-guests rule, has approved it then all members have reason not to challenge that judgement, and that means that they have reason not to act on the reasons for or against bringing a fourth guest. Rather, they should regard the rule as displacing the reasons which the committee was meant to consider in issuing the rule. That is what I mean when I say that the rule is an exclusionary reason.... If this example can be generalised, and I believe that it can, then we have here an explanation why rules are opaque, content-independent, autonomous reasons for action ... More than that, it makes it clear that often rules are valid protected reasons. QED' (Joseph Raz, 'Reasoning with Rules' (2001) 54 Current Legal Problems 1, 15).

Raz suggests, therefore, that in those cases where an authority meets the legitimacy condition of having the capacity to direct subjects to better conformity with reason (elsewhere expressed in his 'normal justification thesis'[20]), it usually does so on account of two main factors: the ability to counteract problems caused by lack of information in virtue of its relative expertise on the regulated matters; and the capacity to establish and secure coordination schemes in cases where coordination is not likely to occur in a spontaneous, self-regulating manner. An authority may overcome these problems by means of its normative force, Raz argues, only if its directives are regarded as exclusionary reasons. For if, instead of letting the authority's requirements supplant their assessments of how to act, subjects were to try following directly the reasons for and against its requirements, those problems that the authority was meant to overcome would simply resurface and the benefit of its guidance would be lost. We can put together on this basis an additional Razian proposition, which will be entitled F2:[21]

> **[F2]** A legal authority can fulfil (by means of its normative force) the functions it is meant to fulfil—e.g. overcoming problems of deficient or incomplete knowledge, helping to solve common difficulties of social coordination, and enabling people to share practices despite deeper disagreements between them—only if it is taken to provide exclusionary reasons.[22]

6.2. The Functional Argument: An Initial Examination

6.2.1. Normative Weighing and Conformity with Reason

Is it really the case that the directives of a legitimate legal authority would fail to fulfil their basic purpose—namely, improving our conformity with reason in the ways mentioned above, or in other similar ways—if they were taken to provide reasons for action that compete with opposing reasons in terms of their weight, rather than excluding them? At first glance the answer may seem, quite straightforwardly, negative. One should not assume a dichotomy under which directives of a legal authority either function as exclusionary reasons or have no effect in terms of practical reason. The weighing model represents a third possibility. It suggests that (when present) personal or institutional attributes that render a legal authority apt to direct us to right conduct do constitute reasons to act as it prescribes—reasons that do and should

---

[20] Raz, *The Morality of Freedom* (n 8) 53.   [21] See clarification in n 15.
[22] On one occasion, in reply to a critique by Gerald Postema, Raz expresses a seemingly different approach to the relation between coordination difficulties and pre-emptive reasons: '[A]uthority can be useful in securing coordination in some circumstances, and since authoritative reasons have

affect our decision-making by means of their weight. Such reasons enter the balance and militate in favour of acting in the prescribed way; and they may tip the balance even in instances where we disagree with the decision behind the directive, and even where the directive is in fact suboptimal as far as an assessment of its particular content is concerned.[23]

As indicated earlier, those attributes of legal authorities that (when present) enable them to direct people to better performance may translate into either epistemic or non-epistemic reasons.[24] At the epistemic level, insofar as lawmakers are better placed than a subject to decide what ought to be done on some matters—as may be the case, for example, if those lawmakers have better access to experts' advice, have more information on hand, or are better acquainted with relevant policy considerations—the subject has a reason to regard the case for doing what they require on those matters as weightier than it would have seemed to him in the absence of a legal requirement.[25] At the non-epistemic level, various considerations may mean that, when the law requires

pre-emptive force, pre-emptive reasons can be useful in securing coordination. But the many examples of coordination without either the law or any other norms with pre-emptive force would give the lie to any suggestion that pre-emption explains the normative force of coordination schemes' (Joseph Raz, 'Postema on Law's Autonomy and Public Practical Reasons: A Critical Comment' (1998) 4 Legal Theory 1, 12). On one possible understanding, Raz might be taken to mean here that in circumstances where authority can help secure coordination, it is able to do so irrespective of its pre-emptive force. That is, while the reasons it provides are pre-emptive, this property is not essential to its ability to secure coordination. This stands in contrast with his arguments cited earlier and encapsulated in F2, as well as with other comments such as these: '[The fact] that mandatory norms are exclusionary reasons is the key to understanding ... the problems involved in justifying them' (Raz, *Practical Reason and Norms* (n 6) 76–77); 'where there are advantages in having authorities ... one needs the protected reason account to show what they are' (ibid 195). The contrast sharpens when one brings to mind the following proviso of Raz: 'In fact, in my view, political authorities are justified primarily on the grounds of coordination, though these are mixed with considerations of expertise' (Raz, 'Facing Up' (n 2) 1164. See also ibid 1180; Raz, *The Morality of Freedom* (n 8) 30–31, 56; Raz, *Ethics in the Public Domain* (n 3) 349). When we combine this proviso with the proposition that pre-emptive force is not essential to the ability of authorities to secure coordination, it follows that authorities could fulfil their primary function without having pre-emptive force. This is incompatible not only with F2 but also with F1. In other words, this would mean that Raz hardly offers any functional argument for the pre-emption thesis. Now, since he himself states that he (inter alia) 'tried to give ... functional reasons' in support of his notion of exclusionary reasons (Raz, 'Facing Up' (n 2) 1164), and since I believe that his functional argument ultimately contains an important element of truth, I will proceed on an interpretation whereby coordination reasons form part of the functional argument, consistently with Raz's previously cited comments.

[23] As previously indicated (p 73, n 2), they can be described as content-independent reasons in a limited sense that implies (relative) independence of the content of the particular directive at hand.

[24] As noted before (p 16, n 65), there is a certain overlap between the attributes that are said here to endow some directives with content-independent *weight* and the attributes that Raz believes to ground content-independent *exclusionary* reasons.

[25] See Donald H Regan, 'Authority and Value: Reflections on Raz's Morality of Freedom' (1989) 62 Southern California Law Review 995, 1004–18, 1086–95; Heidi M Hurd, 'Challenging Authority' (1991) 100 Yale Law Journal 1611, 1667–77. See relevant qualification on p 16, n 66.

performance of an action, the subject has reasons to perform it that she would not otherwise have, at least not in a concrete form that can translate into a specific action;[26] for example, the fact that compliance may help her to coordinate with other actors,[27] the risk that non-compliance would adversely affect social order by stimulating others into breaking the law, and considerations of 'fair play' that apply in mutually beneficial schemes of social cooperation.

To illustrate the modus operandi of this model of practical reasoning, let us draw on a simplified non-legal scenario (borrowing from examples of Raz and Donald Regan).[28] Jones has invested in the stock exchange. From time to time she makes decisions about whether to sell some blocks of shares. Suppose that her past decisions in this context have proved to be successful in 60% of the cases.[29] And further suppose that she has now engaged a financial analyst whose past record of decisions on such matters shows success in 90% of the cases. Jones wants to make use of the analyst's guidance by according his instructions some weight in her decision-making. There is probably more than one strategy by which this could be done, and further details would have to be built into the example before one can select a definite formula to this end.[30] For the sake of simplicity, however, let us assume that the above figures are the only available information, and that having derived from these that the ratio between the analyst's success rate and hers is 1½, Jones decides to adopt the following heuristic: she will always treat the case for doing what the analyst prescribes as 50% stronger than it appears in her independent judgement, so as to factor into her decisions his relative expertise.[31] With this adjustment to the balance, Jones follows the analyst's judgement not only when she agrees with what he says, but also in some cases in which she would have decided differently had it not been for his guidance. She would depart from what he prescribes only when she encounters a compelling and straightforward case[32]—not just any case—against the prescribed action. If she treats the analyst's instructions in this way, surely they can direct her to better conformity with applicable reasons for action. On the face of

[26] See explanation of this last proviso on pp 16–17, n 68.

[27] See Regan (n 25) 1025–31.

[28] Raz, *The Morality of Freedom* (n 8) 67–68; Regan (n 25) 1086–87.

[29] Success in this context is obviously a matter of degree. But imagine that the available information indicates only whether a given decision had a positive or a negative impact on Jones's capital over a certain period.

[30] Regan (n 25) 1086–87 and fn 210.

[31] See ibid 1086. Cf Raz, *The Morality of Freedom* (n 8) 68. Recall that when it comes to *legal* directives there may be some other considerations due to which one should take the case for compliance to be even stronger (see pp 16–17).

[32] That is, compelling and straightforward enough to offset the weight that otherwise tips the balance in favour of the analyst's judgement by virtue of his expertise.

it, therefore, it is hard to see why we should accept the thought that a better decision-maker—outside or within the legal domain—can only lead us to improved conformity with applicable reasons for action if his or her directives operate as exclusionary reasons.

In fact, when Raz discusses an example similar to the case of Jones, his argument sounds more qualified than do his comments quoted in Section 6.1, and appears to be reconcilable with the conclusion I have just drawn.[33] He acknowledges at this point that if we accord the judgement of an expert a certain weight which we factor into the balance, this will change our course of action in some cases, which means that our performance can be improved through this strategy. The only claim he puts forward at this juncture is that the degree of improvement attainable by this strategy remains smaller than that which can be achieved through the method of pre-emption:

In cases about which I know only that his performance [i.e. the financial expert's] is better than mine, letting his advice tilt the balance in favour of his solution will sometimes, depending on my rate of mistakes and the formula used, improve my performance. But I will continue to do less well than he does unless I let his judgment pre-empt mine.

... This procedure will reverse my independent judgment in a certain proportion of the cases. Sometimes even after giving the argument favoured by the authority an extra weight it will not win. On other occasions the additional weight will make all the difference. How will I fare under this procedure? ...

... [O]nly by allowing the authority's judgment to pre-empt mine altogether will I succeed in improving my performance and bringing it to the level of the authority.

... [M]y optimific course is to give his decision pre-emptive force.[34]

This qualified claim, that the weighing model leads to a sub-optimific degree of improvement in one's performance, will be considered in Section 6.2.3. Prior to this, however, it is worth considering another facet of the functional argument which the example of Jones calls into question: the previously mentioned claim that the weighing model requires actors to double-count the merits.

6.2.2. The Charge of Double-Counting the Merits

According to Raz, to count both an authoritative directive and the reasons underlying it—as the weighing model, in some sense, requires—is to be guilty of double-counting the merits.[35] The meaning of this charge seems to

---

[33] Raz, *The Morality of Freedom* (n 8) 67–69.

[34] ibid 68–69.

[35] Raz, *Ethics in the Public Domain* (n 3) 215; Raz, *The Morality of Freedom* (n 8) 58–59. See further discussion of 'double counting' reasons in Christopher Essert, 'A Dilemma for Protected Reasons'

be this: weighing authoritative directives along with all other relevant reasons makes little sense because, this way, the same considerations are in effect factored into subjects' reasons for action twice instead of once. Raz fleshes out this point by reference to an example:

> Consider the rule that, when being with one person and meeting another, one should introduce them to each other. The fact that this rule is a sound, valid or sensible rule is a reason for anyone to act in accordance with it. It is a sound rule because it facilitates social contact. But the fact that introducing people to each other in those circumstances facilitates social contacts is itself a reason for doing so. Do we then have two independent reasons? Clearly not. When considering the weight or strength of the reasons for an action, the reasons for the rule cannot be added to the rule itself as additional reasons. We must count one or the other but not both.... [T]he same reasoning applies to ... [authoritative directives]. Either the directive or the reasons for holding it to be binding should be counted but not both. To do otherwise is to be guilty of double counting.
>
> ... [D]irectives and rules derive their force from the considerations which justify them. That is, they do not add further weight to their justifying considerations. In any case in which one penetrates beyond the directives or the rules to their underlying justifications one has to discount the independent weight of the rule or the directive as a reason for action. Whatever force they have is completely exhausted by those underlying considerations. Contrariwise, whenever one takes a rule or a directive as a reason one cannot add to it as additional independent factors the reasons which justify it.
>
> Hence the pre-emption thesis.[36]

But this passage seems to overlook a crucial distinction between normative factors of two different types.[37] The first type is reasons that concern the relevant conduct per se and apply antecedently to the materialization of a related rule; these are the same reasons that have been referred to here as background or underlying reasons, and which Raz calls dependent reasons.[38] The second type is reasons connected with the fact of there being a rule in place that regulates the conduct in question, rather than with the merits of the conduct itself; such reasons, as has been noted, enjoy a certain (if relative) independence of the particular content adopted by the rule.[39] Take Raz's example of a social rule which says that in the presence of people acquainted with you but unacquainted with each other you should introduce them to each other. As Raz notes, the fact that introducing people to each other facilitates social

---

(2012) 31 *Law and Philosophy* 49, *passim*; Katherine Dormandy, 'Epistemic Authority: Preemption or Proper Basing?' (2017) Erkenn, https://doi.org/10.1007/s10670-017-9913-3.

[36] Raz, *The Morality of Freedom* (n 8) 57–59.

[37] A distinction that Raz does recognize at other points (see, e.g., ibid 30–31, 48–51).

[38] ibid 41, 47.   [39] See p 73, n 2; p 103, n 23.

contacts is itself a reason to do so (the validity of which is antecedent to the materialization of the rule). But such background reasons do not exhaust the reasons to follow the rule (given that there is one); nor does the weight of such background reasons amount to the normative weight of the rule. The rule brings into the normative picture some other considerations, for example, by defining a uniform and conventional fashion of behaviour and attaching to it a certain social meaning. Social contacts could conceivably be facilitated in the above circumstances through alternative methods, such as a practice whereby people introduce *themselves* to others, and it might even be the case that before the materialization of a rule we had little or no reason to prefer one method over the other.[40] But the existence of a social rule that adopts the method whereby one introduces other people brings into play further reasons in favour of following this method; for instance, the fact that following a pattern that is commonly practised by others advances social coordination, and the symbolic significance that our behaviour may have in light of etiquette rules. That is, given the above rule, introducing my acquaintances to each other will probably be perceived as a gesture of politeness, amiability, or respect, whereas refraining from doing so may come across as a sign of the opposite dispositions.

Now consider Raz's above-quoted criticism of the weighing model against the background of the distinction just drawn between reasons that antecede a rule (or any other kind of directive) and reasons that the rule brings into play. Once it is recognized that these two types of reason can and should be distinguished within the framework of a weighing procedure, it becomes apparent that the charge of double-counting is unwarranted. Take, once more, the example of Jones.[41] When the analyst prescribes a certain course of action, Jones treats the case for following that course of action as weightier than it would have seemed to her otherwise. But the weight Jones thus adds is merely a function of the ratio between the analyst's success rate and hers. On the example's premises, given that the analyst's success rate is 90% and Jones's is 60%, she adopts a heuristic strategy of regarding the case for doing what he says as 50% weightier than she would otherwise judge it to be. This supplement of weight is meant to mirror only the comparative expertise of the analyst, that is, the normative significance of the fact that *he prescribes* such and such a course of action, which is, once more, a factor distinct from an assessment of the particular content of the instruction at hand. No extra weight is assigned to the background reasons under this strategy, and the weighing model does not require Jones to double-count the merits in the alleged way.

---

[40] Which would not mean we had little or no reason to make a choice between the two and to regulate our behaviour consistently with that choice.

[41] See p 104.

6.2.3. Insufficient Conformity with Reason?

Proponents of the functional argument can face up to the observations made in the previous subsections without abandoning their position altogether, for, as was indicated earlier, there is a qualified variant of the functional argument to which they can turn. This variant acknowledges that the weighing model enables a legal authority to improve its subjects' conformity with reasons for action *to some degree*. But, the argument contends, it does not enable the authority to facilitate conformity with reason *to a sufficient degree*. At first glance, this argument, too, appears to be incorrect. To start with, the argument as I have just put it is vague: what does the wording 'to a sufficient degree' mean? Sufficient for what? The argument can be made intelligible only if it is understood to be referring to sufficiency in relation to some underlying purposes, values, or standards. The argument, in other words, is that the weighing model fails to require a degree of compliance with legal authority commensurate with sufficient conformity with certain underlying *reasons* for acting as the authority prescribes. This, however, seems to be an unwarranted accusation against the weighing model. According to this model, the normative weight of reasons introduced by a directive reflects the true weight of reasons we have for following the institution or individuals who issued it. Further, and more generally, it maintains that we should follow the directive precisely to the extent that we have actual reasons to do so, that is, to the extent that reasons (both pre-existing reasons and those attached to the directive-issuer's operation) to follow it are weighty enough to win against other reasons in the balance—no more and no less. By definition, therefore, it cannot be true that the degree of compliance the weighing model requires is suboptimal.

Proponents of the functional argument might stand their ground in the following way. True, they might say, normative weight can successfully reflect *some* reasons for compliance with an authority—such as reasons to coordinate with others and to maintain social order—but it fails to reflect at least one important type of reason for compliance: reasons grounded in expertise that an authority may have at its disposal. This line of thought can be fleshed out by reference to the now-familiar example of Jones.[42] If Jones always acts in accordance with the analyst's instructions, she will fare well in 90% of the cases, this being the analyst's general success rate. If, on the other hand, Jones takes into account the analyst's relative expertise by way of according weight to his instructions, there may be a portion of cases in which she will depart

---

[42] The following contention is modelled after an argument of Raz: see Raz, *The Morality of Freedom* (n 8) 67–69.

from them. But her doing so, the claim goes, would be sub-optimific because there is nothing in the example's premises to suggest that her knowledge and understanding in any subclass of cases are better than they are in the entire class of cases involved. Thus, we have no reason to expect that in those cases where Jones departs from the analyst's instructions, she will do better than her usual unaided success rate: 60%. And this, in turn, will pull her overall success rate below 90%, that is, below what she could achieve if she simply allowed the analyst to determine for her what is to be done.

This argument seems to me to be erroneous. If Jones accords the analyst's judgement the additional weight it should be given due to his expertise,[43] she will act contrary to an instruction of his only when the case against it strikes her as *sufficiently clear and conclusive*.[44] Such cases, it should be noted, may arise despite the general competence of an authority. Even generally competent authorities may occasionally make mistakes that are easily recognizable by their addressees—whether such mistakes occur as a result of human, technical, or institutional aspects of their operation that may occasionally go wrong. And even when no such failure is involved, an authoritative instruction that is designed to apply with some level of generality may yield a clearly unacceptable outcome in a particular contingency that arises within its ambit. Once we bring to mind the fact that some such incidents will be clearer than others, we can appreciate that an actor's chances to correctly detect them will not be equally or randomly distributed across the relevant group of cases. For, as Regan has noted, there will normally be some measure of positive relation—even if not linear—between the degree to which the choice seems clear to us and the probability of our deciding rightly.[45] Thus, when the analyst errs and his mistake seems very clear, it can be plausibly anticipated that Jones's chances of recognizing the mistake would be somewhat better than at other times when the case seems close. What is more, we can imagine some cases in which the mistake would be so extremely clear, that Jones's (or any other minimally sensible person's) chances of being right in observing the mistake may well exceed 90%.[46] So, even if on the whole she is more likely to conform to reason by following the analyst than by acting alone, to avoid following him *on those occasions* may well be conducive to her overall conformity with reason.[47]

---

[43] Whether this conditional clause is likely to obtain (*mutatis mutandis*) in the legal context will be discussed in Section 6.3.

[44] See n 32.   [45] Regan (n 25) 1089. See generally ibid 1086–95.

[46] See ibid 1086–89.

[47] See ibid 1089 (the body text and fn 211). See also Stephen R Perry, 'Second-order Reasons, Uncertainty and Legal Theory' (1989) 62 Southern California Law Review 913, 934–36, 941 (where Perry seems to proceed on a similar premise).

None of the considerations discussed so far seems to substantiate the functional charge against the weighing model. This, however, does not conclude the matter: as will become clear shortly, there are certain functional problems that the weighing model suffers from after all.[48]

6.3. Biases, Epistemic Deficiencies, and the Weighing Model

6.3.1. The Problem Introduced

In the previous section, the weighing model has been examined from the point of view of an objective observer who possesses correct data about normatively relevant attributes of the decision-makers and institutions involved: for example, their knowledge, ignorance, abilities, and fallibilities. Figures such as the rate of successful decisions of the relevant actor and of a guiding expert were simply a given in the above illustrations. It should be remembered, however, that the conditions of real-life decision-making are different in at least two respects. First, normatively relevant attributes of the decision-makers and institutions involved, such as their relative expertise or their conduciveness to fair social arrangements, are in reality hardly ever quantifiable in the precise numerical forms used in the foregoing illustrations. Normally, the only type of evaluation we can form as to these factors consists in a rough and intuitive estimation. Second, insofar as the weighing model is understood as a method of practical decision-making to be employed by individual actors, it is the actors themselves, and not an objective omniscient bystander, who would be required to identify such personal or institutional attributes and to correctly evaluate their weight. This begins to emerge as a problem for the weighing model once it is recalled that the very discussion of legitimate authority presupposes conditions in which subjects can benefit from practical guidance, partly because their own information or judgement about the substantive matter addressed by the authority is incomplete or otherwise suboptimal. The problem seems to be that, insofar as an actor is uninformed or prone to error regarding the substantive matter regulated by the authority, it may also become harder to safely rely on his assessment of relevant institutional or personal attributes, and in particular on his ability to recognize the fact that, and the degree to which, he is uninformed or prone to error on the matter.[49]

---

[48] These problems have been left out of my analysis thus far in order to facilitate a sufficiently discriminating treatment of the functional argument which, I hope, will help distinguish what part of this argument is well grounded and what part of it is not.

[49] See Frederick Schauer, *Playing by the Rules: A Philosophical Examination of Rule-Based Decision-Making in Law and in Life* (Clarendon Press 1991) 98; Larry Alexander, 'Law and Exclusionary Reasons' (1990) 18 Philosophical Topics 5, 9–10. Cf Scott J Shapiro, 'Authority' in Jules L Coleman

For however genuine the actor's attempt to assess his relative fallibility may be, it is nonetheless possible that his assessment will be subject to the very fallibility he tries to assess.

But how deep and pervasive is this problem? Is it merely a problem of isolated informational deficiencies with no pattern or regularity, or is it, instead, rooted in some deeper and more general phenomenon? It will be argued, by recourse to empirical studies in psychology, that the problem is partly rooted in some biases to which we are systematically susceptible in certain contexts of activity. These biases, it will be observed, are involved in some of the central practical problems that law typically addresses and is comparatively well suited to address[50] (Sections 6.3.2–6.3.5).[51] I should be quick to clarify, however, that the argument will *not* be that law is capable of providing practical solutions in the face of those biases because lawmaking officials tend to be persons less amenable to them (which is, of course, not the case). Instead, law's comparative advantage in this regard—though dependent for its realization on the reasonable personal competence of lawmakers—will be attributed to certain structural characteristics of legal norms and of the settings and mode of decision-making in which lawmakers typically operate. It will then be argued that the frequent presence of those biases in situations or domains of activity which law regulates—and the notion that law has a pivotal role in counteracting them—strongly militate against the weighing model (Section 6.3.6). Finally, the bearing of those biases on the pre-emption thesis will be discussed (Section 6.3.7).

Before turning to the relevant biases, notice should be taken of two distinctions that can inform the discussion. These are, more specifically, two structural differences between the typical environment and mode of decision-making of subjects in everyday activity on the one hand, and of lawmakers operating in their capacity as such on the other. The qualifier 'typical' is important because

---

and Scott J Shapiro (eds), *The Oxford Handbook of Jurisprudence and Philosophy of Law* (OUP 2002) 382–439, at 420–23 (where Shapiro argues that Bayes' theorem entails that an agent who follows the above method of decision-making under conditions of uncertainty would not be able to harness the epistemic benefits of authority).

[50] My emphasis on the relevance of biases in this context is consistent in its general spirit with some of Hume's arguments in his essay 'Of the Origin of Government' (see David Hume, *A Treatise of Human Nature* (first published 1740, LA Selby-Bigge and PH Nidditch eds, Clarendon Press 1978) bk III, pt II, s VII).

[51] Grounding the argument against the weighing model in biases that *law* aims to counteract means that the argument's scope is confined to the legal domain (though some elements of it might be applicable to rules in general). This signifies that, insofar as those biases have lesser relevance, for example, in the context of using the opinions of a financial analyst (which featured in some of the foregoing illustrations), the weighing model might be more appropriate in that context than in the legal domain.

the differences I am about to highlight mark no more than approximate tendencies, ones that shade into each other in more than one way. But they are tendencies that nonetheless have significant implications for our discussion. (1) In the course of everyday activity as ordinary citizens, many (though not all) of our decisions are, in the operative sense, decisions about *our* actions. Lawmakers operating in their capacity as such, on the other hand, typically decide about actions of a general class of people. There is, if you like, a directional difference between these modes of decision-making: the former often consists in a decision whose operative content is first-personal, whereas the latter's operative content (e.g. a rule drafted or voted on) is paradigmatically addressed to a general class comprised almost entirely of other actors.[52] (2) Private decision-making, especially in the course of everyday activity, is often (though, again, not always) *particularistic* in character. Decisions made by a citizen in the practical settings of day-to-day life are often decisions about how to act here and now. The private decision-maker in these settings is therefore placed in relatively close proximity to situational stimuli. On the other hand, the type of decision-making in which legislative and regulatory authorities are engaged is primarily *non-particularistic*. Decisions made by legislators and regulators are characteristically general (not only in the aforementioned sense of their class of addressees, but also regarding the class of circumstances encompassed)[53] and prospective in application—they are intended to apply to future action.[54] Such public officials are placed in decisional settings that are relatively distant from the specificities of each and every case that falls within the purview of their decisions. These distinctions provide relevant background for the argument below, as they will make it easier to appreciate

---

[52] There is an obvious sense in which a lawmaker's decision is also self-personal, in that it can be framed in terms such as: 'should I (i.e. the lawmaker) put forward this or that rule?' or 'how should I vote in a parliamentary proceeding?' However—and this is the sense in which it is not self-personal—the rule she is putting forward or voting on is addressed to a general class comprised almost entirely of other actors. This latter fact has significant implications for our purpose.

[53] See, e.g., Aristotle, *Nicomachean Ethics*, 1137b, in *The Complete Works of Aristotle* (Jonathan Barnes ed, Princeton University Press 1984); HLA Hart, *The Concept of Law* (3rd edn with an introduction by Leslie Green, OUP 2012) 21; Lon L Fuller, *The Morality of Law* (2nd edn, Yale University Press 1969) 33–34, 46–49. The case of judicial decisions is more complicated in this respect. Unlike private decisions, they are exclusively addressed to others; but unlike typical legislative and regulatory acts, they are particularistic in that they are primarily addressed to specific, named individuals (or corporations) and concern specific disputes. However, to the extent that judicial decisions have binding force as precedents for future cases, their function bears some resemblance to that of legislative or regulatory acts. Another relevant difference between judicial and private decision-making is that the former is paradigmatically about past events. In this sense, it takes place in conditions more conducive to careful and reflective decision-making than are the normal conditions in which daily decisions on immediate actions are made.

[54] See, e.g., Fuller (n 53) 35, 51–52.

how, in certain contexts of activity where individual decision-making tends to be affected by certain types of bias, legal modes of regulation offer a suitable remedy, and why this fact undermines the weighing model.

6.3.2. Self-enhancement Bias

The directional difference highlighted above between modes of decision-making—i.e. decisions directed at self/others—brings into play two types of bias with special pertinence to this inquiry. They will be discussed in turn in this and the following subsection. The first type, known to psychologists as the *self-enhancement bias*,[55] tends to emerge when people evaluate their own performance and skills in comparison with those of others. In this context, more often than not, judgement seems to be compromised by inner motives for upholding one's self-esteem,[56] resulting in a pattern documented in several empirical studies under the label 'the better-than-average effect': most people rate their performance and skills as better than those of the average person, with a disproportionately large percentage placing themselves towards the top end of the comparative scale.[57] Thus, for instance, experimental evidence suggests that the majority of drivers take themselves to be more skilful and less risky than most other drivers.[58] And a similar pattern of self-appraisal inflation has been found in surveys pertaining to other personal traits and skills, and across different domains of activity, such as self-assessment of ethical

[55] See, e.g., Raymond Baumhart, *An Honest Profit: What Businessmen Say About Ethics in Business* (Holt, Rinehart and Winston 1968) 20–25; Laurie Larwood and William Whittaker, 'Managerial Myopia: Self-Serving Biases in Organizational Planning' (1977) 62 Journal of Applied Psychology 194; Ola Svenson, 'Are We All Less Risky and More Skillful Than Our Fellow Drivers?' (1981) 47 Acta Psychologica 143; Jonathon D Brown, 'Evaluations of Self and Others: Self-Enhancement Biases in Social Judgments' (1986) 4 Social Cognition 353; Justin Kruger and David Dunning, 'Unskilled and Unaware of It: How Difficulties in Recognizing One's Own Incompetence Lead to Inflated Self-Assessment' (1999) 77 Journal of Personality and Social Psychology 1121. See also K Patricia Cross, 'Not Can, But Will College Teaching Be Improved?' (1977) 17 New Directions for Higher Education 1, 8–12.

[56] Along with other, cognitive and situational factors—see David Dunning, Judith A Meyerowitz, and Amy D Holzberg, 'Ambiguity and Self-Evaluation: The Role of Idiosyncratic Trait Definitions in Self-Serving Assessments of Ability' (1989) 57 Journal of Personality and Social Psychology 1082; Mark D Alicke et al, 'Personal Contact, Individuation, and the Better-Than-Average Effect' (1995) 68 Journal of Personality and Social Psychology 804; Kruger and Dunning (n 55); Justin Kruger, 'Lake Wobegon Be Gone! The "Below-Average Effect" and the Egocentric Nature of Comparative Ability Judgments' (1999) 77 Journal of Personality and Social Psychology 221; David Dunning et al, 'Why People Fail to Recognize Their Own Incompetence' (2003) 12 Current Directions in Psychological Science 83.

[57] See citations in n 55.

[58] Svenson (n 55). See also Caroline E Preston and Stanley Harris, 'Psychology of Drivers in Traffic Accidents' (1965) 49 Journal of Applied Psychology 284.

conduct in business,[59] managerial abilities,[60] academic teaching perform-ance,[61] and logical reasoning.[62]

One important implication of these findings is that they help explain why legal systems need to regulate some of the matters they commonly regulate. The fact that most drivers tend to overestimate their driving skills and under-estimate their dangerousness as drivers, for example, is part of what makes it sensible to have the road traffic safety laws that we find in so many jurisdic-tions. If no legal speed limit, overtaking restrictions, and other similar rules were in force, and drivers were to individually decide on these matters by weighing applicable reasons for action, they would frequently fail to take into account the full extent of their shortcomings and the actual limits of their abilities as drivers. In such a state of affairs, there would be too many wrong decisions on the part of too many drivers. This problem can be overcome by recourse to legal regulation, partly because the judgement exercised by law-makers will turn on how *they* estimate the driving skills of *other people* (i.e. the ordinary driver), rather than on how any given driver estimates his or her own skills. The next step of my argument—contending that law could not adequately counteract such biases if people were to treat its requirements as the weighing model suggests—will be pursued in Section 6.3.6, following a discussion of other relevant biases.

6.3.3. Self-serving Bias

The second type of relevant bias—self-serving bias—tends to emerge when people exercise moral judgement about matters that bear on their own interest. In these situations, more often than not, people perceive relevant facts and moral principles in a manner somewhat beneficial to themselves.[63]

---

[59] Baumhart (n 55).   [60] Larwood and Whittaker (n 55).   [61] Cross (n 55).

[62] Kruger and Dunning (n 55) 1124–25. This may evoke Hobbes's remark that 'such is the nature of men, that howsoever they may acknowledge many others to be more witty, or more elo-quent, or more learned; Yet they will hardly believe there be many so wise as themselves: For they see their own wit at hand, and other mens [*sic*] at a distance' (Thomas Hobbes, *Leviathan* (first pub-lished 1651, Richard Tuck ed, CUP 1991) 87).

[63] David M Messick and Keith P Sentis, 'Fairness and Preference' (1979) 15 Journal of Experimental Social Psychology 418; David M Messick, 'Social Interdependence and Decision Making' in George Wright (ed), *Behavioral Decision Making* (Plenum 1985) 87–109, at 94–100; Leigh Thompson and George Loewenstein, 'Egocentric Interpretations of Fairness and Interpersonal Conflict' (1992) 51 Organizational Behavior and Human Decision Processes 176; Linda Babcock and George Loewenstein, 'Explaining Bargaining Impasse: The Role of Self-Serving Biases' (1997) 11 Journal of Economic Perspectives 109; Erica Dawson, Thomas Gilovich, and Dennis T Regan, 'Motivated Reasoning and Performance in the Wason Selection Task' (2002) 28 Personality and Social Psychology Bulletin 1379. See further, Greg Pogarsky and Linda Babcock, 'Damage Caps, Motivated Anchoring, and Bargaining Impasse' (2001) 30 Journal of Legal Studies 143.

Thus, even if the decision emanates from a process of reasoning that is not wittingly egoistic, excessive weight is nonetheless likely to be assigned to those considerations that coincide with the decision-maker's needs and wants at the expense of other relevant considerations. As Albert Venn Dicey once described it:

[M]en come easily to believe that arrangements agreeable to themselves are beneficial to others. A man's interest gives a bias to his judgment far oftener than it corrupts his heart.[64]

Consider, as relevant evidence, the results of an experiment in which students were asked to make fair judgements as to the payment that should be given to them and to others for different amounts of working hours as exam readers.[65] The questionnaires administered to one group of participants premised that they had worked seven hours, whereas another student had worked ten hours (Self=7, Other=10). The questionnaires administered to another group of participants premised the reverse, namely that they had worked ten hours, whereas another student had worked seven hours (Self=10, Other=7). The results exhibited a clear bias towards overpayment to self. For instance, there was a significantly higher rate of participants in the former (Self=7, Other=10) group than in the latter (Self=10, Other=7) group who consistently replied that fairness requires that equal payments be made to themselves and to the other student (despite the difference in working hours).[66] Moreover, among participants who did not consistently opt for an equal payments outcome as the fairest, the gap between payment to self and payment to other was significantly larger in the latter (Self=10, Other=7) group than in the former (Self=7, Other=10) group.[67]

The tendency instantiated in such findings ties in with some of most important functions law fulfils in social life. Consider, for example, laws protecting and regulating the use of public goods such as parks, beaches, rivers, and other parts of the environment, or laws levying taxes to finance the provision of public goods such as national defence, sanitary services, roads, and railways. If these matters were left unregulated and each citizen were to decide what she ought to do by way of protecting the relevant public goods and how much to contribute to their sustenance, there would arise, among various other problems,[68] the problem of self-serving biases. That is, many citizens, even those who would not act in a deliberately selfish way, would tend to

---

[64] Albert Venn Dicey, *Lectures on the Relation Between Law and Public Opinion in England During the Nineteenth Century* (2nd edn, Macmillan 1914) 15.
[65] Messick and Sentis (n 63).   [66] ibid 428, 432.   [67] ibid 428–29, 432.
[68] For example, coordination difficulties, lack of information about collective needs, and deliberate egoism.

perceive the facts and to balance reasons for actions in a manner somewhat overly sensitive to their individual circumstances and needs, and thus tend to exempt themselves too often from sharing collective burdens.[69] Legal regulation suggests itself as a potential way out of the problem, not least because of its typically generic character—that is, because the paradigmatic mode of decision associated with it is decision directed at the public at large.[70]

There is a relevant counter-argument that will be discussed later in this chapter but is worth noting at this point. Lawmakers and other legal officials, it may be argued, are themselves systematically susceptible to certain forms of bias associated with their position and power. As famously noted by Lord Acton, 'power tends to corrupt', and, as argued by critical legal theorists— such as members of the critical legal studies (CLS) movement, feminist legal theorists, and critical race theorists—legal doctrine and reasoning often suffer from a tilt in favour of traditionally powerful groups in society and work to preserve their domination over weaker groups. While the existence of these forms of bias will not be denied and will help inform the conclusion of this book, it will be argued that they do not undermine the truth or relevance of the observations made in the previous paragraph. For reasons of expositional convenience, however, I defer this argument to a later point in the analysis.[71]

6.3.4. The Availability Heuristic and its Biasing Effect

Another type of bias with particular relevance to our discussion emanates from a cognitive mechanism labelled by Amos Tversky and Daniel Kahneman *the availability heuristic*.[72] These two eminent psychologists have shown that people's intuitive estimations of the probability of events are influenced by availability, that is, the ease with which instances or associations

---

[69] Cf John Locke's comment that in the state of nature 'though the law of Nature be plain and intelligible to all rational Creatures; yet Men being biassed by their Interest ... are not apt to allow of it as a Law binding to them in the application of it to their particular Cases' (John Locke, *Two Treatises of Government* (first published 1689, P Laslett ed, CUP 1967) bk II, ch IX, para 124). See further on law and self-serving bias, Ward Farnsworth, 'The Legal Regulation of Self-Serving Bias' (2003) 37 UC Davis Law Review 567.

[70] This is not to deny that, in some contexts, 'the invisible hand' of the market can effectively operate so that self-interested individual behaviour will incidentally promote collective welfare. The above discussion, however, focuses on other types of situation, in which a regulatory vacuum is not likely to produce collectively desirable results.

[71] pp 123–25.

[72] Amos Tversky and Daniel Kahneman, 'Availability: A Heuristic for Judging Frequency and Probability' (1973) 5 Cognitive Psychology 207; Amos Tversky and Daniel Kahneman, 'Judgment under Uncertainty: Heuristics and Biases' (1974) 185 Science 1124.

of the relevant event come to one's mind.[73] Availability is indicative of the probability of events, since frequently occurring events have, *ceteris paribus*, better chances to be noticed than infrequent ones, and, to this extent, they are likely to be better recalled and easier to imagine.[74] Availability, therefore, can function as a heuristic device that reduces complex tasks of probability computation to simpler mental operations.[75] However, despite its general usefulness, the availability heuristic is subject to serious limitations.[76] First, there is an obvious sense in which the connection between frequency of occurrence and availability is merely a probabilistic connection, rather than a conclusive one: while a frequently occurring event is likely to be discerned by people and register in their minds, it is always possible that some individuals have never, or rarely, or not recently, experienced or witnessed it, which means that it may have low availability from their perspective.[77] For example, young people may be underexposed to incidents of death from diseases linked with age.[78] If availability exerts powerful influence on probability judgements, it may render them, as it were, prisoners of their own experience and lead them to underestimate the likelihood of developing such diseases in the future.[79] Second, availability is affected by additional variables not related to frequency of occurrence, such as whether, and to what degree, the relevant event is a vivid and salient one.[80] For example, terrorist attacks are more dramatic and tend to make more of a news item than do road accidents, and thus may well have increased cognitive availability.[81] By allowing such variables to impinge on how we perceive the likelihood of events, the availability heuristic leads

---

[73] Tversky and Kahneman, 'Availability' (n 72) 207–08.

[74] ibid 208; Tversky and Kahneman, 'Judgment under Uncertainty' (n 72) 1127.

[75] Tversky and Kahneman, 'Judgment under Uncertainty' (n 72) 1124. This may be especially useful in everyday dealings where people only have a limited amount of time and energy for investigation prior to action and may not have relevant statistical data on hand.

[76] ibid.

[77] There are, of course, also indirect means of communication by which impressions can be conveyed, e.g., television and social media. But it is not clear how much these do to correct the potentially distorting influence of availability, and it is possible that they sometimes even reinforce it. For one thing, frequency of occurrence does not seem to be one of the leading criteria by which television broadcasters select their reported items (see body text accompanying n 81). And it is also conceivable that some of the phenomena observed in the context of social media, such as the so-called echo chamber effect, have availability-limiting/distorting effects.

[78] Sarah Lichtenstein et al, 'Judged Frequency of Lethal Events' (1978) 4 Journal of Experimental Psychology: Human Learning and Memory 551, 575.

[79] ibid; Tversky and Kahneman, 'Availability' (n 72) 230; Cass R Sunstein, *Risk and Reason: Safety, Law and the Environment* (CUP 2002) 33.

[80] Tversky and Kahneman, 'Availability' (n 72) 228–29; Tversky and Kahneman, 'Judgment under Uncertainty' (n 72) 1127.

[81] Sunstein (n 79) 50–52. See generally ibid 33–35, 78–98.

to systematic deviations from correct statistical assessment.[82] It has, in other words, a biasing effect.

That these biases permeate people's evaluations of probability has been demonstrated in several experimental studies. In one experiment, for example, participants were given one of the letters K, L, N, R, V in each trial, and were asked whether it is likelier that a word selected at random from a standard English text will be a word beginning with that letter, or a word wherein that letter appears third.[83] Each of the above letters is, in fact, likelier to appear as the third letter in a word. However, it is easier to think instantly of words that begin with these letters; that is, they have greater cognitive availability. The results attested to a biasing influence of this factor: of 152 participants, 105 thought that the majority of the above-listed letters are likelier to appear at the beginning of a word.[84] In another experimental study, in which participants were asked to estimate the frequency of deaths from various causes,[85] significant over- and under-estimations, many of which seem to mirror a biasing effect of availability, were made by the participants.[86] Overestimated items tended to be dramatic and vivid causes of death—for example, floods, tornadoes, and venomous bites or stings—while underestimated items tended to be 'quiet killers' that hardly attract public attention—for example, death from leukaemia, emphysema, diabetes, and heart disease.[87]

The notion of availability-related bias can offer further insight into the type of practical difficulties law aims to overcome in various domains of regulation. We often rely in daily reasoning on subjective assumptions or intuitive estimations about the likelihood of desirable outcomes, potential ramifications, and possible harms associated with alternative courses of action. So it should be clear in light of the above discussion that bias linked with the availability heuristic may work its way into practical decision-making and lead us to suboptimal action. And when the subject of our decision or the setting in which we make it is highly susceptible to such bias, this may significantly strengthen

[82] Tversky and Kahneman, 'Availability' (n 72) 209; Tversky and Kahneman, 'Judgment under Uncertainty' (n 72) 1127.

[83] Tversky and Kahneman, 'Availability' (n 72) 211–12.

[84] ibid 212. Furthermore, each of these letters was thought by a majority of the participants to be likelier to appear at the beginning of a word than as the third letter in it (ibid). The study included additional experiments denoting a similar tendency.

[85] Lichtenstein (n 78). See discussion in Paul Slovic, *The Perception of Risk* (Earthscan 2000) 106–07; Sunstein (n 79) 34.

[86] Lichtenstein (n 78) 562–71; Slovic (n 85) 106–07.

[87] Lichtenstein (n 78) 562–67; Slovic (n 85) 107. A corresponding tendency appeared when participants were given pairs of lethal events and were asked which is the more frequent event in each pair: the bulk of them, for example, incorrectly judged road accidents to be a more frequent cause of death than stroke, and homicide to be more frequent than suicide (Lichtenstein (n 78) 553–59).

the case for regulatory intervention.[88] Thus, for example, a miner, construction worker, or factory operative may be continually exposed in the course of her work to noise, dust, or other unhealthy substances that, although not causing immediately noticeable harm, have detrimental effects in the long term. Given the gradual and unspectacular manner in which such physical or chemical agents materialize into a perceptible injury, the risks associated with them may have low cognitive availability from the perspective of the worker and her employer.[89] So, if left to their own devices to freely determine what precautions to take or whether to purchase a related insurance policy, the worker and her employer are prone to overlook or give too little weight to the above types of risk, and thus fail to take the appropriate measures.[90] Legal regulation provides a suitable way to avert such failures, partly because the normal design of lawmaking systems and procedures allows them to operate on the basis of probability evaluations that are much less visceral and subjective in character, and thus much less vulnerable to the biasing influence of the availability heuristic. Lawmaking officials who contemplate occupational safety and health requirements, or compulsory insurance schemes for certain work environments, will be expected, and will normally have the time and resources, to initiate a methodical risk assessment that relies on statistical evidence.[91]

6.3.5. Intertemporal Choice and Hyperbolic Discounting

The fourth type of bias worth considering here is the tendency to overvalue imminent rewards at the expense of long-term rewards, also known in behavioural science as *myopic* or *hyperbolic discounting*.[92] Manifestations of this

---

[88] This is not to suggest that people could or should generally dispose of the availability heuristic. The point, instead, is that this heuristic should not be settled for in specific situations where (1) it predictably produces errors that are consequential or common enough (or both), and (2) more accurate assessment methods can be relied upon with comparatively small costs and minimal adverse effects.

[89] Moreover, if they have not witnessed instances of the relevant physical damage or disease, cognitive availability may further diminish.

[90] There are also cases in which availability produces the opposite effect. For example, a recent experience of an accident, or overly dramatic news reports about a certain peril, may lead to exaggerated fears and unduly deter people from engaging in a normal activity (Sunstein (n 79) 33–35, 50–52, 78–98).

[91] The availability heuristic is not the only source of errors in people's intuitive perception of risks and probabilities. For a discussion of related error-producing cognitive and emotional phenomena, see ibid 28–49. See also Ehud Guttel and Alon Harel, 'Matching Probabilities: The Behavioral Law and Economics of Repeated Behavior' (2005) 72 University of Chicago Law Review 1197.

[92] See, e.g., George Ainslie, 'Specious Reward: A Behavioral Theory of Impulsiveness and Impulse Control' (1975) 82 Psychological Bulletin 463; Richard J Herrnstein, 'Rational Choice Theory: Necessary but Not Sufficient' (1990) 45 American Psychologist 356; Gordon C Winston and

tendency abound in daily life. 'Imagine', as Richard Herrnstein writes, 'that we could always select meals for tomorrow, rather than for right now. Would we not all eat better than we do? We may find it possible to forgo tomorrow's chocolate cake or second helping of pasta or third martini'.[93] When it comes to the meal at hand, however, this becomes harder, and often the temptation of such instant gratifications prevails over concerns for our health and figures. As David Hume put it in his essay 'Of the Origin of Government':

> In reflecting on any action, which I am to perform a twelve-month hence, I always resolve to prefer the greater good ... But on my nearer approach ... [a] new inclination to the present good springs up, and makes it difficult for me to adhere inflexibly to my first purpose and resolution. This natural infirmity I may very much regret, and I may endeavour, by all possible means, to free myself from it.[94]

This tendency has been tested empirically with quantifiable rewards, such as monetary payments. In this context, the mere observation that people discount value from delayed monetary payments—i.e. that they count them as less valuable than immediate payments of the same amount—is not regarded as evidence of irrational tendencies.[95] For this behaviour is sometimes justifiable by factors like the risk of future frustration or default (due to the debtor's death, bankruptcy, forgetfulness, etc.) and the prospect of interest gains on capital in one's possession.[96] However, the fashion in which people discount confirms that irrational tendencies are also at work here. Experiments have shown that the fashion of discounting usually approximates hyperbolic curves,[97] which is to say that the rate of discounting diminishes with time.[98] By way of illustration, people who discount hyperbolically, at a given point in time (t), discount more for the time interval between t and $t + 2$ than for the time interval between $t + 2$ and $t + 4$, and more for the time interval between $t + 2$ and $t + 4$ than for the time interval between $t + 4$ and $t + 6$, although all of these are intervals of precisely the same length. This manner of discounting leads to incidents of choice inconsistency such as this: people who, at time point t, make a rational choice between future rewards—e.g. opting for some (sufficiently) larger reward payable at $t + 6$ instead of a smaller reward payable

---

Richard G Woodbury, 'Myopic Discounting: Empirical Evidence' in Stanley Kaish and Benjamin Gilad (eds), *Handbook of Behavioral Economics*, vol 2B (JAI Press 1991) 325–42; Kris N Kirby and Richard J Herrnstein, 'Preference Reversals due to Myopic Discounting of Delayed Reward' (1995) 6 Psychological Science 83; Kris N Kirby, 'Bidding on the Future: Evidence Against Normative Discounting of Delayed Rewards' (1997) 126 Journal of Experimental Psychology: General 54.

[93] Herrnstein (n 92) 359.   [94] Hume (n 50) 536.
[95] Herrnstein (n 92) 358; Kirby (n 92) 54–55 and fn 2.   [96] Kirby (n 92) 55 fn 2.
[97] ibid 59–68; Ainslie (n 92); Herrnstein (n 92) 359; Kirby and Herrnstein (n 92).
[98] Herrnstein (n 92) 360; Kirby and Herrnstein (n 92) 83–84; Kirby (n 92) 54–55.

at $t + 4$—would often fail to make such a choice when they are at, say, $t + 3$.[99] Such experimental findings help explain how, when we express a preference or form an intention as to a future course of action, temptations pulling in an opposite direction may become harder to resist as the relevant occasion approaches, and we sometimes find ourselves departing from what we earlier held to be, and what may indeed be, the optimal course of action.[100]

Common tendencies of hyperbolic discounting, and the resulting phenomenon of preference reversal, have key implications for this inquiry. Private decision-making in the course of everyday activity, as was noted earlier, is to a large extent particularistic, in the sense that the decision is often taken by the actor about how to act here and now. Decisions of legislative or regulatory authorities are structurally different in that here it is not the immediate actor but someone else who makes the decision, and who does so prospectively. These differences render the latter decisions structurally less prone than the former to hyperbolic discounting. And, in turn, they help explain the role played by rules of law, with their relative persistence through time, in counteracting this bias. This role is performed, in different ways and to different degrees, by a large variety of legal rules, but, for illustrative purposes, one domain in which it is particularly evident can be mentioned: pension and social security policy. Human patterns of hyperbolic discounting suggest that many young adults tend to underestimate the importance of saving money for old age, as it comes at the expense of payoffs they can receive in the present. Policymakers are placed at a vantage point that allows them more easily to appreciate the full picture of people's old-age needs and changing earning capacities throughout a lifetime, and to formulate adequate responses, this being part of the reason why in many different jurisdictions pension matters are not left wholly unregulated and certain funds for retirement are insured by statutory social security schemes.

6.3.6. Common Biases and the Case Against the Weighing Model

Four types of common bias—i.e. self-enhancement, self-serving, availability, and myopic discounting bias—have been discussed above. It has been

---

[99] See Kirby and Herrnstein (n 92) (reporting a series of experiments in which individuals were presented with choices of the above form) and Herrnstein (n 92) 358 (discussing a similar example). See also Jay V Solnick et al, 'An Experimental Analysis of Impulsivity and Impulse Control in Humans' (1980) 11 *Learning and Motivation* 61; George Ainslie and Varda Haendel, 'The Motives of the Will' in Edward Gottheil et al (eds), *Etiologic Aspects of Alcohol and Drug Abuse* (Charles C Thomas 1983) 119–40; Andrew Millar and Douglas J Navarick, 'Self-Control and Choice in Humans: Effects of Video Game Playing as a Positive Reinforcer' (1984) 15 *Learning and Motivation* 203, 213–17.

[100] Kirby (n 92) 54–55; Kirby and Herrnstein (n 92) 83.

observed that some of the typical problems that law is structurally well suited to address are problems intimately connected with the operation of these biases in practical settings.[101] Law's comparative advantage at addressing these problems, it has been argued, lies partly in the fact that its characteristic conditions and modes of decision-making are structurally less susceptible to the above biases than the conditions and modes of decision-making typical of day-to-day individual activity. Now, suppose that in some situations where individual decision-making is affected by those biases law steps in so as to counteract their influence, but subjects, when faced with legal requirements, employ the weighing model as their decision-making procedure. Practical error could be effectively prevented in this manner only if private actors accord the requirements of law such weight that is sufficient to counterbalance the effect of the foregoing biases. That is, only if those actors are apt to weigh correctly the structural advantages of the relevant institution and form of regulation—and particularly the fact that, and the extent to which, the relevant authority may be better situated to decide than they are due to its lesser susceptibility to those biases—can the method of weighing enable law to function optimally as a guide to right action. The crucial difficulty for the weighing model, however, is that when the weight of those structural advantages is assessed by the actor in situations of bias that made law necessary in the first place, this assessment itself is liable to be biased too.

The difficulty just noted is, in fact, two-pronged. First, in some of the instances considered above, the *same* type of bias that tends to influence the actor's judgement of the action on its merits is liable to compromise her assessment of whether, and to what extent, she is biased. Thus, for example, her assessment of whether and how much she is influenced by self-serving bias is itself an assessment that bears on her own interest, because it may tip the balance for or against her adherence to restrictions and burdens laid down by the law (e.g. tax requirements)—so it, too, may be affected by a self-serving bias. Second, and more generally, it is part of the nature of biases that they tend to operate at an unconscious or not fully conscious level. They colour our perception of things while leaving us under the impression that we see things as they are. And, thus, in situations where individuals are affected by biases, they tend not to recognize the fact that, or the degree to which, they are thus affected. This much is not only implied by the very notion of bias; it

---

[101] These biases have been discussed here separately. In practice, however, the situations that law typically regulates are often situations where some or all of these biases may operate together in a mutually reinforcing manner. Note further that the foregoing discussion does not purport to have exhaustively covered all the biases implicated in social problems addressed by law, nor does it suggest that those social problems can be fully explained in terms of biases.

is also a pattern that finds empirical support in relevant experimental studies, where the tendency for people to overlook their own biases or underestimate their extent has been borne out and given the name *the bias blind spot*.[102]

The observations made above strongly militate against the weighing model. Since action through this model requires assessments by the actor of the normative force of rules against the particularities of each situation of his daily activity, it clearly runs the risk of eliciting, instead of restraining, human propensities such as short-sightedness and self-favouritism. This mode of practical reasoning with rules is, in effect, likely to stand in the actor's way to making optimal use of the potential benefits of rule-guided action. And if we abstract from the mode of decision-making of an individual subject and take account of the dynamic of interacting subjects, the possibility of an even worse outcome emerges into view. For each person's recognition that other people are less than disposed to comply with legal requirements may itself operate as a stimulator of non-compliant behaviour, which would, in turn, further deepen and reinforce a disinclination to comply. It thus seems highly questionable whether orderly social life and the essential goods that hinge on it would be attainable if the weighing model were to socially prevail. (And, as previously noted, I set aside here the neither-practically-sustainable-nor-morally-palatable scenario of a government wielding a level of coercion that would be so extensive, frequent, and severe as to 'solve' by itself the problem, let alone durably solve it. I will discuss the limitations of coercion and the perils of overreliance on it in Section 8.2.)[103]

At this point, however, it is appropriate to consider an objection that was mentioned and set aside earlier. The objection, to reiterate, is that lawmakers and other legal officials are themselves systematically susceptible to certain

---

[102] Emily Pronin, Daniel Y Lin, and Lee Ross, 'The Bias Blind Spot: Perception of Bias in Self Versus Others' (2002) 28 Personality and Social Psychology Bulletin 369; Emily Pronin, Tomas Gilovich, and Lee Ross, 'Objectivity in the Eye of the Beholder: Divergent Perceptions of Bias in Self Versus Others' (2004) 111 Psychological Review 781; Joyce Ehrlinger, Thomas Gilovich, and Lee Ross, 'Peering Into the Bias Blind Spot: People's Assessment of Bias in Themselves and Others' (2005) 31 Personality and Social Psychology Bulletin 680; Cynthia McPherson-Frantz, 'I AM Being Fair: The Bias Blind Spot as a Stumbling Block to Seeing Both Sides' (2006) 28 Basic and Applied Social Psychology 157. See also James Friedrich, 'On Seeing Oneself as Less Self-Serving Than Others: The Ultimate Self-Serving Bias?' (1996) 23 Teaching of Psychology 107. Note that the observation is not that people never acknowledge their biases or always underestimate their extent. Rather, what has been observed is a general tendency: a pattern that characterizes most people's self-perception in most of the cases where they show biases. Further, it is possible that education about biases can improve people's ability to recognize their own biases in retrospect or even reduce their effect in the future. What remains doubtful is, first, whether such an improvement is easy to attain or sustain; second, whether setting up a society-wide, bias-related educational scheme is a feasible project; and, third, whether people can eliminate their biases altogether by means of knowledge and reasoning alone.

[103] Also relevant, if less directly, is the empirical discussion in Section 8.5.

forms of bias associated with their position and power. 'Power tends to corrupt', as the famous maxim goes, and, as some critical legal theorists have observed, there are patterns of legal thought and practice that work to perpetuate social injustice through their tendency to preserve or even reinforce the domination of traditionally powerful groups in society (e.g. in terms of economic class,[104] gender,[105] or race[106]). Now, real as they are, these forms of bias do not, I think, undermine the present argument against the weighing model. To start with, it should be borne in mind that any worthwhile legal and political system will have in place several safeguards that help curb the effect of structural biases associated with legal and political power. These include, for example, constitutional protection of civil and political rights (including rights that facilitate social and political change, such as freedom of speech and assembly), institutional checks and balances between separate branches of government, a reasonable degree of adherence by officials to 'rule of law' constraints on the exercise of arbitrary power, and a reasonable level of compliance with rules of due process, transparency, and accountability. However, such safeguards, and rights in particular, have themselves been a target of critique by several CLS scholars,[107] in the light of which it becomes especially important to delineate the modest claim made at this point: it is readily conceded that such safeguards are effective only up to a point, and may even have certain negative effects (e.g. insofar as their associated rhetoric can work to conceal or blind us to existing patterns of social injustice). It is only claimed here that, on balance, such safeguards make a beneficial contribution towards constraining and reducing the possibility for power abuse. Or, to put the point differently, if I had to choose between living with these safeguards or living without them, I would emphatically choose to live *with* them, despite their shortcomings. Now, this qualified claim does not

---

[104] See, e.g., Morton J Horwitz, *The Transformation of American Law, 1780–1860* (Harvard University Press 1977); Mark Tushnet, 'A Marxist Analysis of American Law' (1978) 1 Marxist Perspectives 96; Richard L Abel, 'Torts' in David Kairys (ed), *The Politics of Law: A Progressive Critique* (3rd edn, Basic Books 1998) 445–70.

[105] See, e.g., Nadine Taub and Elizabeth M Schneider, 'Women's Subordination and the Role of Law' in David Kairys, *The Politics of Law* (n 104) 328–55; Catharine MacKinnon, 'Feminism, Marxism, Method and the State: Toward Feminist Jurisprudence' (1983) 8 Signs 635; Catharine MacKinnon, *Feminism Unmodified: Discourses on Life and Law* (Harvard University Press 1987); Mary J Mossman, 'Feminism and Legal Method: The Difference it Makes' (1987) 3 Wisconsin Women Law Journal 147. Cf Rosemary Hunter, 'The Power of Feminist Judgments?' (2012) 20 Feminist Legal Studies 135.

[106] See, e.g., Derrick A Bell, *Race, Racism and American Law* (6th edn, Aspen Publishers 2008); Kimberlé Crenshaw et al (eds), *Critical Race Theory: The Key Writings That Formed the Movement* (The New Press 1995); Richard Delgado and Jean Stefancic (eds), *Critical Race Theory: The Cutting Edge* (3rd edn, Temple University Press 2013).

[107] See, e.g., Mark Tushnet, 'The Critique of Rights' (1993) 47 SMU Law Review 23.

conclude the matter. For it prompts a further question, which focuses on the *remaining extent* to which even those worthwhile legal and political systems I refer to fall short. Does not the remaining extent to which even such systems preserve or reinforce existing power relations mean that the weighing model should be adopted as an appropriate remedial measure? I believe the answer is 'no' on a number of counts, of which I will mention two. First, for the opposite answer to be warranted it must be true that the negative consequences expected if the weighing model were to prevail are 'the lesser evil' compared to the degree of injustice the relevant legal systems (i.e. those with appropriate institutional safeguards) tend to preserve or generate. This, however, seems questionable, particularly if one accepts the claim made earlier that a scenario in which the weighing model were to socially prevail would doubtfully be compatible with an acceptable level of social order and the vital goods it enables.[108] Second, and perhaps more pertinently, there is fortunately no need to make the difficult choice between those two 'evils': there is a third alternative that will be put forward in the following chapters, and which offers a way out of this predicament. In a nutshell, the proposed solution consists of a normative attitude whose holders, on the one hand, are more firmly committed to law-abidance than actors who follow the weighing model, but, on the other hand, remain responsive to case-specific reasons against compliance and ready to disobey seriously iniquitous laws. Further explanation and defence of this alternative is left for the next chapters.[109]

Another comment should be made by way of clarification. The foregoing analysis revolves around biases that tend to be present in certain decision-making environments. Clearly, however, those biases are not generated simply and only by the *environment* of decision-making. At least some of them may be prompted partly by the actor's own *motivational weaknesses*. But it is essential to remain clear about what type of motivational weakness is relevant to the present inquiry, and to distinguish it from other types that fall outside its ambit. Some motivational problems on people's part are of a kind or intensity that no conception of legal normativity can effectively solve. This is probably what Raz has in mind when making the following remark:

How does the pre-emption thesis solve the problem of motivation? People can have reason to do what they are not motivated to do, and they may be motivated to do what they have no reason to do. So even if the law's subjects have a pre-emptive reason to comply with the law, it is not clear how that can contribute to the solution of the problem of motivation.

[108] Including those rule-of-law benefits, and the level of protection for rights, that the relevant legal systems *do* provide.
[109] chs 7–9.

Postema may have in mind people who are motivated to act as they are morally required, and who believe that they are morally required to comply with the law. But if they are so motivated, then they would obey the law (assuming that they know what it is) whether or not the law has pre-emptive force. Of course, if it has pre-emptive force then they will recognize its pre-emptive force. But that does not solve the problem of motivation. The problem of motivation has been solved by the original stipulation that people are motivated to obey the law.

On the other hand, if people are not motivated to obey the law then the fact that the law has pre-emptive force will do little to motivate them; at least it will do nothing more to spur their motivation than would be done by any other normative force the law may have, or may have had.[110]

Motivational problems of a sufficiently serious kind will persist and emerge regardless of how law's bearing on practical reason is understood. It can be reasonably assumed, for example, that most murderers and rapists will not be dissuaded from their wrongdoing by the notion that law has pre-emptive normative force or by the notion that it carries normative weight. The means more likely to be effective in such cases are, if any, punishment or moral rehabilitation. But the world does not comprise only individuals who are not at all motivated to act as they should and individuals who are fully motivated to do everything they ought to. Even generally well-intentioned agents who are appalled by serious wrongdoings, as most of us presumably are, may sometimes face motivational difficulties to avoid certain *mala prohibita* or to comply with legal requirements whose breach appears to have relatively remote moral implications, as may be the case, for example, with an easily evadable tax obligation or certain road traffic restrictions (where the relevant traffic risk is less than conspicuous). Motivational difficulties of this kind, as seen above, tend to manifest themselves, inter alia, in the form of biases in one's judgement, bona fide as it may be.[111] Such biases, then, mark the point

---

[110] Raz, 'Postema on Law's Autonomy' (n 22) 12.

[111] See discussion in Sections 6.3.2–6.3.5. On the role of motivational factors in biased reasoning, see, e.g., Tom Pyszczynski and Jeff Greenberg, 'Toward an Integration of Cognitive and Motivational Perspectives on Social Inference: A Biased Hypothesis-Testing Model' in Leonard Berkowitz (ed), *Advances in Experimental Social Psychology*, vol 20 (Academic Press 1987) 297–340; Ziva Kunda, 'The Case for Motivated Reasoning' (1990) 108 Psychological Bulletin 480; Peter H Ditto and David F Lopez, 'Motivated Skepticism: Use of Differential Decision Criteria for Preferred and Nonpreferred Conclusions' (1992) 63 Journal of Personality and Social Psychology 568; David Dunning, 'On the Motives Underlying Social Cognition' in Norbert Schwarz and Abraham Tesser (eds), *Blackwell Handbook of Social Psychology*, vol 1 (Blackwell 2001) 348–74; Dawson, Gilovich, and Regan (n 63); Emily Balcetis and David Dunning, 'See What You Want to See: The Impact of Motivational States on Visual Perception' (2006) 91 Journal of Personality and Social Psychology 612; David Dunning, 'Motivated Cognition in Self and Social Thought' in Mario Mikulincer and Phillip R Shaver (eds), *APA Handbook of Personality and Social Psychology*, vol 1 (American Psychological Association 2015) 777–803.

at which motivational difficulties connect, and become relevant, to the issue we are concerned with, namely, law's functionality under different models of practical reasoning. As we have seen, by requiring actors to regularly engage in weighing of legal requirements in their daily setting of activity, the weighing model would undermine law's ability to counteract those common biases.[112]

6.3.7. Common Biases and the Pre-emption Thesis

Does the pre-emption thesis, as viewed in the broader context of Raz's conception of authority, provide a normative framework that better enables law to counteract the biases discussed above? I believe it does, but not in the right way and not to a satisfactory degree. While other parts of this book have criticized the *way* in which the pre-emption thesis 'mediates' between people and reasons,[113] this subsection focuses only on the *degree* of its potential success in counteracting the above biases. When read in conjunction with Raz's normal justification of authority,[114] the pre-emption thesis leads to something like the following proposition: once an authority is recognized as more competent to decide in a certain domain, a subject is expected to follow its directives in that domain regardless of what he considers to be right on the balance of (first-order) reasons for action. Within that domain, a subject need not decide on matters that have been resolved by the authority, and to this extent he can avoid the influence of biases that would otherwise affect his decisions. To this extent, then, the pre-emption thesis succeeds where the weighing model fails. But the pre-emption thesis, as figuring in Raz's theory of authority, might still leave subjects too exposed to the biases discussed here. This is so primarily due to the piecemeal character of Raz's conception of the conditions of legitimate authority (i.e. the only authority that, by his understanding, exercises pre-emptive force) and particularly the condition stated in his normal justification thesis.[115] There are two senses in which the Razian test for the legitimacy of authority is piecemeal. First, the legitimacy

---

[112] Nothing in what I have said is meant to suggest that people should *generally* refrain from evaluating the law and from weighing its merits and demerits (if for theoretical purposes or for practical ones, such as exercising their democratic rights in order to bring about a change in the law or the regime or, when necessary, resorting to other forms of resistance). The fulcrum of my argument has been biases and fallibilities connected with the *environment and mode* of decision-making in which we operate as subjects of the law in the course of our everyday activity. And the above environment and mode of decision-making also demarcate the scope of my objection to the weighing model: it is only an objection against using this model as our ordinary method of reasoning for purposes of everyday activity under the law.

[113] chs 2–4.   [114] Raz, *The Morality of Freedom* (n 8) 53.

[115] See Raz, *The Morality of Freedom* (n 8) 53, 70–80, 99–104; Raz, *Ethics in the Public Domain* (n 3) 347, 350.

of the authority exercised by government over its citizens is tested, according to Raz's normal justification thesis, on an individual basis—that is, afresh for each citizen, taking into account his knowledge, understanding, personal or professional skills, etc.[116] Second, the question of legitimacy is tested, on this conception, in a domain-specific manner, that is, independently and separately with regard to each domain of activity regulated by the relevant legal system, rather than in a system-wide manner, whereby the system's operation across its various regulatory areas is viewed as a whole.[117] Consequently, the typical scope of legitimate governmental authority is envisaged from a Razian perspective to be considerably patchy. Thus, for instance, according to Raz, '[a]n expert pharmacologist may not be subject to the authority of the government in matters of the safety of drugs, [and] an inhabitant of a little village by a river may not be subject to its authority in matters of navigation and conservation of the river by the banks of which he has spent all his life'.[118]

There are two types of decision that, under this conception, subjects are expected to make in unfavourable conditions that involve potential exposure to biases. First, each subject should judge regarding each regulated domain of activity in which he is engaged (where the domain's proper limits are to be identified by the subject himself) whether the authority is more competent to decide than he is in that domain.[119] The pharmacologist or the villager, instead of generally ascribing normative force to the directives of their government by virtue of its overall operation as a reasonably just and sensible government (provided this is the case), are asked to assess whether their own knowledge and expertise in pharmacology or in matters of conservation of the river are superior or inferior to the authority's. This very assessment,

---

[116] Raz, *The Morality of Freedom* (n 8) 73–74, 77–78, 104; Raz, *Ethics in the Public Domain* (n 3) 347, 350.

[117] Raz, *The Morality of Freedom* (n 8) 68–69, 73; Raz, *Ethics in the Public Domain* (n 3) 350; Raz, 'The Problem of Authority' (n 11) 1027.

[118] Raz, *The Morality of Freedom* (n 8) 74. See also ibid 77–78. Cf Timothy Endicott, 'The Subsidiarity of Law and the Obligation to Obey' (2005) 50 The American Journal of Jurisprudence 233, 244–48 (featuring an example of a 'wise electrician' faced with regulations regarding home wiring insulation); and see contra Gerard V Bradley, 'Response to Endicott: The Case of the Wise Electrician' (2005) 50 The American Journal of Jurisprudence 257.

[119] It might be objected that the conditions expressed in Raz's 'service conception of authority' concern only the *justification* of authority, as distinct and separate from the criteria to which citizens should have recourse in their practical decision-making. But it would be difficult to theoretically defend that separation given the premises of Raz's conception of authority. Raz maintains that the legitimacy of an authority is correlated with a duty to obey it (Raz, *The Morality of Freedom* (n 8) 23–37). For him, if (and only if) A has legitimate authority over B, B has a duty to obey A. So Raz would not be able to sever the connection between citizens' decision-making and the justification of authority without thereby implying that whether B has a duty to obey A is not relevant for B's practical decision-making—which seems to be an unsupportable proposition.

however, is liable to be distorted by the assessor's partiality and particularly by the type of self-enhancement bias that frequently leads people to overestimate their ability and skill.[120] Second, if in a certain domain a subject is better informed than the authority, then within that domain he is left to his own devices and may depart from legal rules as he deems fit. This is unsatisfactory, because individual expertise and knowledge regarding a substantive matter do not avert the effect of various biases that are essentially connected with the conditions in which daily life decision-making takes place—for example, the stimuli surrounding a decision-maker—and have little to do with lack of information. For instance, it is doubtful that an expert in pharmacology, even the best one, should not be subject to drug safety regulations or that a villager, however well versed in her local environment, should not be subject to regulations concerning its conservation. When performing private or occupational tasks in real-life conditions they, like most human beings, are susceptible to the tendency to hyperbolically discount the value of future goods, to self-serving biases, to bias linked with the availability heuristic, and to other unwanted influences of their decisional environment.[121] It is reasonable to suppose, therefore, that their being subject to regulations concerning their own practices has an important role in ensuring that they perform optimally or, at any rate, in improving their performance.

One might, of course, say that such common biases should be taken into account in the application of Raz's test for the legitimacy of authority;[122] such common biases, one might say, signify that in fact the expert pharmacologist and the villager well acquainted with his surroundings are in all likelihood subject to the government's legitimate authority in matters that concern their own expertise. But if this is so, the typical scope of legitimate authority no longer appears to be piecemeal in character and is therefore quite different from how Raz pictures it. So long as he maintains his piecemeal conception of authority, there remains an extent to which the argument from common biases militates not only against the weighing model, but also against his model.[123] And yet, none of this should detract from the fact that the pre-emption thesis provides a normative framework which better enables law to

---

[120] See Section 6.3.2.

[121] For example, also relevant here is the phenomenon dubbed in French *déformation professionnelle*, namely the tendency for people to view things from the narrow perspective of their own profession, while failing to give sufficient attention to the wider picture.

[122] Raz, at least at one point, alludes to this possibility (Raz, *The Morality of Freedom* (n 8) 75).

[123] Could a proponent of pre-emption seek to retain this notion while opting for a non-piecemeal test of legitimacy? This could mean that our practical judgement may be pre-empted over a scope which is as wide as the ambit of typical legal systems—an outcome that seems hardly palatable in terms of its implications for individual autonomy.

counteract those biases than the weighing model does, since the latter, unlike the former, invariably requires subjects to act through all-things-considered balancing exercises, whether or not the matter at hand falls within their area of expertise.

6.4. Conclusion

The argument examined in this chapter—the functional argument as applicable to the legal context—says, in a nutshell, this: legal authorities would not be able to fulfil the function of directing their subjects to better conformity with reasons for action if subjects were to respond to their requirements by acting on the balance of reasons for and against compliance (i.e. what has been dubbed here the weighing model), instead of treating their directives as pre-emptive reasons.[124] More particularly, the argument contends that the weighing model robs authorities (including legal authorities) of their ability to fulfil basic functions such as overcoming common problems caused by lack of information, facilitating coordination between people, and enabling them to share practices in spite of moral disagreements.

In Section 6.2, the functional argument has been subjected to a prima facie examination, which led to the following observations: if weighable reasons for and against compliance included only reasons for and against the particular content of the relevant directive (what has been referred to here as background or underlying reasons), the functional argument would be warranted. In fact, however, they may include also normatively significant attributes of the relevant legal institution, such as its ability to facilitate coordination in virtue of its salience, its access to relevant expertise, or other relevant qualities it may possess. Thus, the extent to which the relevant institution possesses attributes that make compliance with it worthwhile can be represented in the form of reasons for action that bear corresponding weight. And the weightier they are, the likelier it is that they would tip the balance in favour of acting as the law requires. On the face of it, therefore, it is hard to see why one should accept the claim that the weighing model would systematically undermine law's ability to adequately function as a normative guide to right conduct.

These prima facie observations were later revisited and found to be crucially incomplete. Their main utility, however, has been in facilitating a sufficiently discriminating treatment of the functional argument so as to distinguish what

---

[124] The argument, as previously noted, refers to the function authorities are meant to perform by means of normative guidance, rather than by coercive measures or the threat to use them.

part of this argument is well grounded and what part of it is not. In Section 6.3, the spotlight has been directed onto a specific type of functional difficulty that the weighing model actually encounters. A functional assessment of a model of practical reason should take into account the real-life conditions under which reasoning actors operate. In real life, however, an actor may lack not only substantive information regarding the matters law regulates (be it safety issues, environmental matters, finance, or any other matter), but also information about relevant characteristics of the decision-makers involved, and particularly about the fact that, and the degree to which, he is comparatively fallible or uninformed on the matter.

The scale and depth of this difficulty, I have claimed, is best appreciated in light of its connection with the operation of certain biases. Drawing on relevant empirical studies in psychology, I have sought to highlight the relevance of four types of bias: self-enhancement, self-serving, availability, and hyperbolic discounting biases. These biases, I have observed, are implicated in some of the characteristic practical problems which legal systems address and, more importantly, which law is structurally well suited to address. The operation of these biases, I have further argued, has critical implications for the weighing model. It means that subjects whose practical attitude towards the law is dominated by the weighing model—by the idea that, when faced with a legal requirement, they should weigh the reasons for and against compliance as applicable to the case at hand and act accordingly—are prone to error that would lead to sub-optimific and unjustified law violations. Such biases, I have concluded, show that the weighing model fails to provide a framework of practical reasoning within which legal authority could adequately fulfil its function as a normative guide to right conduct.[125]

---

[125] See relevant comments regarding the limitations of coercive force and sanctions on pp 100, 123 and in Section 8.2.

PART III

THE DISPOSITIONAL MODEL

7

The Dispositional Model Expounded

7.1. Introduction

If the observations made in Parts I and II are correct, then, for all their different valuable insights, both the pre-emption thesis and the weighing model suffer from significant flaws that call for their rejection. This part of the book builds on my previous observations in an attempt to develop and defend an alternative model. I begin, in this section, with a brief introduction of my proposed model, which will be followed by a more elaborate explanation in Sections 7.2–7.4. Before I proceed, I should only ask my reader to bear in mind that, in keeping with this structure of presentation, my initial comments will be somewhat skeletal, but I will gradually build more details into my proposal and beef it up with more arguments in the subsequent sections and chapters.

The model I propose—which I call *the dispositional model*—is centred on a triadic intersection between *law*, the domain of *practical reasons*, and the *attitudes* that shape and influence our behaviour. According to this model, a crucial aspect of law's potential normative significance lies with reasons that are neither exclusionary reasons nor ordinary reasons for action, but rather reasons to adopt a certain attitude towards the legal system. More specifically, the model makes the following contention: the fact of there being a legal system in place which meets certain competence and quality prerequisites—namely, a system whose substantive laws, procedures, and design generally exhibit a reasonable level of conformity with morality as well as with principles of legality (also known as the rule of law),[1] and are in general reasonably apt to secure valuable goods—is a reason for its subjects to adopt an attitude

---

[1] By referring here separately to morality and to the rule of law I do not intend to take sides in the debate over whether the rule of law embodies moral values. See, e.g., Lon L Fuller, *The Morality of Law* (2nd edn, Yale University Press 1969); Jeremy Waldron, 'Why Law—Efficacy, Freedom, or Fidelity?' (1994) 13 Law and Philosophy 259; Nigel E Simmonds, *Law as a Moral Idea* (OUP 2007); Kristen Rundle, *Forms Liberate: Reclaiming the Jurisprudence of Lon L Fuller* (Hart Publishing 2012). See contra, e.g., HLA Hart's review of Fuller, *The Morality of Law* in (1965) 78 Harvard Law Review 1281; Joseph Raz, *The Authority of Law: Essays on Law and Morality* (2nd edn, OUP 2009) ch 11; Matthew H Kramer, 'On the Moral Status of the Rule of Law' (2004) 63 Cambridge Law

Legal Directives and Practical Reasons. Noam Gur. © Noam Gur 2018. Published 2018 by Oxford University Press.

which I will refer to as a law-abiding attitude and will characterize in detail in the course of this chapter.[2] Most pertinently, the conative (or behavioural) component of this attitude is a *disposition*, a standing inclination, to comply with legal requirements. So, those who adopt a law-abiding attitude, as I characterize it, thereby adopt a disposition to comply with the law. Henceforth, I will frequently refer to the model as claiming that (under the above conditions) we have a reason to adopt a disposition to comply with the law. This is a terminological shortcut that I employ for expositional convenience—it should not be taken to detract from anything said here about other elements of a law-abiding attitude and their relevance to my model.

At this point, two core characteristics of what I call a disposition to comply with the law should be highlighted. First, as is normally the case with dispositions that become part of the agent's attitudinal profile, it has a degree of deep-seatedness and persistence. It is not a mere momentary response to a particular situation or a fleeting state of mind, but rather an inclination that acquires some degree of embeddedness in the relevant agent and thus tends to endure through time.[3] To this extent and in this sense, therefore, the motivational force it exerts gains *independence* of specific reasons for action as applicable to particular situations; it makes its force felt in a manner not conditional on those reasons and on how the agent assesses them in a given situation.

However, and this is the second core characteristic of the advocated disposition, since it reflects no more than an *inclination*, its influence on one's actions remains provisional in character. It is less than determinative of how one acts in a given situation, but rather remains an *overridable* force, a force amenable to be overridden in situations where sufficiently powerful reasons against compliance crop up. This means that, despite its independence of reasons for action that apply to the case at hand, it does not exclude those reasons from the range of factors that influence the decision how to act—it has a content-independent but non-exclusionary nature. Adopting the above disposition, therefore, implies (inter alia) following a habit or pattern of action without showing *absolute* commitment to it (i.e. such that cannot be overridden),

---

Journal 65. I have briefly expressed some of my thoughts on this question elsewhere (Noam Gur, 'Form and Value in Law' (2014) 5 Jurisprudence 85).

[2] By 'a reason' I mean here, more precisely, a reason that in the final analysis—after considering reasons that speak in favour of adopting other attitudes towards the law—establishes that we should adopt a law-abiding attitude; in other words, a reason that wins against reasons for adopting other attitudes towards the law.

[3] I say 'tends' because the advocated disposition is not a permanent disposition that can never be abandoned or changed. Rather, its relative fixedness only means that abandoning or changing it does not normally occur overnight or on a case-by-case basis.

neither in general nor within certain domains of activity. It means that one is in general more likely than not to comply, but not that one will comply in every case, come what may—not even within the scope of an authoritative rule. To forestall possible doubts, it should be emphasized that, by referring to a habit, I do not mean to suggest that there is nothing more to the advocated disposition than a habit. The disposition I am arguing for is part of a normative attitude, whereas mere habits, as HLA Hart famously highlighted, can be devoid of normative character.[4]

I should be quick to make another clarification: It is not claimed by the dispositional model that reasons to adopt a disposition to comply with the law are the only type of reason that can materialize through the operation of legal institutions. The model acknowledges that directives issued by legal institutions sometimes, or even often, also give rise to ordinary reasons for action, namely, reasons to perform the action they require or avoid the action they forbid.[5] For instance, in contexts of activity where coordination is desirable, legal requirements may convert this abstract desideratum into specific reasons for performing the actions they require in virtue of their ability to affect the likely behaviour of actors with whom we wish to coordinate. However, the model contends that law has some further attributes that (subject to satisfaction of the above-stated prerequisites)[6] invest it with normative force qualitatively different from ordinary reasons for action. Notably, as we have seen in Part II, law has certain structural attributes that enable it to solve social problems caused or aggravated by fallibilities and biases operative in our daily environment of activity. This fact recommends private actors *not* to act on simple assessments of the balance of (pre-existing and law-related) reasons for action. For such assessments will often be tainted by biases that work towards non-compliance. However, this fact does *not* go as far as excluding otherwise applicable reasons for action. What it recommends, instead, is that subjects act on the basis of determinations that are predisposed to compliance with law (to such an extent that will, by and large, suffice to counteract opposing situational biases).[7] I have just now alluded to some

---

[4] HLA Hart, *The Concept of Law* (3rd edn with an introduction by Leslie Green, OUP 2012) 55–61.

[5] I will elaborate on the difference between ordinary reasons for action and reasons to adopt a disposition in Section 7.4. Further relevant comments will be made in Section 9.2, where the distinction between state-given and object-given reasons will be discussed.

[6] p 135.

[7] Another benefit of the advocated disposition is that, to some extent, it abates deliberation burdens and saves time in the course of daily activity. This itself, however, could be done by simple heuristics or presumptions. What explains the need for a settled attitude with motivational purchase and persistence is my argument about the relevance of common situational biases. I will say more about the difference between presumptions and dispositions in Section 9.1.

aspects of my justificatory case for the dispositional model, but my primary aim at this stage remains merely to introduce and elucidate its claims. A direct argument in support of the model will be offered in Chapter 8.

As is apparent from my earlier comments, the dispositional model does not endorse a law-abiding attitude under *any* legal system, but only under a legal system that meets certain prerequisites of competence and quality: the system's laws, procedures, and design must generally exhibit an at least reasonable (as distinct from perfect or ideal) level of conformity with relevant moral standards, as part of which they must be at least reasonably just and fair; they must generally exhibit a reasonable level of adherence to rule-of-law principles of governance; and they must, in general, be reasonably apt to secure valuable goods whose attainment is typically dependent on the operation of law and which are suitable for legal regulation. Here I should add that, as I see these prerequisites, they cannot be met by a system that fails to give reasonable protection to basic human rights: for example, freedoms of movement, speech, assembly, and association, and rights of political participation, such as the right to vote and run for office. For ease of reference, I will hereafter be using somewhat abridged phrases to refer to systems that meet the above prerequisites, phrases such as *reasonably just and apt to serve valuable purposes* or *reasonably just and well-functioning*.

Two further comments are worth making regarding these prerequisites. First, as the reader may have noticed, there is an extent to which some or all of them overlap—for example, the extent to which the valuable goods referred to in the last prerequisite are such that they have *moral* significance.[8] The overlap between these prerequisites—whose exact extent is a debatable matter that need not be addressed here—is merely a reflection of my effort to prevent anything from unduly slipping through their net. Second, I should clarify that these prerequisites are deliberately cast at a relatively high level of generality, such that it provides latitude for further specification. This seems to me warranted given the focal purpose of this book, which is to inquire into a modal aspect of the relationship between law and practical reasons, rather than to search or establish a theory about the justificatory underpinnings of legal legitimacy.[9] Accordingly, some scope is left for divergence of opinion as to whether this or that legal order meets those prerequisites, which would not be disagreement about the correctness of my argument, but only on how it applies to some particular instances.

---

[8] See also my comment in n 1 regarding the relation between morality and the rule of law.

[9] There is, of course, an extent to which these two lines of inquiry shade into each other. But the difference in focus between them is real.

It is worth pausing at this point to briefly demonstrate how a desirable behavioural disposition of the kind envisaged here is thought to operate.[10] For this purpose, consider the following set of premises. Suppose I will be faced in the near future with a sequence of cases where I will have to choose whether or not to perform a certain action (φ).[11] In 80% of the cases the reasons in favour of φ-ing will be weightier than the reasons against it. In 20% of the cases the reasons against φ-ing will be weightier than the reasons in favour of it. Also suppose that certain stimuli that are often present in the setting in which I decide whether to φ render me biased against φ-ing. The bias has the following effect: if I decide what to do purely by weighing reasons for action, I would end up choosing not to φ in more than 20% of the cases—say, in 40%. This means that in at least 20% of the cases I would be making the wrong choice. Let us now say that when situated in a more neutral environment, away from the above stimuli, I recognize my suscepti-bility to bias against φ-ing. So I decide to habituate myself to the opposite pattern of action: I accustom myself to φ-ing regularly.[12] In addition, I ask a close friend to strongly encourage me to stick to my φ-ing whenever he sees me. As a result of these (and perhaps some other similar) measures, I become disposed to φ. It turns out that when I am thus disposed, the proportion of cases in which I avoid φ-ing decreases, and, with it, the proportion of cases in which I make the wrong choice. My disposition to φ allows me to perform better than I would without it. So I had good reason to adopt this disposition and I have good reason to retain it.

The counterparts of both core characteristics of the dispositional model can be found in the above example, and may serve to further elucidate the model. First, my disposition to φ need not be, and is not likely to be, such that it renders me entirely irresponsive to the weight of opposing reasons that may crop up in a particular situation. Instead, it may fulfil its beneficial role even as an inclination whose force remains overridable, namely a force that may yield in the presence of case-specific reasons of a *certain* weight which militate against φ. Second, despite being overridable, its character as part of an internalized attitude means that it acquires some independence as a cona-tive and motivational force in my decision-making, and that it has a degree

---

[10] By 'behavioural disposition' I mean a disposition that tends to manifest itself in its possessor's behaviour. This wording is not intended as an allusion to the approach known as behaviourism.

[11] The body text above does not cite specific actions in order to keep the illustration general enough, but φ could be readily replaced with a more concrete example, say, 'going for a morning jog'.

[12] Which does not mean a completely automaton-like mode of action that is utterly oblivious to its normative surroundings.

of persistence in its influence on my actions.[13] As such, it can make its force felt even in particular situations where the reasons for adopting it (in this example, the conditions that tend to give my judgement a bias against φ) are absent. It follows from this that, although a desirable disposition such as the above allows me to perform, on the whole, better than I would without it, there may be *specific situations* in which its effect is counterproductive, leading me to an error that I would not have made without the disposition. For example, there may be cases in which the reasons against φ-ing are only slightly stronger than the reasons for it and my judgement happens not to be subject to a bias against φ-ing. In such circumstances, were it not for my disposition to φ, I would be likely to choose (correctly) not to φ, but, being disposed in favour of it, I am likely to choose (erroneously) to φ. These implications, and their specific instantiation under the dispositional model, will be further elaborated and illustrated in Section 7.4. Prior to that, however, more should be said about attitudes and dispositions in general, and about a law-abiding attitude in particular. This will be my focus in the following two sections.

7.2. Attitudes and Dispositions

I will not attempt here anything like a formal definition of an attitude or a disposition. But I will offer some explanations, which, I hope, may sufficiently elucidate the sense in which I am using these notions. To make a first step, let us say that an attitude is a mindset or a mental posture towards some thing or things, for example, inanimate objects, persons, or states of affairs. And let us call the thing or things at which an attitude is directed *the attitude object*. By way of example, the attitude object of Michael's highly professional attitude is his work. This characteristic of attitudes—namely, the fact of their being specifically directed at another thing, the attitude object[14]—is part of what distinguishes them from another type of mindset: moods. Claire's cheerful or grumpy mood is a mindset that may project on her perception of (and interaction with) her entire surroundings, rather than being directed at one specific feature thereof.

Another particularly relevant characteristic of the idea of an attitude is this: attitudes typically influence their possessor's interaction with the world. More precisely, an attitude disposes its possessor to respond to the attitude

---

[13] The fact that the disposition was overridden in a specific case that presented me with weighty reasons against φ does not by itself mean that I have ceased to be generally disposed to φ.

[14] This quality can also be referred to as 'intentionality', but I refrain from using this term to avoid confusion with 'intentionality' in the sense of being deliberate or purposive.

object (and to other relevantly connected objects) in some way or ways typical to the attitude in question. Thus, Michael's professional attitude disposes him to perform occupational tasks in certain ways characteristic of professionalism, for example, to a high standard, in a timely manner, without letting extraneous personal interests impinge on his work, and so on. And it may also dispose his responses to other (relevantly connected) objects, such as the manner in which other people perform their work. It may, for example, dispose him to respond with disapproval to unprofessional behaviour on the part of others. There is, then, an intimate connection between the ideas of an attitude and a disposition. The connection is this: the operative significance of an attitude—that is, the way in which it affects its possessor's interaction with the world—is best understood in terms of a disposition: namely, a disposition of the attitude's possessor to respond to the attitude object (and other relevantly connected objects) in ways characteristic of the relevant attitude.[15] A clear manifestation of this relationship between attitudes and dispositions is found, for example, in the typical forms of locution in which 'disposition' and 'attitude' respectively feature. Disposition locutions frequently employ the word 'to' followed by a verb ('He is disposed to ... ', 'She has a disposition to ... '), which denotes their operative focus. Attitude locutions, on the other hand, frequently employ, instead of the above terminology, the words 'towards' or 'for' followed by a noun designating the attitude object ('He has a favourable attitude for ... ', 'Recent years have seen a change in public attitudes towards ... '). The latter locutionary form does not directly express the operative significance of attitudes. At most, it contains implicit reference to it.

I will have more to say about attitudes later in this section. But the preceding point provides a useful background for some comments on dispositions, to which I now turn. It is neither possible nor necessary to embark here on a survey of the extensive philosophical literature on the metaphysics of dispositions.[16] As was noted, I will confine myself to explanatory comments essential for elucidating the sense in which I am using this notion. A disposition, in the sense relevant to my argument, can be generally characterized as an inner tendency of a person to behave in a particular way when certain conditions, 'stimulus conditions' as they are commonly referred to in the relevant philosophical parlance, are present. Thus, if P, C, and B are,

---

[15] This is not to say that dispositions and attitudes are fully correlative. As will be noted later, not all dispositions are linked with attitudes (p 144).

[16] See, e.g., Elizabeth W Prior, *Dispositions* (Aberdeen University Press 1985); David Armstrong, Charlie B Martin, and Ullin T Place, *Dispositions: A Debate* (Routledge 1996); Stephen Mumford, *Dispositions* (OUP 1998). For an overview, see Sungho Choi and Michael Fara, 'Dispositions' in Edward N Zalta (ed), *Stanford Encyclopedia of Philosophy* (2012) <http://plato.stanford.edu/entries/dispositions> accessed 2 November 2017.

respectively, the disposition's bearer, the disposition's stimulus conditions, and the disposition's behavioural manifestations, then P is likely to B in C (absent countervailing forces). Now, let us take a closer look at some aspects of this general characterization. First, it will be noted that this characterization does not refer to dispositions in general, but rather focuses on a particular subclass of dispositions. It focuses on dispositions of *human beings* (human dispositions, if you like), and, more specifically, on human dispositions that tend to manifest themselves in their possessor's *behaviour* (which I will refer to as behavioural dispositions).[17] This latter supplement is called for because people can have dispositions that are hardly classifiable as behavioural dispositions, for example, viral susceptibilities, food or dust allergies, or the like.

Second, I speak of '*inner* tendencies' in order to emphasize the difference between dispositional statements and other statements on probable occurrences or factual patterns. There are statements about probable occurrences or factual patterns which are attributable to factors external to their subject matter, and which are not naturally construed as implying a disposition thereof. Thus, for example, to say that X is likely to get wet if left out in the rain is not naturally understood to imply that X has a disposition to get wet when out in the rain (X could be anything, as pretty much anything that is left out in the rain gets wet[18]), in contrast to, for example, statements about what is likely to happen to X when it gets wet given some physical or psychological features thereof (e.g. if X is a sugar cube, it is likely to dissolve when in contact with water—it has a disposition to dissolve in such conditions).[19]

Third, the above characterization of dispositions may help clarify what I earlier referred to as *the operative focus* of dispositions. It makes it clear that, by speaking of the operative focus of dispositions, I do not mean that dispositions must actually manifest themselves in actions. This is so due to two facts associated with the characteristic modality of dispositions.[20] The first is that dispositions, as mentioned above, have stimulus conditions for their manifestations.[21] If the stimulus condition of a disposition is absent, its manifestation will remain a mere potentiality, rather than an actuality. Jack's friendly disposition, for example, depends for its manifestation on the fact of there being other people (or other creatures towards whom one can display friendliness) in Jack's surroundings or within his reach. If Jack is the only

---

[17] See comment in n 10.   [18] Even if only on its surface, as waterproof material does.

[19] That dispositions are intrinsic to their bearer is widely, but not unanimously, accepted among philosophers writing on dispositions (see discussion and references in Choi and Fara (n 16) s 5).

[20] On the modality of dispositions, see, e.g., Stephen Mumford and Rani Lill Anjum, 'Dispositional Modality' in Carl F Gethmann (ed), *Lebenswelt und Wissenschaft: Deutsches Jahrbuch für Philosophie*, vol 2 (Meiner 2011) 468–82.

[21] See, e.g., Choi and Fara (n 16) s 1.1.

survivor of a shipwreck who lives on a desert island, his friendly disposition is not likely to manifest itself under his present life circumstances, at least not in his outward behaviour and in the normal way it manifests itself.[22] Second, few dispositions (if any at all) are sure-fire dispositions which always necessarily manifest themselves when their stimulus conditions obtain.[23] This is particularly true of human behavioural dispositions, such as the one advocated herein. Our behavioural dispositions rarely (if ever) amount to absolute, exceptionless determinants of our behaviour. Even when their stimulus conditions obtain, they might not result in the relevant behaviour—whether because of the presence of overriding factors or due to an arbitrary deviation of the actor from her ordinary pattern of behaviour. An altruist, for example, is disposed to assist others in need, but might refrain from doing so in a given situation, say, where she herself is in dire straits.

I have already noted that attitudes are intimately connected to dispositions, in that the latter express the operative significance of the former. Two further clarifications are called for, however, with regard to this relationship. First, while saying that the operative significance of attitudes is best encapsulated in terms of dispositions, I wish to express no view on whether dispositions encapsulate not merely the operative significance of attitudes, but also the very concept of an attitude. Something like this question, it is worth noting, is subject to a debate in the philosophy of mind between what may be called 'the representational approach' and 'the dispositional approach' to attitudes.[24] While much of the debate has revolved around one type of attitude, namely belief, it carries over to other types of attitude.[25] According to the representational approach, having an attitude is, ultimately, a matter of having some specific internally stored mental representation (tokened in a manner appropriate to the attitude in question).[26] Thus, for example, to believe that humidity is congenial to orchids is to have an internally stored mental

---

[22] Or, to borrow an example in a similar vein from Julia Driver, '[i]n a society of plenty, some people may have the disposition to help those in need, yet never exercise it because it just so happens that no opportunities to do so present themselves' (Julia Driver, *Uneasy Virtue* (CUP 2001) 74).

[23] See, e.g., Jennifer McKitrick, 'Dispositional Pluralism' in Gregor Damschen et al (eds), *Debating Dispositions: Issues in Metaphysics, Epistemology and Philosophy of Mind* (Walter de Gruyter 2009) 186–203, at 190–91.

[24] See, e.g., Eric Schwitzgebel, 'A Dispositional Approach to the Attitudes: Thinking Outside of the Belief Box' in Nikolaj Nottelmann (ed), *New Essays on Belief: Constitution, Content and Structure* (Palgrave 2013) 75–99; Eric Schwitzgebel, 'Belief' in Edward N Zalta (ed), *Stanford Encyclopedia of Philosophy* (2015) <http://plato.stanford.edu/entries/belief> accessed 2 November 2017.

[25] Schwitzgebel, 'A Dispositional Approach to the Attitudes' (n 24).

[26] See, e.g., Jerry A Fodor, *Psychosemantics* (MIT Press 1987) 16–21. Fodor invokes a metaphor of mental 'boxes' wherein tokens of different attitudes are stored—a 'belief box', a 'hope box', and so on (ibid 17).

representation or symbol which stands for 'humidity is congenial to orchids' (tokened in a manner appropriate to beliefs). According to the dispositional approach to attitudes, on the other hand, having an attitude is, ultimately, a matter of having certain dispositions.[27] Thus, for example, to believe that humidity is congenial to orchids is to be disposed to respond with assent to the utterance 'humidity is congenial to orchids',[28] to be disposed to act as though humidity is congenial to orchids when engaged in a relevant pursuit such as growing orchids,[29] and to have other similar dispositions. Now, interesting as it is, this debate is not material to my argument herein. What is material to my argument is that the operative significance of attitudes (the manner in which they shape their possessor's actions and reactions) is best captured in dispositional terms. But this much is compatible not only with the dispositional approach to attitudes, but also with the representational approach. For the latter does not deny that attitudes have the effect of disposing our actions and reactions; it only denies that our being thus disposed is the very thing that constitutes our having an attitude.

A second clarification about the relationship between attitudes and dispositions is that, while every attitude implies or results in a disposition, not every disposition is an implication or a product of an attitude. For one thing, some dispositions can be ascribed to things that are not capable of having attitudes in the sense relevant to our discussion, such as inanimate objects.[30] Thus, for example, the fragility of a glass, the elasticity of a rubber band, and the solubility of a pill are all dispositions without attitudes. And even human beings, who are obviously capable of having attitudes, can have certain dispositions which do not match any attitude—as is the case, for example, with Tom's susceptibility to flu or Jane's sensitivity to sunlight. Attitudes and dispositions, therefore, are not perfectly correlative notions.

In Section 7.1, it was noted that there is a degree of persistence (or, relative stability and endurance) which characterizes what I call a law-abiding attitude and a disposition to comply with law. Is this type of persistence characteristic of attitudes (and their concomitant dispositions) in general?

---

[27] See, e.g., Schwitzgebel, 'A Dispositional Approach to the Attitudes' (n 24), and, in the context of beliefs, Ruth B Marcus, 'Some Revisionary Proposals about Belief and Believing' (1990) 50 Philosophy and Phenomenological Research 133.

[28] Assuming conditions such as comprehension of the language used, sincerity, and physical capacity to communicate.

[29] Or, to be disposed to act this way *ceteris paribus*.

[30] I add the qualifier 'in the sense relevant to our discussion' because the word 'attitude' is sometimes used with the meaning of a physical posture or orientation of a body. In aviation terminology, for example, 'attitude' is commonly understood to mean an aircraft's orientation relative to the direction of travel.

I think it is, even if its degree varies quite considerably. But I should clarify the point I am making here. While it seems to me that many of the things we call attitudes do, in fact, exhibit some degree of persistence, the exact point I am making is different. My point here is not an empirical one about the actual modus operandi of things that we call attitudes,[31] but rather a point about the common meaning and connotation of the notion of an attitude as it features in ordinary usage and understanding. The notion is normally invoked to signify mental states that enjoy some degree of continuing hold in their possessor's mind. It is not normally employed to denote a mere fleeting state of mind, such as a short-lasting mood or a momentary thought. Thus, for example, we would not normally make a statement of the form 'Anna had an attitude problem this morning'. If what we are referring to is Anna's state of mind *this morning*, we are much more likely to say something like 'Anna was in a foul mood this morning'. Or, if what we are referring to is an attitude after all, we are much more likely to say simply that 'Anna has an attitude problem', which is naturally understood to imply that her problem is ongoing.

I have claimed that the notion of an attitude ordinarily implies *a degree of* persistence or *relative* stability. My claim is couched in these non-absolute terms because, although we normally take attitudes to be more persistent and stable than ephemeral mental states, attitudes are not (and are not normally regarded as) entirely permanent or immutable. If attitudes *were* entirely permanent or immutable, political cultures and social mores would be far less changeable than history actually suggests they are, and many common practices—such as psychological counselling, campaigns, advertising, and public relations—would be rendered a near or complete futility, making their widespread use in modern society hard to explain. Some of the most conspicuous facts about our social world, then, suggest that attitudes have (and are commonly understood to have) the capacity to form, develop, change, and be abandoned over time. What is more, attitudes are not even taken to be the most persistent and stable precursor of human behaviour; notably,

---

[31] Empirically, the stability of attitudes is a debated matter. Empirical support for attitudes' stability can be found, e.g., in Steven R Brown, 'Consistency and the Persistence of Ideology: Some Experimental Results' (1970) 34 The Public Opinion Quarterly 60; Gerald Marwell, Michael T Aiken, and NJ Demereth, 'The Persistence of Political Attitudes Among 1960s Civil Rights Activists' (1987) 51 Public Opinion Quarterly 359; Duane F Alwin, Ronald L Cohen, and Theodore M Newcomb, *Political Attitudes over the Lifespan: The Bennington Women after Fifty Years* (University of Wisconsin Press 1991). For evidence casting certain doubts on attitudes' stability, or at least on the extent to which attitudes are stable, see, e.g., Timothy D Wilson and Dolores Kraft, 'Why Do I Love Thee?: Effects of Repeated Introspections about a Dating Relationship on Attitudes toward the Relationship' (1993) 19 Personality and Social Psychology Bulletin 409.

personality traits are normally understood to be more persistent and less changeable than attitudes.[32]

My claim about the persistence of attitudes has focused on ordinary usage and understanding of the notion of an attitude. It is worth noting, however, that there exist some technical modes of expression in which 'attitudes' may bear different meanings. When philosophers of mind or action talk about propositional attitudes, for example, they refer to a range of mental states which includes, inter alia, mental states that have no intrinsic tendency to persist, but come and go in response to present circumstances—for instance, one's present belief that there is now a pizza in the oven or one's current desire to eat it. Such mental states are sometimes referred to in philosophical discourse as 'occurrent' beliefs or desires, which are contrasted to 'dispositional' beliefs or desires, namely those that have the tendency to endure through time.[33] Now, I take no issue with the use of 'attitude' as a category inclusive of occurrent mental states. But, irrespective of its possible merit within the specific technical context where it is customary, it remains the case that, outside that context, the notion of an attitude ordinarily connotes a state of mind that enjoys some continued existence and relative tendency to endure. And these connotations are, to my mind, part of what makes the notion of an attitude apt to convey the idea I am propounding here.[34]

I have earlier pointed out that, when speaking of 'reasons to adopt a disposition to comply with the law', I am in fact using a certain terminological shortcut. Although this wording captures what is, in practical terms, most significant about the proposed model, it does not fully express the notion I have in mind. To reiterate, what I have in mind is, more fully and precisely, reasons to adopt a *composite attitude* whose primary mode of influence on our behaviour takes shape in a disposition to comply with law. That attitude— which I have called a law-abiding attitude—consists of some elements other than the above disposition, whether we ultimately define those elements as mental representations (as the representational approach to attitudes would have it)[35] or as other, concomitant dispositions (as the dispositional approach to attitudes would have it).[36] In the following section, I will say more about the advocated law-abiding attitude and its elements.

---

[32] This is not to suggest that personality traits, in contrast to attitudes, are permanent or virtually permanent. Whether they are is a question that need not be discussed here.

[33] For a critical view on this terminology, see Schwitzgebel, 'A Dispositional Approach to the Attitudes' (n 24) 92–94.

[34] Even if the distinction between occurrent and dispositional attitudes were to be assumed here, no alteration to my argument would be required, apart from stipulating that when referring to attitudes I should be understood to mean dispositional attitudes.

[35] Body text accompanying n 26.   [36] Body text accompanying n 27.

7.3. A Law-Abiding Attitude: Components and Formation

The aim of this section is to shed light on the notion I call a law-abiding attitude, with a particular focus on the components and formation of that attitude. For this purpose, I will, inter alia, draw on relevant resources in social psychology and sociology, though this will be done only to the limited extent possible given the scope of this work. Let me begin with a structural distinction frequently utilized in psychological discourse about attitudes. Attitudes, according to this distinction, comprise three different components: a cognitive, an affective, and a conative or behavioural component.[37] It will be noted that users of this distinction in psychological discourse have not uniformly aligned themselves with one contending view in the philosophical debate between the representational and the dispositional approach to attitudes.[38] With this in mind, I will set this debate to one side when using the above tripartite distinction, and, as before, I should not be read as taking sides in it.

The cognitive component of an attitude includes perceptions, concepts, and beliefs about the attitude object[39]—for instance, Claire's belief that Rachel is a sincere and good-hearted person. The affective component of an attitude consists in emotions or feelings evoked by the attitude object—for example, Claire's feelings of fondness and respect towards Rachel. The conative or behavioural element of an attitude consists in a disposition to act in a certain way towards the attitude object—for example, Claire's disposition to maintain contact with Rachel and to spend time in her company. I will not assume that attitudes invariably consist of all three components—that anything that does not contain all of them is not an attitude.[40] I will, however, draw on the above tripartite distinction in order to highlight and distinguish between the different possible elements of which a law-abiding attitude may consist.

[37] See, e.g., Daniel Katz and Ezra Stotland, 'A Preliminary Statement to a Theory of Attitude Structure and Change' in Sigmund Koch, *Psychology: A Study of a Science*, vol 3 (McGraw-Hill 1959) 423–75, at 428–32; Milton J Rosenberg and Carl I Hovland, 'Cognitive, Affective, and Behavioral Components of Attitudes' in Milton J Rosenberg et al (eds), *Attitude Organization and Change: An Analysis of Consistency Among Attitude Components* (Yale University Press 1960) 1–14, at 1.

[38] Note in this connection that cognitive and affective features of an attitude could, in principle, be characterized in terms of either the representational or the dispositional approach. And also worth mentioning is the fact that at least *some* of the key propounders of the above tripartite distinction have used a dispositional definition of attitudes (see, e.g., Katz and Stotland (n 37) 428; Rosenberg and Hovland (n 37) 1).

[39] Rosenberg and Hovland (n 37) 4.

[40] For comments in support of this assumption, see Alice H Eagly and Shelly Chaiken, 'The Advantages of an Inclusive Definition of Attitude' (2007) 25 Social Cognition 582, 589–91, 596.

Much of what I say in the present chapter concerns the *behavioural component* of the law-abiding attitude endorsed here. So the question may be asked: what do, or may, the other two components—the cognitive and affective components of the relevant attitude—consist of? My answer will refer to what these components *may*, or *are likely to*, consist of—as I do not maintain that there is just one unique cognition or sentiment that must accompany the disposition advocated here. Let us begin with the cognitive level. The likeliest cognitive companion of the advocated disposition is a belief (whose degree of explicit and salient presence in one's consciousness may vary from one individual to another) that legal institutions are *entitled* to issue directives and require that we abide by those directives (at least insofar as their directives do not run counter to especially weighty moral reasons). This perceived entitlement need not be conceptually isomorphic to a Hohfeldian claim-right with a correlative duty owed specifically to the right holder.[41] The law-abider may conceive of legal officials as exercising a power entrusted to them by the public, and may view herself as accountable (in relation to breaches of law) first and foremost to her fellow citizens. But let me abstract away from the directionality issue, and turn to a relevant comparison. The belief just mentioned, as I see it, shares something with the belief Max Weber called *Legitimitätsglaube* (legitimacy-belief). According to Weber, 'the basis of every system of authority, and correspondingly of every kind of willingness to obey, is a belief, a belief by virtue of which persons exercising authority are lent prestige'.[42] The word 'prestige' in this statement should receive a rather inclusive rendering, capable of accommodating all three authority types that make up Weber's famous typology of authority: namely, traditional authority,[43] charismatic authority,[44] and—most pertinent to modern legal systems and, thus, to our own discussion[45]—legal-rational authority.[46] The specific belief relevant to the latter type of authority is, in Weber's words, 'a belief in the "legality" of patterns of normative rules and the right of those elevated to authority under such rules to issue commands'.[47]

---

[41] For arguments against the assumption of a claim-right type of directionality in this context, see, e.g., David Enoch, 'Authority and Reason-Giving' (2014) 89 Philosophy and Phenomenological Research 296, 324–28.

[42] Max Weber, *The Theory of Social and Economic Organization* (Talcott Parsons ed, AM Henderson and Talcott Parsons trs, Free Press 1964) 382.

[43] An authority that rests 'on a belief in the sanctity of immemorial traditions' (ibid 328).

[44] An authority that rests 'on devotion to the specific and exceptional sanctity, heroism, or exemplary character of an individual person' (ibid).

[45] Though, as will be noted below, Weber's classification refers to *ideal types*, which, on his understanding, do not empirically exist in their *pure* form (ibid 382).

[46] ibid 328–41.   [47] ibid 328.

Here, however, a further question may be raised: is it assumed (by Weber's analysis or by my own arguments) that the law-abider's belief in the right of legal institutions to dictate behaviour emerges from an underlying evaluative perception regarding moral attributes of law or the legal system in question? On Weber's understanding of the legitimacy of a legal authority (with 'legitimacy' meaning here the fact of there being a general belief of the above type), the answer seems to be negative. Weber talks in this connection not about the *moral* character of a legal order, but about its *rational* character. More specifically, he talks about *formal* attributes of a legal order[48] which, he believes, enable people to pursue what he calls *purpose-rational action* (action orientated towards the attainment of the actor's chosen ends),[49] as distinct from the law's conformity with *substantive* norms[50] which guide what Weber calls *value-rational action* (action orientated by a conscious belief in relevant values, such as ethical values).[51] For Weber, then, even insofar as the acceptance of a legal order as authoritative ensues from individuals' assessment of the legal order's functioning, that assessment characteristically engages an instrumental type of rationality, which he conceives of as distinct and separate from moral evaluation.

It bears noting that Weber's analysis does not purport to mirror or fully correspond to the empirical reality of people's attitudes towards law or their legal system. For his methodological focus is on what he calls 'ideal types', that is, analytical constructs 'formed by the one-sided *accentuation* of one or more points of view'.[52] As such, they are designed to throw light on some true elements of the phenomenon under investigation, but, in their pure form, as Weber puts it, 'cannot be found empirically anywhere in reality'.[53] And, indeed, relevant empirical work, such as studies carried out by Austin Sarat and Tom Tyler, show (if indirectly) that Weber's association of legal legitimacy with purpose-rationality alone does not correspond to the reality of people's attitudes towards the law.[54] These studies indicate that *moral* perceptions

---

[48] Primarily, the extent to which it operates through enacted, general rules applied by recourse to 'unambiguous general characteristics of the facts of the case' (Max Weber, *Economy and Society: An Outline of Interpretive Sociology* (Guenther Roth and Claus Wittich eds, University of California Press 1978) 656–57).

[49] For the full definition and an explanation, see ibid 24, 26.

[50] Norms that include, for example, 'ethical imperatives' or 'political maxims' which are not derived from the law itself (in the sense noted in n 48 above)—see ibid 657.

[51] See Weber's full definition and explanation in ibid 24–25.

[52] Max Weber, 'The Meaning of "Ethical Neutrality" in Sociology and Economics' in his *The Methodology of the Social Sciences* (Edward A Shils and Henry A Finch eds and trs, Free Press 1949) 90.

[53] ibid.

[54] Austin Sarat, 'Legal Obligation: A Survey Study' (1977) 9 Polity 384; Austin Sarat, 'Studying American Legal Culture: An Assessment of Survey Evidence' (1977) 11 Law and Society Review

about a legal order (such as the perception that its laws and procedures are generally fair and just) often contribute to the formation in people's minds of a belief in the legitimacy of that order.[55] This finding seems highly plausible when we bear in mind the moral import of some of the typical operations of law, such as the moral significance of some of the matters law typically regulates and the morally consequential nature of some of its enforcement measures (e.g. incarceration, fines, or confiscations of assets). Given the moral gravity attached to these typical operations of legal systems, it would be rather surprising if we found that moral perceptions about valuable aspects of the legal order have no part in the formation of common beliefs about its legitimacy.

While the point made in the previous paragraph is primarily empirical, its subject matter—the role of morality in the formation of legitimacy belief—is relevant for the (normative) model proposed here, the dispositional model. The model readily accepts that adherence by a given legal system to moral values and principles (e.g. justice, fairness, and respect for persons) should play a central role in the formation of legitimacy belief; and that, if the legal system descends to a pattern of repeated failures to live up to these moral standards, the result should be an erosion of legitimacy belief. And yet, the question may be asked: is the clarification just made about the dispositional model really compatible with the model's core claim? And, in particular, is it compatible with the earlier noted sense in which the envisaged disposition exerts a *content-independent* influence on one's behaviour? I believe it is. For there is a difference between, on the one hand, the factors that contribute to the formation of an attitude and a concomitant disposition, and, on the other hand, the conditions that trigger behavioural manifestations of that disposition in a particular case. Suppose, for example, I have acquired, through a relatively prolonged assimilation of the view that 'gambling generally tends to have destructive effects on one's life', a general and firmly embedded disposition against gambling. Having materialized, my disposition (if strong enough) may lead me to refrain from gambling even on an occasion where I am presented with arguments, which I find persuasive, as to why gambling on that particular occasion would be desirable and harmless, and why my assessment of these arguments is not prone to error in the present conditions. I have acquired the disposition through recourse to a relevant rationale, but, once the disposition is in place, it may exert its influence even when

427; Tom R Tyler, *Why People Obey the Law* (with a new afterword by the author, Princeton University Press 2006) 71–178; Jason Sunshine and Tom R Tyler, 'The Role of Procedural Justice and Legitimacy in Shaping Public Support for Policing' (2003) 37 Law and Society Review 513.

[55] See citations in n 54.

the rationale for its acquisition is absent.[56] A similar distinction is applicable to the law-abiding disposition envisaged here, thus making it possible for the disposition to be content-independent in one sense (concerning the conditions for its activation) and content-dependent in another sense (concerning the process of its formation). This distinction, as applicable to the dispositional model, will be further illustrated and elaborated in Section 7.4.

Is there an affective component to the envisaged law-abiding attitude? A preliminary caveat worth making here is that 'affective' is not to be confused with 'affection'. The intimate type of emotions that the latter word connotes could well be regarded as misplaced in the context of attitudes towards the law. 'Affective', by contrast, is a broader category that includes, inter alia, less intimate feelings that seem more relevant to our context, such as respect, satisfaction, and allegiance. Thus, the affective component of a law-abiding attitude may consist, for example, in respect and gratitude for legal officials, such as judges, magistrates, prosecutors, or police officers,[57] for what is viewed as their service to society and (especially in the case of police officers) for incurring the personal risk involved in their work; or, some pride in what is seen as political and moral virtues of the legal system of one's country, such as its enduring commitment to democratic values and the rule of law, the spirit of respect for human rights embodied in its constitution, and its ethically progressive and enlightened laws;[58] or, feelings of allegiance to and support for the law and legal system of one's society,[59] which are possibly

---

[56] The influence of attitudes on behaviour has been empirically questioned in the past by a number of social psychologists and sociologists (see, e.g., Richard T LaPiere, 'Attitudes vs. Actions' (1934) 13 Social Forces 230; Allan W Wicker, 'Attitudes versus Actions: The Relationship of Verbal and Overt Behavioural Responses to Attitude Objects' (1969) 25 Journal of Social Issues 41). But an extensive body of subsequent research has compellingly shown that—while attitudes are only one among various factors that shape people's behaviour, while attitudes vary in their strength, and while their operation is subject to certain conditions—attitudes do influence behaviour (see, e.g., Martin Fishbein and Icek Ajzen, 'Attitudes Towards Objects as Predictors of Single and Multiple Behavioral Criteria' (1974) 81 Psychological Review 59; Mark Snyder and William B Swann, 'When Actions Reflect Attitudes: The Politics of Impression Management' (1976) 34 Journal of Personality and Social Psychology 1034; Martin Fishbein and Icek Ajzen, 'Attitude–Behavior Relations: A Theoretical Analysis and Review of Empirical Research' (1977) 84 Psychological Bulletin 888; Lynn R Kahle and John J Berman, 'Attitudes Cause Behaviors: A Cross-Lagged Panel Analysis' (1979) 37 Journal of Personality and Social Psychology 315; Christopher J Armitage and Mark Conner, 'Efficacy of the Theory of Planned Behavior: A Meta-Analytic Review' (2001) 40 British Journal of Social Psychology 471). It may be added, anecdotally, that radical scepticism about the connection between attitudes and behaviour seems hardly plausible given some conspicuous facts about our social world, such as the effort and time parents invest in educating their children.

[57] See Tyler (n 54) 48.

[58] Cf Raz, *The Authority of Law* (n 1) 251 (where Raz mentions similar sentiments, but does so as part of an argument substantially different to the one advanced here).

[59] See Tyler (n 54) 47.

related to a more general sentiment of membership of one's society; or, some combination of these or similar feelings. Now, let me clarify that I am not making here the claim that such affective orientations *must* form a part of the law-abiding attitude at issue. I do, however, suggest that they may conceivably be present in association with a disposition of the type advocated here; and it even seems to me likely (and consistent with empirical evidence)[60] that some such affective sentiments—even if only mild or relatively weak—are involved in the ordinary materialization of such a disposition.

My focus in this section has so far been on the components of a law-abiding attitude. A further issue, which will be commented on more briefly, is its formation. Attitude formation and change are the subject of a vast body of social science literature.[61] A considerable part of this literature is concerned with the process whereby people form socially accepted attitudes requisite for their operation in social settings, a process commonly referred to as *socialization*.[62] And, especially since the 1970s, a specific strand of socialization literature has emerged which focuses on the formation process of normative attitudes towards the law, a process that has been termed *legal socialization*.[63]

I will not attempt to provide here a summary or a detailed analysis of this body of literature. Nor will I argue for any one specific scheme or strategy by means of which a law-abiding attitude should be acquired or nurtured. Instead, I will confine myself to emphasizing two points of particular relevance to my argument. The first point is the multiplicity of factors that may contribute to the formation of the attitude endorsed here, and, in particular, the mutual role of external factors, such as the agent's social and educational milieu, and of the agent herself. Starting with the role of external factors: as is made clear by legal socialization literature, many law-abiding citizens have

---

[60] See, e.g., David Easton and Jack Dennis, *Children in the Political System: Origins of Political Legitimacy* (McGraw-Hill 1969) 128–36, 177–83, 233–36, 255–60, 356–79; Tyler (n 54) 48, 176–77; Tom R Tyler and Yuen J Huo, *Trust in the Law: Encouraging Public Cooperation with the Police and Courts* (Russell Sage Foundation 2002) 105, 109–11.

[61] See, e.g., Martin Fishbein and Icek Ajzen, *Belief, Attitude, Intention, and Behavior: An Introduction to Theory and Research* (Addison-Wesley 1975) 216–87; Richard J Crisp and Rhiannon Turner, *Essential Social Psychology* (2nd edn, Sage 2010) 92–102, 111–25; Gerd Bohner and Michaela Wanke, *Attitudes and Attitude Change* (Psychology Press 2002) 69–186; Greg Maio and Geoff Haddock, *The Psychology of Attitudes and Attitude Change* (Sage 2009) 87–170.

[62] See, e.g., David A Goslin (ed), *Handbook of Socialization Theory and Research* (Rand McNally 1969); Joan E Grusec and Paul D Hastings, *Handbook of Socialization: Theory and Research* (Guilford Press 2007).

[63] See, e.g., June L Tapp and Lawrence Kohlberg, 'Developing Senses of Law and Legal Justice' (1971) 27 Journal of Social Issues 65; June L Tapp and Felice J Levine, 'Legal Socialization: Strategies for Ethical Legality' (1974) 27 Stanford Law Review 1; Ellen S Cohn and Susan O White, *Legal Socialization: A Study of Norms and Rules* (Springer-Verlag 1990); Jeffrey Fagan and Tom R Tyler, 'Legal Socialization of Children and Adolescents' (2005) 18 Social Justice Research 217.

acquired their attitude, in large part, as a result of the way they were brought up and shaped by their social environment, for example, by socialization agents such as the family, the school, peers, the media, and indeed the law itself.[64] They may have absorbed that attitude in a variety of ways: for instance, by observing the way other people, such as their parents and peers, behave and following their example; by being taught from early years that they ought to comply with the instructions of people in roles of authority, such as their parents, kindergarten nurses, and teachers—a message that may, in some form and degree, diffuse into their later attitudes towards other authorities, including legal ones; through exposure to educational content about the value of law and order or to narratives that tend both to present the guardians of law and order in a positive light and to attach negative connotations to the outlaw; through the influence of the characteristically normative language used in and about the law (featuring, for example, terms such as authority, rules, duties, obligations, breach, violation, and punishment); and so forth.

On the other hand, there is normally at least a certain extent to which we can influence and contribute to the development and change of our own attitudes—and our attitudes towards law are no exception to this. This, too, can be done in a variety of ways: for instance, through reflection on the value of the attitude in question which may gradually lead to its internalization; by adopting certain habits which tend to breed the relevant attitude (in our context, a habit of compliance with the law); by choosing to associate with people who possess and exhibit that attitude; by removing from our close environment, inasmuch as we can, sources of influences prone to negatively affect our attitudes; and so on.[65] Our ability to influence the development of our attitudes has not been ignored by socialization theorists.[66] Indeed, several theorists have highlighted an aspect of socialization which they call 'self-socialization', denoting the way in which people take part in shaping their own social development by selecting, focusing on, and emulating certain socialization influences (e.g. particular peers or particular media sources)

---

[64] See, e.g., Tapp and Kohlberg (n 63) 87–89; Tapp and Levine (n 63) 4–5, 9–10, 54–72; Fagan and Tyler (n 63) 217–42; Cohn and White (n 63) 12–16.

[65] I should clarify that the word 'adopt' as featuring in the dispositional model ('a reason to adopt a law-abiding attitude') is intended in a sense capacious enough to accommodate measures taken by the agent to facilitate the formation or internalization of an attitude even if these measures are indirect and even if their effect is gradual. I will say more about this in Section 9.2.

[66] See, e.g., Eleanor E Maccoby and Carol N Jacklin, *The Psychology of Sex Differences* (Stanford University Press 1974) 277–302; Jeffrey J Arnett, 'Adolescents' Uses of Media for Self-Socialisation' (1995) 25 Journal of Youth and Adolescence 519; Walter R Heinz, 'Self-Socialization and Post-Traditional Society' in Richard A Settersten and Timothy J Owens (eds), *Advances in Life Course Research: New Frontiers in Socialization* (Elsevier 2002) 41–64; Desiree D Tobin et al, 'The Intrapsychics of Gender: A Model of Self-Socialization' (2010) 117 Psychological Review 601.

among a wider variety of available influences.[67] With this in mind, it seems likely that the process of developing and retaining a law-abiding attitude is, or at least can be, an interactive process, wherein a mutual role is played by the individual and by her social environment.[68]

Once noticing the mutual roles of, on the one hand, the individual adopting a law-abiding attitude and, on the other hand, external factors that help cultivate this attitude, we may introduce into the dispositional model a further refinement which takes account of this distinction. In its refined version, the model consists of two facets: one referring to reasons for individuals to adopt a law-abiding attitude, and the other referring to reasons for a society to nurture a law-abiding attitude in its members. The fact of there being a legal system in place which is reasonably just and apt to serve valuable purposes is, according to the model, a reason for its subjects to adopt a disposition to comply with the law, and a reason for socialization agents in the relevant society to foster such a disposition among its members.

We may now turn to a second point, which introduces another qualification into the dispositional model. The dispositional model contends that, under a legal system that is reasonably just and apt to serve valuable purposes, a law-abiding attitude should be cultivated. In the background of this claim, however, there is a tacit supposition that, along with a law-abiding attitude, certain other desirable attitudes and dispositions, particularly moral ones, should be fostered—including, for example, sensitivity to the suffering of others, a sense of and commitment to justice, and respect for people's autonomy, dignity, and physical integrity. That moral attitudes and dispositions ought to be fostered is, of course, not a *distinctive* claim of the dispositional model, and may even seem like a truism—a claim that is already implicit in the adjective 'moral' and needs no separate statement. However, in addition to their general significance, moral attitudes and dispositions assume a specific role and significance within the context of the dispositional model. Their specific role and significance relate to what was earlier referred to as

---

[67] See citations in n 66.

[68] It follows from the above that there is an extent to which a person's attitude and disposition regarding the law may be affected by factors beyond her control, and that her ability to affect her own attitude will sometimes be limited. On pp 169–70, I will discuss a related qualification for my model by reference to the principle of 'ought implies can'. Here I will only add that ability limitations of this sort are not unique to law-related attitudes and dispositions; they pertain to many, and perhaps all, of our (moral and other) attitudes and dispositions. And, in any case, the involvement of agent-external influences should hardly tempt us to impoverish our picture of reasons by overlooking the whole dimension of reasons that concern attitudes and dispositions. On the contrary, it reinforces the case for a discussion of these reasons by reminding us of the importance of doing what we can to shape and secure (for ourselves and for others) a social and educational milieu which breeds and fosters desirable attitudes and dispositions.

the *overridable* nature of the advocated law-abiding disposition. For this overridable quality to ever come into effect—namely, for the disposition to ever be actually overridden—there must be some potentially countervailing force capable of influencing our actions. And, in the case of conflicts between law and morality, that countervailing motivational force is most likely to come in the form of moral dispositions. Moral dispositions can, therefore, be regarded as a prerequisite for the type of equilibrium the dispositional model seeks to generate between our obedience and disobedience in appropriate cases.[69] This type of equilibrium will be further elucidated in the following section, where my main aim will be to explain how the dispositional model differs from both the pre-emption thesis and the weighing model; and it will be defended in Chapter 8, where I will explain, inter alia, why the possession of ordinary moral dispositions does not eliminate the need for a law-abiding disposition.

7.4. The Dispositional Model, Pre-emption, and Weighing

I begin this section by highlighting what I regard as the most notable difference between the dispositional model and the pre-emption thesis.[70] As I consider this difference to be relatively straightforward, and have mentioned it in Section 7.1, my comment will be brief. A pre-emptive reason to perform an action (φ) is a reason to φ that excludes some of the reasons that would otherwise militate against φ. This means that however weighty those contra-φ reasons might be, they should not be acted upon. Insofar as I comply with the pre-emptive reason, then, those contra-φ reasons cease to play a role in determining whether I perform φ or refrain from it. Matters are different under the dispositional model, in that the exclusionary element just

---

[69] Henry Thoreau famously remarked: 'It is not desirable to cultivate a respect for the law, so much as for the right' (Henry Thoreau, *Walden and Civil Disobedience* (first published 1849, Paul Lauter ed, Houghton Mifflin Company 2000) 18). If this is taken to mean that we should never cultivate any respect for the law, there is an extent to which the position I am advocating here disagrees. If I were to frame my position in those terms, I would probably say that it is desirable to cultivate respect for some legal systems—namely, those that are reasonably just and apt to serve valuable purposes—but even greater respect for the right itself.

[70] There are other significant differences between them. For one thing, exclusionary or pre-emptive reasons do not have the attitudinal focus that the reasons cited by the dispositional model have. Exclusionary reasons, as Raz has made clear, are reasons against acting for some reasons (see, e.g., Joseph Raz, *Practical Reason and Norms* (2nd edn, Princeton University Press 1990) 39; Joseph Raz, 'Facing Up: A Reply' (1989) 62 Southern California Law Review 1153, 1156–57). Whether John Doe has complied with a pre-emptive reason to φ is, thus, a question of what reasons he was acting for in performing φ (assuming he has performed it), not a question of what settled attitudinal profile he has, or what measures he has taken to change it.

noted is absent from this model. The attitude envisaged by this model implies a behavioural disposition, which is no more than a *tendency* or *inclination* to comply with legal requirements. As such, it remains overridable (or defeasible) by the weight of opposing reasons that might apply in particular cases, rather than exclusionary of opposing reasons. It does not exclude any reason against compliance, at least not in a sense that is not conditional on that reason's weight,[71] which is the sense of exclusion Raz endorses.[72] Although such a disposition entails that one is generally more likely to comply with legal requirements than to contravene them, if a particular situation arises in which very weighty reasons against compliance present themselves, one may be compelled by the force of these reasons[73] to depart from one's habitual compliance.[74] One's being disposed in this way means that one shows an increased degree of resistance to reasons against compliance, but it does not mean that one becomes (in conative terms) completely irresponsive to those reasons or impervious to their influence, not even within a defined scope of human pursuits. Under the dispositional model, then, subjects' readiness to comply with the law in any given situation remains conditional on there being some degree of conformity or proximity between what they are told to do and what they have reasons to do. Compliance, by this understanding, remains provisional in a way that the pre-emption thesis cannot accommodate.[75]

The difference between the dispositional and weighing models requires a somewhat more extensive explanation. According to the weighing model, people should act on the balance of reasons for and against following the law in a given situation (i.e. pre-existing reasons as well as law-related ones, such as the destabilizing effect that an act of disobedience might have on law and order). The dispositional model, on the other hand, contends that the subjects of a legal system that is reasonably just and apt to serve valuable purposes have a reason to adopt (and, by implication, to operate with) a disposition to comply with the system's requirements. One of the main differences between these models is rooted in properties of the disposition which I earlier referred to by terms or phrases such as 'embeddedness', 'independence as a

---

[71] Cf Christian Piller, 'Kinds of Practical Reasons: Attitude-Related Reasons and Exclusionary Reasons' in Sofia Miguens, João Alberto Pinto, and Carlos E Mauro (eds), *Analyses* (Porto University 2006) 98–105, at 102–03, where the author draws a similar distinction between attitude-related reasons and exclusionary reasons. I will elaborate on the relationship between my proposed model and what Piller calls attitude-related reasons in Section 9.2.

[72] Raz, *Practical Reason and Norms* (n 70) 36, 40, 189, 190.

[73] Or by the force of related behavioural dispositions.

[74] On the overridability of dispositions, see n 23 and accompanying body text.

[75] This limitation of the pre-emption thesis has been explained at length in Part I.

conative and motivational force', and 'persistence'.[76] These properties mean that, once the disposition is adopted, it tends to endure and exert its influence in a manner that is not contingent on reasons for action as applicable to the specific case at hand. The disposition is a behavioural inclination that makes its force felt independently of our reasons for action—it is not a sheer reflection of some or all of the reasons for action that apply to us in a given situation. And this, in turn, implies that those who are disposed to comply with the law may be led to perform actions that they would not perform if they were guided solely by the balance of reasons for action (even after allowing for law-related reasons for action).

This last implication manifests itself in two different ways. First, by exerting its influence on our practical decisions and actions, a disposition may have an error-averting effect. The possibility of its having such an effect is explicable by the conjunction of two facts: (1) the fact that fallible agents sometimes misjudge the balance of reasons for action, and (2) the fact that a behavioural disposition may lead them, by dint of its independent and persistent force, to avoid actions they would consider to be warranted if they were weighing reasons for action without being disposed as they are. Of course, not all dispositions have the capacity to avert error. If I am disposed to φ and φ-ing is invariably wrongful, then my disposition to φ would not avert error; on the contrary, it would produce it. If, however, φ-ing is the right thing to do in at least some circumstances, my disposition to φ may have a corrective influence on my action in those circumstances; it may prevent mistakes I would otherwise make. And that is also true of my disposition to comply with the law, insofar as the law itself prescribes right conduct.[77]

While this error-averting effect holds great practical significance, it does not instantiate divergence between the actions ensuing from a law-abiding disposition and the actions required by the balance of reasons for action. What it instantiates, instead, is divergence between the actions ensuing from a law-abiding disposition and the actions ensuing from a *mistaken assessment* of the balance of reasons for action. However, there is another manifestation of the difference between the dispositional and the weighing models, which does show how their practical outcomes can diverge even when the balance of reasons of action is *correctly* assessed. There are—necessarily, even under the best possible legal system—some cases in which an agent who acts on a correct assessment of the balance of reasons for action will break the law, whereas an agent with a disposition to comply may well act as the law requires. This

---

[76] pp 136, 139–40, 144–45.

[77] Or, conduct that one ought to perform given relevant facts about the law, such as its ability to facilitate coordination.

will be so in cases where the weight of applicable reasons against following the law exceeds the weight of applicable reasons for it, but only by an amount that is not sufficiently large to override a disposition to comply with the law (and here I am referring to a disposition of an appropriate strength). In such cases, a correct assessment of the balance of reasons points to non-compliance, but the law-abiding citizen may well comply.

Let us call the above cases *divergence cases*. The clearest examples of divergence cases are likely to be found in circumstances where the weight of applicable reasons against following the law exceeds the weight of applicable reasons for it, but only by a slight amount. I will offer one example of what I (consistently with several other legal philosophers who have cited this example) believe to be such a case: the example of a driver who comes upon a red traffic light where the road is clearly empty of other vehicles and pedestrians.[78] To render the example more concrete, imagine this scenario: when driving on a lonely road in the desert you come to an intersection with a traffic light showing red. The visibility is very good, the surrounding landscape is free of visual obstructions, and you can tell that there are no other vehicles or pedestrians within miles in any direction. It is evident that an act of non-compliance on your part will not be seen or discovered by anyone else. So it will not result in your being punished and will not stimulate other actors into disobedient behaviour. Also suppose that—given how discerning and strong-willed you are, or given other features of your personality or condition—running a red light in this special situation will not weaken your resolve to comply with the law in other circumstances. Several writers have noted (and many others seem to concur) that in this type of situation there is no reason (whether antecedent or law-related) for you to stop and wait for the light to turn green.[79] And even if any such reason for action could be said to apply to the case, we may plausibly suppose that it is too remote and weak to make it rational to perform an act that is, in all other respects, sharply inconsistent with common sense: stopping and waiting when there is absolutely no traffic and not a single soul for miles around. If so, assuming that your action is guided purely by a correct assessment of the balance of reasons for action, you will violate the law in these circumstances. The case may well be different,

---

[78] See, e.g., MBE Smith, 'Is There a Prima Facie Obligation to Obey the Law?' (1973) 82 Yale Law Journal 950, 971; Donald H Regan, 'Law's Halo' (1986) 4 Social Philosophy and Policy 15, 18–19; Heidi M Hurd, 'Challenging Authority' (1991) 100 Yale Law Journal 1611, 1614; William A Edmundson, *Three Anarchical Fallacies: An Essay on Political Authority* (CUP 1998) 12–34.

[79] See, e.g., Smith (n 78) 971 and Regan (n 78) 18–19. See also Larry Alexander, 'Law and Exclusionary Reasons' (1990) 18 Philosophical Topics 5, 8 (noting: '[I]n situations where I predict no effect on others' behavior, no detection of my disobedience, and no sanctions, my reasons against *A* [i.e. a legally prohibited action] remain exactly as they were before the law was enacted').

however, if you have a general disposition to comply with the law. If such a disposition is in place, and if it is sufficiently strong and deep-seated, it may lead you to stop and wait for the light to change after all.

It bears emphasizing that the point made here about the possibility of divergence cases does not boil down to, or entirely rest upon, my assessment of the desert traffic light case.[80] Nor is this point limited to cases in which one has little or no reason to comply. It is a more general point: namely, that cases can exist (be their specific factual descriptions as they may) in which the reasons against compliance with a legal requirement are stronger than the reasons for compliance with it, but only by an amount that yields to the force of a given disposition to comply with the law.

Furthermore, I do not wish to deny that there is *a certain sense* in which an act of compliance in what I call divergence cases *could* be described as a rational act (though that is not the sense we commonly use when referring to an act as rational): if an agent acquired a disposition, such that it is rational to acquire, and this disposition leads her, inter alia, to comply in what I refer to as divergence cases, one might suggest that her act of compliance is rational in the sense that it ensues from a disposition whose acquisition was rational.[81] But this sense of 'rational act' does not mean that the act is supported by the balance of reasons for action, at least not as understood by the weighing model. Reasons for action, in this sense, are facts connected with qualities of the action itself or its consequences (including consequences it has qua an act of compliance or non-compliance). On this understanding, to establish that one has a reason to perform a certain action, we must show how performance

---

[80] Incidentally, note that the dispositional model offers a way of accounting for different intuitions about cases such as the lonely traffic light case, namely the intuitions reflected, respectively, in the view that we have no reason to obey in this case and the opposite view that we do. Writers such as Smith (n 78) or Regan (n 78) correctly deny that stopping at the red light is supported by applicable reasons for action, but what is missed by their view is the fact that, prior to the case, we have reasons to adopt an attitude (and a disposition) that is likely to result in compliance in that case. The latter fact, on the other hand, might be part of what motivates the opposite view; but, if that is so, its own error, as I see it, is to confound that fact with a reason for action.

[81] This line of thought may be reminiscent of the way Kant approaches the moral assessment of an action, namely, by asking whether the action was performed on the basis of right maxims, i.e. those derived in accordance with the categorical imperative (Immanuel Kant, *Groundwork of the Metaphysics of Morals*, 4:421, *Critique of Practical Reason*, 5:72, and *The Metaphysics of Morals*, 6:389, in Immanuel Kant, *Practical Philosophy* (Mary J Gregor ed and tr, CUP 1996)). It also has parallels with the positions of David Gauthier and Thomas Pink, who have argued, respectively, that acts ensuing from a rationally formed intention or from a rationally arrived-at decision are necessarily rational acts (David Gauthier, 'Afterthoughts' in Douglas MacLean (ed), *The Security Gamble: Deterrence Dilemmas in the Nuclear Age* (Rowman and Allanheld 1984) 159–61; David Gauthier, 'Rethinking the Toxin Puzzle' in Jules L Coleman and Christopher W Morris (eds), *Rational Commitment and Social Justice: Essays for Gregory Kavka* (CUP 1998) 47–58; Thomas Pink, *The Psychology of Freedom* (CUP 1996) 93).

of that specific action, given the specific circumstances in question, would genuinely serve or satisfy a specific value. Thus, the mere fact that an action ensues from a rationally adopted disposition is not a reason for action.[82]

But, merely for the purpose of this discussion, let us momentarily assume that actions ensuing from a rationally acquired disposition *are* necessarily rational in the sense that they are supported by the balance of reasons. Even this overly generous assumption would fall short of threatening the claim made above, that is, the claim that action with a disposition to comply with the law and action on a correct assessment of the balance of reasons will occasionally diverge. At best, the postulated assumption casts doubt on the possibility of practical divergence between action with a disposition to comply with the law and action based on a correct assessment of the balance of reasons *given that the actor has rationally acquired a disposition to comply with the law.* The weighing model, however, says nothing about a disposition to comply with the law or the reasons for adopting it. These, by way of reminder, are core elements of *the dispositional model.*

---

[82] It is not denied that the above fact, when combined with others, may, under certain conditions, indirectly give rise to a reason for action—e.g. a reason that stems from a concern that by deviating from a beneficial disposition, the agent would frustrate the legitimate expectations of other agents or would weaken her own disposition. However, even such a reason need not be of a weight that renders the action warranted *on the balance of* reasons for and against the action.

8

The Dispositional Model Advocated

Some of what I have said thus far about the dispositional model implicitly points to my argument in support of this model. In this chapter, however, I will engage more directly with the task of advocating the model and considering possible objections to it. I will first put forward my basic argument for the model (Section 8.1), which endorses it as an optimal middle path between the two alternative models discussed in previous parts of the book. I will then consider a number of other related issues and their bearing on the case for the dispositional model, including the possibility of inducing compliance with law through punishment or reward (Section 8.2), the contribution of moral dispositions to law compliance (Section 8.3), and pathways of principled disobedience under the dispositional model (Section 8.4). Finally, phenomenological and empirical arguments that bear on my case for the dispositional model will be discussed (Section 8.5).

8.1. The Basic Case for the Dispositional Model

Suppose you are asked to choose a decision-making procedure to be prevalently used by subjects of the law in your society, under the assumption that its legal system is reasonably just and apt to serve valuable purposes. The following alternatives are given to you. (1) *The Weighing Model*: When faced with a legal directive, subjects will accord it a degree of normative force that is meant to reflect the weight of considerations for following it as applicable in the relevant situation, while weighing it against reasons for taking alternative courses of action. (2) *The Coherent Pre-emption Thesis*: Subjects will

Legal Directives and Practical Reasons. Noam Gur. © Noam Gur 2018. Published 2018 by Oxford University Press.

act in accordance with a coherent reading of the pre-emption thesis.[1] That is, they will obey legal authorities to the exclusion of their own judgement on the merits of the action, with the following exceptions: (a) cases where the pre-emption thesis is inapplicable because the relevant directive was issued without legitimate authority, and (b) cases where there are compelling reasons for disobedience that are not within the directive's scope of exclusion, *provided* that condition (a) or (b) can be substantiated in a manner consistent with the pre-emption thesis itself, namely, without rendering the conclusion that a reason is excluded dependent on its weight.

The analyses in Chapters 2–4 and 6 have shown that each of the above alternatives suffers from serious normative deficiencies. A brief overview of these deficiencies will place us in a good position to appreciate the merit of the dispositional model. Consider, first, the weighing model. This model requires individual agents faced with legal directives—even those issued by institutions that the Razian would consider legitimate authorities—to always act on the basis of an assessment of the reasons for and against compliance as applicable to the case at hand (including reasons that were not in play before the directive was issued, such as coordination benefits or reliance interests of other parties, if and insofar as they bear on the action at hand). It envisages, in other words, full-on exercises of judgement on the part of individual actors which they are supposed to carry out by reference to a specific practical situation and the reasons applying to it. At the same time, it effectively denies that legal directives, even those regarded by the Razian as authoritative, have binding normative force within their scope: they may be indicative of what is independently right, wrong, wise, or foolish to do, and they may bring into play certain other reasons for action (by affecting the factual landscape in normatively relevant ways), which the actor ought to take into account, but they do not, in any other sense, normatively restrict the deciding actor or her decision-making process—they do not, in virtue of their status or source, bind her. These characteristics are represented in Figure 8.1, subject to one limitation: the figure focuses on *authoritative* legal directives, not any legal directives, in order to form a common frame of reference for a later comparison with the pre-emption thesis.[2]

---

[1] It is self-explanatory why the only reading I regard as relevant for the purposes of this inquiry is the coherent reading.

[2] Figure 8.1 displays a simple scale ranging from maximum bindingness of authoritative directives within their scope (or minimum latitude for case-specific assessment by subjects) at the right end of the scale, to minimum bindingness of authoritative directives within their scope (or maximum latitude for case-specific assessment by subjects) at the left end of the scale. The weighing model is placed at the left end of the scale.

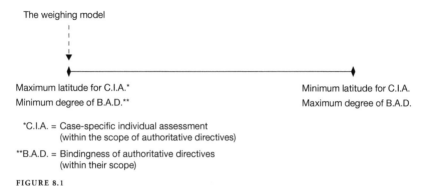

The weighing model

Maximum latitude for C.I.A.*   Minimum latitude for C.I.A.
Minimum degree of B.A.D.**   Maximum degree of B.A.D.

*C.I.A. = Case-specific individual assessment
          (within the scope of authoritative directives)

**B.A.D. = Bindingness of authoritative directives
           (within their scope)

FIGURE 8.1

The normative shortcomings of this model have been explained at length in Chapter 6. I have observed that an important part of the justification for using legal forms of social ordering lies in their suitability to address practical problems that involve the operation of certain common biases, such as self-serving biases, availability-related bias, and hyperbolic discounting of the positive or negative value of future outcomes. Law's comparative advantage to that effect (though dependent for its realization on the reasonable personal competence of lawmakers) has been attributed to some structural characteristics thereof—such as its directional focus, generality, prospective application, and relative endurance through time—which make its directives, *ceteris paribus*, less amenable to the said biases than private decisions in daily settings of activity often are. Against this background, I have highlighted what I consider to be the critical normative defect of the weighing model: by requiring individual subjects to act upon situational assessments of the normative force of legal directives, this model opts for a mode of reasoning fully exposed and highly susceptible to precisely the same biases that made it necessary and justified to use legal forms of regulation in the first place. It thus undermines law's ability to perform its beneficial and essential conduct-guiding function.

I have also observed that, in comparison with the weighing model, the pre-emption thesis offers a normative framework that better enables law, or at least law that meets Raz's conditions of authority, to fulfil its conduct-guiding function. The pre-emption thesis ascribes to the directives of a (legitimate) legal authority full normative bindingness within their scope. Within that scope, it normatively bars action on a case-by-case assessment of what Raz calls first-order reasons.[3] A visual expression of these features can be found in Figure 8.2.

[3] Or, according to some of his formulations, first-order reasons *against* the directive.

FIGURE 8.2

By carving out certain domains in which it allows (and requires) subjects to operate without recourse to case-by-case assessments of the merits of the action, the method of pre-emption provides a mode of practical reasoning relatively insulated from the types of situational bias mentioned above. So why not opt for the alternative I entitled 'the coherent pre-emption thesis'? The conclusions arrived at in Chapters 2–4 explain the crucial problem that rules out this alternative too. The problem is that even generally competent authorities, which meet the normal justification thesis, may, on occasion, direct their subjects to an action clearly identifiable as morally wrong or even grossly immoral—whether this occurs due to their own (human, technical, or other) localized error (Situation 1)[4] or due to the generality of rules, which means that even a good rule may occasionally yield a highly objectionable outcome in a particular contingency (Situation 2).[5] Some such situations, then, would feature among the cases in which the 'coherent pre-emption thesis' requires compliance—and that is a defect serious enough to make this alternative unacceptable. It will be recalled that my various attempts at reconciling the pre-emption thesis with disobedience in these situations—by narrowly demarcating either the domain in which the pre-emption thesis is meant to apply or the range of reasons that it regards as excluded—were unsuccessful. For it is only by recourse to the balance of reasons for action, a route of reasoning that runs counter to the main thrust of the pre-emption thesis, that one can distinguish the entire category of cases that I entitle Situations 1 and 2 from cases in which exclusionary force is said to apply. Conceding that subjects should disobey in Situations 1 and 2, therefore, entails a rejection of what I call the coherent pre-emption thesis,[6] and, vice versa, adopting the

---

[4] pp 22–23.   [5] pp 23–24.
[6] The same cases do not seem to pose a problem for the weighing model, as this model regards law's normative force as defeasible by sufficiently weighty moral reasons.

coherent pre-emption thesis leads to the morally intolerable inference that reason warrants obedience in some Situations 1 and 2.

With this as a background, let us revert to the dispositional model. The dispositional model is preferable to either of the two foregoing alternatives because it strikes a better balance between, on the one hand, considerations in favour of treating legal directives (of a reasonably just and well-functioning system) as normatively binding, and, on the other hand, considerations in favour of leaving normative latitude for case-specific assessments of legally required actions. An agent who is disposed to comply with legal directives in the manner advocated herein shows a commitment to compliance that is, on the one hand, more steadfast than that of an agent who merely follows the balance of reasons for and against acting as the law requires, and, on the other hand, less conclusive than that of an agent who lets authoritative laws pre-empt her judgement within their scope of application (at least insofar as pre-emption is coherently construed).[7] As we have seen, such an agent does not operate through free and active weighing of the reasons for and against compliance, but rather follows a behavioural pattern of fairly habitual compliance with the law.[8] Thus disposed, she is less susceptible to the influence of biases that are part of what made the use of legal regulation necessary in the first place. Since the disposition is adopted prior to a decision on whether to comply with this or that law in this or that situation, and since it exerts its force independently of whether reasons support any particular act of compliance, it is able to operate effectively as a counter-force to the foregoing biases. At the same time, the envisaged disposition represents a mere inclination or tendency of behaviour, which implies a type of provisionality that cannot be found in the notion of pre-emption, and which thus leaves the agent responsive to case-specific reasons against compliance when these are very weighty.[9] So, although such an agent may well comply with the law in some cases where the reasons against compliance are *slightly* or *moderately* weightier than the reasons for it, when the case involves reasons of *serious gravity* against compliance she may well be compelled to break the law. The

---

[7] The discussion here has certain parallels with the ethical debate between act-utilitarianism and rule-utilitarianism. But a number of qualifications should be added in this connection. First, my arguments are not committed to, or limited by, premises of utilitarian ethics. Second, my arguments focus on *legal* rules, not rules in general. Third, I offer an analysis of rival models of practical reason, not an analysis of rival ethical theories. Fourth, even ignoring the above qualifications, the dispositional model can be seen as the counterpart of neither act-utilitarianism nor rule-utilitarianism, but of some middle ground between them (one that has certain affinities with Richard Hare's position in his *Moral Thinking: Its Levels, Method and Point* (Clarendon Press 1981)).

[8] pp 136–37, 139–40.

[9] pp 136–37, 139, 143.

foregoing characterization of the dispositional model can be represented dia-grammatically, once more, by reference to a scale ranging from maximum normative bindingness to maximum latitude for case-specific assessments by subjects. Here too, in order to facilitate comparison with the pre-emption thesis the diagram can be read as referring to directives that the Razian would consider to be authoritative. As can be seen in Figure 8.3, in contrast to the preceding models the dispositional model lies at neither the left nor the right end of the scale, but in the intermediate area.[10]

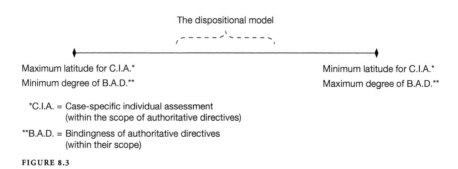

FIGURE 8.3

The following query might be raised at this point. Dispositions vary in their strength, that is, in how strong an influence they exert over their possessor's actions. So, does the case I am making for the dispositional model depend for its cogency on how strong the disposition to comply with the law is? It does, though only in a limited sense. The strength of a disposition to comply with the law bears on the type of balance the disposition attains between bindingness of directives and latitude for case-specific assessment. It bears, in other words, on whether the disposition is one that strikes an optimal balance between these attributes and, if not, how far it is from the

---

[10] We could also try to characterize the dispositional model through the figurative talk of degrees of opacity/transparency between directives and the reasons behind them. (Cf, for example, Schauer's use of a similar terminology: Frederick Schauer, *Playing by the Rules: A Philosophical Examination of Rule-Based Decision-Making in Law and in Life* (Clarendon Press 1991) 97, 173, 200; Frederick Schauer, 'Rules and the Rule of Law' (1991) 14 Harvard Journal of Law & Public Policy 645, 649. I will compare my position with Schauer's in Section 9.1; see also pp 174–75 and Section 8.5). But recourse to this phraseology should come with the caveat that the dispositional model does not object to critical reflection on directives and their background reasons, but only prevents the type of mindset that makes an actor too ready to channel his dislike of, or disagreement with, a specific directive into an act of non-compliance. Under this caveat, we might say, in the above figurative vein, that the dispositional model gives legal directives (under a system that meets the previously mentioned prerequisites) a level of translucency that constitutes a middle ground between complete opacity and complete transparency to contrary reasons in their background.

optimum. But a disposition need not be of *optimal* strength for it to be preferable to both a pre-emptive and a weighing mode of practical reasoning. It can be suboptimal—whether too weak or too strong—and still be preferable to either of these alternatives. This should be inferable from the fact that the pre-emption thesis and weighing model represent the two end points on the sliding scale appearing above, such that they give, within their scope, full priority to one of the relevant attributes (authoritative bindingness or latitude for case-specific assessment) over the other.

Now, it is not my purpose here to try to pin down the exact strength of an optimally balanced disposition. My purpose, instead, is to establish that the dispositional model is a practical and conceptual framework within which that optimally balanced attitude can be found; and that it offers a better answer to our conundrum than both the pre-emption thesis and the weighing model. Having said that, some rough and general indication as to the strength of the disposition I envisage should and can be given. Thus, for example, it may be noted that the envisaged disposition is not remotely as forceful as are certain moral dispositions many of us have, such as the dispositions many of us have against killing, torturing, intentionally causing bodily harm to others, or sexually assaulting them. A disposition to comply with legal requirements (qua legal requirements) that is as, or nearly as, forceful as these moral dispositions typically are would likely produce an undue level of subservience in its possessor, which could undermine her readiness to disobey even gravely immoral requirements. On the other hand, the envisaged disposition to comply with the law is strong enough to be able to have an appreciable influence on our actions in the face of tangible temptations to break rules, such as temptations to avoid personal inconvenience, loss of time, and monetary or other material costs that compliance may involve (as may be the case, for example, with tax requirements, anti-pollution regulations, road traffic rules, and many other laws). This is not say that the motivational force exerted by the disposition must be equal to or greater than the pull of such temptations to break the law. The disposition need not be such that it is able to overcome contrary motivations *alone*. What I mean to say, instead, is that the disposition must be such that it makes an appreciable contribution to a set of motivational factors—which also includes, for example, the wish to avoid legal sanction as well as law-independent moral dispositions—which, together, often (though not necessarily always) overcome contrary motivations. More will be said in the following sections about other contributors to this motivational set (mainly, legal sanctions and law-independent moral dispositions), where I will argue that these motivational contributors, too, are necessary but not sufficient, and cannot generally provide an adequate substitute for a law-abiding disposition.

The dispositional model, I have argued above, is capable of striking a better balance than either of its rivals between authoritative bindingness on the one hand and latitude for case-specific assessment on the other. But a Razian might pose the following objection. True, he or she might say, the pre-emption thesis entails a greater degree of bindingness (and less latitude for case-specific assessment) than the dispositional model *within the scope of authoritative directives*. However, Raz considers the scope of legitimate governmental authority to be much narrower and patchier than that which governments usually claim to have and are commonly taken by their subjects to have.[11] The dispositional model, by contrast, lacks that piecemeal nature, as it contends that, given a legal system that is reasonably just and apt to attain valuable purposes, we should adopt a general disposition to comply with the law.[12] It follows that, although the pre-emption thesis entails a greater degree of bindingness within the scope of authoritative directives, it may well implicate a *lesser* degree of bindingness on the whole. So whatever the negative side effects of authoritative bindingness are, it is doubtful that the pre-emption thesis implicates them to a greater extent (taking into account both their rate of occurrence and gravity) than the dispositional model does.

I will not examine whether the last statement is correct on its own terms, as it can be rejected on another ground: it invokes a conception of the scope of governmental authority that has been found to be inadequate in an earlier part of this book.[13] Raz's piecemeal conception of the scope of governmental authority is, as I have argued, unsatisfactory since, in reality, the need to organize, and place constraints on, the operation of individuals in a political society through governmental regulation is significantly more general than that which is envisaged by this conception. Raz, for instance, believes that '[a]n expert pharmacologist may not be subject to the authority of the government in matters of the safety of drugs, [and] an inhabitant of a little village by a river may not be subject to its authority in matters of navigation and conservation of the river by the banks of which he has spent all his life'.[14] But the idea that people may not be subject to rules of law in domains they know well or specialize in—domains which are likely to embrace a large part of their daily activity and potential impact on other people—strikes me as counterintuitive. The problem with that idea has been explained in Chapter 6.[15] I have argued there that Raz's piecemeal conception of governmental authority places

---

[11] See Joseph Raz, *The Morality of Freedom* (Clarendon Press 1986) 70–80, 99–104; Joseph Raz, *Ethics in the Public Domain: Essays in the Morality of Law and Politics* (rev paperback edn, Clarendon Press 1995) 347, 350; Joseph Raz, 'The Problem of Authority: Revisiting the Service Conception' (2006) 90 Minnesota Law Review 1003, 1008.

[12] But see qualification on pp 154–55.   [13] pp 127–29.

[14] Raz, *The Morality of Freedom* (n 11) 74. See also ibid 77–78.   [15] pp 128–29.

too much emphasis on considerations of expertise and insufficiently takes account of structural features of legal rules and institutions, of differential decision-making environments, and, therefore, of the extent to which the justification of legal regulation is linked with the operation of common situational biases which law is structurally well suited to counteract. Once we recognize (as, for example, David Hume did)[16] the extent and importance of the link between situational biases and the operation of law, we can appreciate that the desideratum of subjecting human conduct to legal rules applies in a considerably broader fashion than Raz suggests. We can then see that an attempt to alleviate the problematic implications of pre-emptive force by curtailing the scope of governmental authority—whether or not it is actually successful at alleviating those problematic implications[17]—has the effect of throwing the baby out with the bathwater.

I wish to turn now to a possible query which centres on the principle of 'ought implies can'. In Section 7.3, it was noted that there is normally an extent to which an agent can contribute to, and affect, the internalization or change of her own attitudes—for example, through reflection on the relevant attitude and the goods or values associated with it, by adopting habits that tend to breed that attitude, and by avoiding, as much as possible, sources of influences liable to negatively affect her attitudes. But it was also noted that factors external to the agent, such as elements of her social milieu, tend to play an important part in shaping her attitudes. And such factors, needless to explain, are to a certain extent beyond the agent's control. What follows from this is that an agent's ability to affect her own attitudes will sometimes, or even often, be subject to limitations. And it is at this point that the 'ought implies can' principle emerges as (arguably) relevant to the scope of my claim about reasons to adopt a law-abiding attitude.

Before I come to crux of this matter, however, the following three points should be noted: first, the 'ought implies can' principle is more frequently discussed in relation to obligations and duties than in relation to reasons,[18] which are our primary focus here; second, time-honoured and foundational though it is, the principle is not uncontested;[19] and, third, it is arguable that

---

[16] David Hume, 'Of the Origin of Government' in his *A Treatise of Human Nature* (first published 1740, LA Selby-Bigge and PH Nidditch eds, Clarendon Press 1978) bk III, pt II, s VII.

[17] Part I of the book argues that the notion of pre-emption is morally unsound even in a fragmented and limited scope of governmental authority.

[18] But see, e.g., Bart Streumer, 'Reasons and Impossibility' (2007) 136 Philosophical Studies 351. Contra Streumer, see Ulrike Heuer, 'Reasons and Impossibility' (2010) 147 Philosophical Studies 235.

[19] See, e.g., Wayne Martin, 'Ought but Cannot' (2009) 109 Proceedings of the Aristotelian Society 103; Peter A Graham, '"Ought" and Ability' (2011) 120 The Philosophical Review 337;

the principle has some exceptions and limitations.[20] Against this background, my position should be clarified as follows. First, the minimum that I wish to claim about a reason to adopt a law-abiding attitude is that (under systems of the relevant description) a person (*p*) has such a reason *insofar as p can* adopt that attitude—in other words, that *p* has a reason to adopt a law-abiding attitude *to the extent that p* is able to take effective steps that would contribute to its formation or internalization, or would make its formation or internalization likelier. Second, whether a reason to adopt (or, to have) a law-abiding attitude applies to *p even beyond the extent* of *p*'s ability to take effective steps to this end is a question that I leave open. Addressing this question would require us to embark on a discussion of 'ought implies can' (e.g. the principle's validity, scope of application, and possible exceptions) that extends beyond the confines of this book. Third, it is worth recalling that, along with its claim about reasons for individuals to adopt a law-abiding attitude, the dispositional model makes a second claim, which refers to reasons for a society (or, for its socialization agents) to nurture a law-abiding attitude in its members.[21] The importance of the latter claim is partly explained by the limits of one's ability to affect one's own attitudes. In this sense, then, these two claims of the dispositional model should be seen as complementary. Fourth and last, there is an extent to which the empirical reality of people's law-related attitudes already corresponds with the attitude I am advocating here, and the empirical evidence I will discuss in Section 8.5 suggests that this extent is significant. Now, insofar as *p* already possesses a law-abiding attitude, the dispositional model can be understood to refer not to *adopting* a new attitude, but to *maintaining* a present attitude (namely, it can be understood to imply that *p* has a reason to maintain her attitude); and insofar as *p*'s ability to maintain her attitude is less limited than her ability to adopt a new one, this, too, extends the scope of the dispositional model.

8.2. Inducement of Compliance through Punishment or Reward

For law to be able adequately to operate as a normative guide of action, I have argued, it is necessary that its subjects have a disposition to comply with legal

Brian Talbot, 'The Best Argument for "Ought Implies Can" is a Better Argument Against "Ought Implies Can"' (2016) 3 Ergo 377.

[20] See, e.g., John Kekes, ' "Ought implies Can" and Two Kinds of Morality' 34 Philosophical Quarterly 459; John Broome, 'Normative Practical Reasoning' (2001) 75 Proceedings of the Aristotelian Society 175, 188–89.

[21] p 154.

requirements, rather than acting simply through weighing of reasons for and against compliance as applicable to their particular situation. This argument, however, may prompt the following query: why should law's ability to operate by means of its normative force concern us, or at least why should it concern us when the sense of normativity spoken of does not include inducement of compliance by punishment or reward? After all, law enforcement institutions have the capacity to generate prudential reasons for compliance by means of punishing law violations or rewarding acts of compliance. Techniques of punishment or reward can induce compliance without making it the case that subjects act on anything other than the balance of reasons for action. All that these techniques do is lead subjects to act on a balance that takes into account the weight of a new, prudential reason. These techniques, therefore, seem compatible with the weighing model. The gist of my response to this query will be this: while the creation of prudential reasons for compliance (at least those associated with punishment) is necessary for the general efficacy of a legal system in ordinary conditions, so is the presence of a disposition to comply with the law. The former cannot, on a general basis, adequately replace the latter.

Consider, first, the possibility of inducing compliance through reward. A scheme of rewards may form a suitable technique for inducing compliance with the law in some specific contexts of regulation. But I see strong reasons to believe that, far from forming a significant part of law's characteristic ambit of application, such contexts are very limited.[22] Before we come to what I consider to be the main reason, namely economic feasibility, it is worth noting an additional reason that has to do with the symbolic significance of reward. Rewards tend to be associated with a high level of performance or achievement, and with moral standards of particularly virtuous behaviour, subsumable under what Lon Fuller called 'the morality of aspiration', more than with mandatory standards of behaviour or the type of morality Fuller

---

[22] Cf Jeremy Bentham's remark that '[b]y reward alone, it is most certain that no material part of that business [i.e. the business of government] could be carried on for half an hour' (Jeremy Bentham, *Of Laws in General* (HLA Hart ed, The Athlone Press 1970) s 135). While my claim here is cast in a more moderate formulation and does not rely on the same reasons invoked by Bentham, it substantially agrees with his remark. For a recent discussion of rewards as a means of governance, and of Bentham's position in this regard, see Frederick Schauer, *The Force of Law* (Harvard University Press 2015) ch 8. Schauer offers several critical insights in this chapter, but his conclusion regarding the limits of governance through reward seems largely consistent with Bentham's above remark. Schauer thus notes: '[I]t is hard to imagine a system by which people who did not commit robbery, or did not have unsafe workplaces, or did not discriminate in employment, received rewards for their law-abiding behavior. And so, although tax deductions and various other reward schemes are plausible alternatives to punishment or other negative sanctions in some narrow contexts, it is understandable why the law can be expected to continue to make far more use of sticks than it does of carrots' (ibid 119).

called 'the morality of duty'.[23] However, a substantial part of what legal systems typically regulate consists in forms of behaviour more suitable for mandatory standards than for optional ones[24]—and by this I do not refer only to paradigmatic forms of *mala in se*, but also to matters on the fringes of (or arguably outside) that category, such as driving at a high speed, polluting the environment, providing employees with unsafe work equipment, operating food outlets with poor level of hygiene, and so on. Rewarding people for not acting in such ways could create the false impression that their conduct is, like performance that lives up to the morality of aspiration, a specifically virtuous conduct that is not necessarily expected of them as a matter of course.

As indicated above, however, the main ground for denying the possibility of a widely applicable scheme of rewards for law compliance is its cost.[25] A reward scheme could produce effective incentives for compliance only insofar as the expected value, namely value times probability, of rewards for compliance would be significant enough.[26] But since rewards (unlike punishments) would be due to those who *comply* with the rules, and since we see compliance as the common and normal response to legal rules[27]—as something to be done by each person numerous times a day—the scale of expenditure required for the scheme in question would be astronomical.[28] Just imagine, for example, how much it would cost to provide drivers with effective rewards for actions as common and frequent as stopping at stop signs, fastening their seatbelts, or parking where they are allowed to park. And road traffic is only

---

[23] Lon L Fuller, *The Morality of Law* (2nd edn, Yale University Press 1969) 3–32.

[24] This is said without intention to play down the importance other kinds of legal norms, such as power-conferring norms (HLA Hart, *The Concept of Law* (3rd edn with an introduction by Leslie Green, OUP 2012) 26–42).

[25] By which I mean not only the value of the rewards, but also other administration costs, such as the cost of monitoring a vast number of law compliance acts and transferring rewards to the relevant actors.

[26] It might appear that the system could reduce the number of rewards so long as it increases the value of a given reward proportionally. I suspect, however, that there is only a limited extent to which the system could do so. For once the conferral of a reward, even of a high value, becomes an improbable and intangible event, the danger exists that it would be undercounted or disregarded by citizens.

[27] Indeed, Austin famously regarded a widespread habit of obedience (to what he characterized as a determinate and common superior) as a necessary conceptual condition for there being a political society (and, thus, positive law), and Hart famously treated general compliance of the citizenry (with rules of behaviour valid according to the rule of recognition) as a necessary conceptual condition for the existence of a legal system. See John Austin, *The Province of Jurisprudence Determined and the Uses of the Study of Jurisprudence* (first published 1832, Hackett 1998) 193; Hart (n 24) 116.

[28] The problem seems even worse when one takes into account actors whose preference pattern conforms to the economic principle of diminishing marginal utility. The greater the reward sums such actors accumulate, all else being equal, the less they would value any additional given reward. This means that in order to maintain incentives for compliance at a steady level of effectiveness, the relevant legal system may need to constantly increase the rewards it grants.

one of the many law-regulated spheres of activity that can furnish similar examples. We must reject, therefore, the reward scheme in question as economically unfeasible.[29]

What about punishment for non-compliance with legal requirements? Could it generally substitute for the role ascribed here to a disposition to comply with the law? This is a less extravagant idea than the reward scheme discussed above, but its realization would still be too costly. Even in existing political communities where a significant part of the populace *is* disposed to comply with law—including, for example, the United States[30] and Britain[31]—it is not without difficulty that the legal system finds the resources needed for its law enforcement tasks. Thus, for instance, law enforcement institutions are often forced to settle for cheaper solutions such as plea bargaining, which, from a rule-of-law point of view, represent a pragmatic second best; and in large parts of the law—including, for example, laws prohibiting or regulating drug-related activity (e.g. sale, possession, or use), cyber law, copyright and other intellectual property laws—the proportion of violations actually monitored, investigated, prosecuted, and punished is small.[32] Now, in a society whose members have *no* disposition to comply with the law, enforcement institutions would have to operate much more vigorously and frequently than they do in those familiar societies. This would obviously require a substantial increase in the resources allocated to law enforcement, and one is

---

[29] As indicated above, I do not deny that there exist specific regulative contexts in which reward for compliance may be a feasible technique of inducing compliance. For instance, regulators seeking to enforce a waste recycling policy might opt for a scheme whereby rewards are given for bringing used bottles to collection points or a scheme whereby households that separate types of waste are given a certain reduction of municipal tax (reflecting the recycling services cost saved through their action).

[30] See Tom R Tyler, *Why People Obey the Law* (with a new afterword by the author, Princeton University Press 2006) esp 45–46; Austin Sarat, 'Legal Obligation: A Survey Study' (1977) 9 Polity 384. In Section 8.5, I will discuss Tyler's work and critical responses to it by Frederick Schauer, Leslie Green, and Laurence Claus, and will conclude that the statement made in the body text above withstands these critiques.

[31] Marta Orviska and John Hudson, 'Quiet in the Cathedral: Who is the Law Abiding Citizen?' (2006) 23 Homo Oeconomicus 129.

[32] See, e.g., 'Drugs swoops "have little impact"' BBC News (UK, 30 July 2008) <http://news.bbc.co.uk/1/hi/uk/7531860.stm> accessed 10 April 2017; Ulf Wolf, 'Cyber-Crime: Law Enforcement Must Keep Pace With Tech-Savvy Criminals' (2009) <http://www.govtech.com/dc/articles/Cyber-Crime-Law-Enforcement-Must-Keep-Pace.html?page=1> accessed 10 April 2017; 'National Crime Agency Strategic Cyber Industry Group: Cyber Crime Assessment 2016' <http://www.nationalcrimeagency.gov.uk/publications/709-cyber-crime-assessment-2016/file> accessed 10 April 2017; The Intellectual Property Office, 'Online Copyright Infringement Tracker: Latest wave of research Mar 16–May 16: Overview and key findings' <https://www.gov.uk/government/uploads/system/uploads/attachment_data/file/546223/OCI-tracker-6th-wave-March-May-2016.pdf> accessed 10 April 2017.

left wondering: Is such an increase practically realizable? If so, how would the necessary reallocation of financial resources affect people's lives? And, in any case, why should one opt for such a costly solution when a far less expensive alternative—namely, compliance underpinned by a mixture of motivational forces that consists partly of a law-abiding disposition, as is normally found in our actual societies[33]—is attainable?[34] Finally, even when we ignore the economic constraints that give rise to these questions, there remains another major problem with the contemplated punishment scheme. Imagine how life would be in a society where law's efficacy relied upon punishment institutions as heavily as envisioned by the scheme in question. Legal punishments and auxiliary enforcement measures, such as surveillance, searches, and arrests, would have to be used with frequency and intensity so great that they keep people constantly alert to and intimidated by the possibility of punishment. Surely, however, this highly oppressive state of affairs is not one in which we wish to find ourselves.

Now, in his recent notable book on law's coercive character, *The Force of Law*,[35] Frederick Schauer has voiced some views that might be in tension with my last argument. Schauer's primary aim in the book is to show that law's effectiveness relies on its coercive apparatus to an extent that makes coercion crucial to understanding and explaining the phenomenon of law. This aim does not conflict with my argument and I take no issue with it. But some of Schauer's arguments go beyond what is needed for establishing the foregoing claim, and are at variance with my argument. For one thing, the part he attributes to coercion in the empirical causal explanation of law compliance is such that it comes at the expense of recognizing the role of a normative attitude of the type advocated here. Indeed, he expresses scepticism about the extent to which such a normative attitude actually exists and causally contributes to compliance rates, suggesting that, at least in American society, its existence is rare and its causal contribution is insignificant.[36] I momentarily leave these empirical claims to one side; they will be critically discussed in Section 8.5. But my disagreement with Schauer includes more than these empirical claims. The degree to which his account emphasizes and routinizes reliance on coercion at the expense of normative internalization of law-abidingness

---

[33] This empirical claim about the actual presence of such a disposition will be discussed in Section 8.5.

[34] For relevant discussion offering further insight into the limitations of legal punishment, see Tyler (n 30) 22–23, 65, and references therein.

[35] Cited in n 22.

[36] See, e.g., Schauer (n 22) 46–48, 52, 55–56, 74, 167–68. At some points his argument sounds more qualified, in that it focuses only on compliance with laws that people disagree with, not on compliance with all laws. More on this on p 188.

has conceptual and normative implications which I am disinclined to embrace. '[C]oercion', Schauer states, 'is law's comparative advantage'[37] (not *one* of law's comparative advantag*es*). 'Law', as pictured by his account, 'is about telling people what to do and threatening them with bad consequences if they fail to comply.'[38] It is a practice that he is content to analogize to the 'gunman writ large',[39] the image HLA Hart famously invoked as a foil for law.[40] And, at the prescriptive level, Schauer proposes that the absence or rare existence of normative attitudes of the type endorsed here should not necessarily be lamented[41] (as I understand him, not even under reasonably just legal and political systems).

I have two interrelated concerns about this approach. First, while the normative attitude advocated here depends for its internalization and endurance on the legitimacy of the legal system, the fear of being subject to coercive sanction does not. So it is unsurprising that regimes of dubious legitimacy (or outright illegitimacy) have often employed, and heavily relied upon, intensive forms and degrees of coercion. Indeed, the very fact that a system resorts to extensive use of harsh punishment should prompt the suspicion that something else, apart from this fact, may be substantially wrong with its laws and policies. But if the conception of law assimilated by a society is as coercion-centred (and a-normative) as that which features in Schauer's account, its members may come to see coercion as so standard and routine that even intense and frequent coercive action would sound no alarm bells in their mind.[42] Second, there is another and more obvious fact about coercion's dangerous potential which reinforces the preceding consideration. High degrees of coerciveness may work to suppress civil resistance to injustice in a way that an overridable disposition to comply with the law does not, in that they create palpable and compelling prudential reasons against disobedient action.[43] It is true, of course, that such prudential reasons are in theory defeasible reasons. But when the severity and likelihood of sanction for disobedience become very substantial, then, with the exception of unique individuals who incarnate extreme levels of selflessness, the chance that people would actually disobey may sharply diminish. For although many people wish to do what is

---

[37] ibid 144. Though he also makes certain qualifications on the place of coercion in law: see, e.g., ibid 167.

[38] ibid, cited from the blurb on the book jacket. To a similar effect, see, e.g., ibid 159–61.

[39] ibid 159–61.   [40] Hart (n 24) 6–7, 19–24, 83, 85.   [41] Schauer (n 22) 152.

[42] Such considerations might be part of what HLA Hart had in mind when pointing out that in a 'healthy society' citizens will often share the normative attitude he called the internal point of view (Hart (n 24) 116, and further related comments at 117).

[43] More will be said about the available pathways of disobedience within the dispositional model in Section 8.4.

right, not nearly as many are ready to do it at a price of seriously adverse personal consequences.

8.3. Can Moral Dispositions Plug the Motivational Gap?

Creating prudential incentives for compliance, I have argued, is a measure that cannot generally provide an adequate substitute for a disposition to comply with the law. This argument, however, might prompt a further query. Many individuals possess moral dispositions independent of (or, at least, not directly dependent on) the law and its requirements. For brevity, I will refer to these simply as moral dispositions.[44] Thus, for example, many individuals are morally (not because the law forbids such actions) disposed not to physically or sexually assault their fellow human beings, not to deceive their fellows or steal from them, and so on. Are those common moral dispositions, together with the prudential incentives for compliance that legal systems can and should produce, not sufficient to secure an adequate overall level of compliance with the directives of a (reasonably-just-and-serviceable-for-good-purposes) legal system? Why should we also adopt and cultivate the law-abiding disposition advocated here? I will offer two principal reasons against the thought that common moral dispositions can do the job that I assign here to a law-abiding disposition.[45]

The first reason is that a large part of what legal systems do and should regulate consists in forms of conduct outside the motivational reach of our moral dispositions or only weakly influenced by them.[46] Clearly within the motivational reach of common moral dispositions are types of conduct that form core instances of *mala in se*, such as murder, rape, robbery, theft, and other such flagrantly wrongful acts. Many of us possess strong and well-embedded moral dispositions against such wrongdoings and need no further incentive or motivational safeguard to ensure that we refrain from them. But there is so much more that legal systems do and should regulate and is not moral as such or is not directly, tangibly, and unambiguously moral. It includes, for example, all or the larger part of what is regulated by health and safety laws,

---

[44] By using this terminological expedient, I do not mean to take issue with those who understand law itself as a moral idea, and are thus likely to say that a law-abiding disposition is a moral disposition.

[45] That is, reasons that militate against the aforementioned thought even after taking into account the extent to which prudential incentives for compliance can feasibly and appropriately be generated.

[46] A largely corresponding point is made in Ian MacMullen, 'Educating Children to Comply with Laws' (2013) 21 Journal of Political Philosophy 1, 7.

tax laws, environmental laws, road traffic laws, regulation of manufacturing standards, regulation of professional conduct and services in different areas (e.g. accountancy, the health sector, and the legal profession), and regulation of trade, commerce, and financial institutions, among other types of legal regulation. Precisely because many of the actions law regulates in those areas are actions at the outer edge of *mala in se* (actions whose moral significance is rather abstract or remote from the individual actor's perspective) or hardly classifiable as moral, they are actions far less, or not at all, amenable to the motivational influence of our moral dispositions. And precisely for this reason, those who are not disposed to comply with the law may find it harder to overcome common temptations to break rules in those contexts of regulation and may be more bent than others on rationalizing their way out from compliant action.

As mentioned above, there is a second reason to doubt that our moral dispositions can fulfil the role I assign to a disposition to comply with the law.[47] One of law's important functions—especially in the more diverse societies we know, but not only in those societies—is to provide a common normative framework that enables peaceful social life notwithstanding significantly differing moral outlooks among members of society, whether their differences track ideological and political orientations, religious beliefs, ethnic backgrounds, or other affiliations. Moral outlooks differing along these lines—and the clusters of moral dispositions attached to each of them—will sometimes lead their respective possessors to different and conflicting practical judgements. Law—both as a set of secondary rules about the procedure of public decision-making and the adjudication of disputes, and as a body

---

[47] My comments in this and the previous paragraph are not oblivious to the fact that law has an expressive function, by which it may help influence social norms and people's moral views about the merits or demerits of this or that conduct. (The relevant body of literature is substantial: see, e.g., Roger Cotterrell, *The Sociology of Law: An Introduction* (2nd edn, OUP 1992) ch 2, esp 53–56; Cass R Sunstein, 'On the Expressive Function of Law' (1996) 144 University of Pennsylvania Law Review 2021; Richard H McAdams, *The Expressive Powers of Law: Theories and Limits* (Harvard University Press 2015).) Law's expressive potential, as I see it, does not undermine my argument for two main reasons. First, the expressive effect of law is subject to significant limitations: e.g. the time lag that typically intervenes between an enactment and the widespread and effective assimilation of its expressive import; the confined range of behaviours that readily lend themselves to such an effect; and the limited ability of law's expressive function to penetrate and change the actor's deep-stead dispositional profile. Second, it is plausible to suppose that part of what enables law to have the expressive influence it has in the first place is the existence of normative attitudes of the type advocated here towards the law. It is true that, after the expressive message of a given legal requirement (insofar as it has one) has been sufficiently internalized, the requirement's efficacy becomes less (or less directly) reliant on people's general attitude towards the law. But what initially gave that legal requirement its normative salience, and set in motion the process of its expressive influence, is, in part, people's law-abiding attitude.

of substantive standards of behaviour—enables society to form and secure practical solutions for such disagreements. And such solutions often involve a degree of compromise, if an inventible compromise, from the standpoints of some or all individual or sectorial moral outlooks involved. But if people generally allowed their moral dispositions not only to be a part of the motivational configuration that shapes their action, but also to displace their disposition to comply with the law, law's ability to secure necessary compromises of the above type would be seriously undermined.[48] Could not, however, the functions of law highlighted in this and the previous paragraph adequately be upheld by prudential incentives for compliance? If these functions of law extended over a relatively narrow scope of human activity, I would perhaps be ready to countenance the possibility that, insofar as these functions are concerned, prudential incentives could exclusively be relied upon despite their high operational costs and normatively problematic implications (which were discussed in the previous section). But since the contexts of activity where law performs those functions are anything but narrow or insignificant, it seems to me that even within their bounds prudential incentives could not and should not shoulder alone the burden of upholding compliance.

8.4. Pathways of Disobedience under the Dispositional Model

Does the dispositional model sufficiently accommodate the possibility of disobedient action in response to legal immorality? I anticipate some doubts in this respect, not least because similar concerns have been voiced in the past regarding a normative attitude of commitment to comply with the law, leading some notable theorists to reject such an attitude or at least the version thereof they have considered.[49] This section offers a number of additional comments on the possibility of disobedience under the dispositional model, which are intended to allay such doubts.

---

[48] In a similar vein to my comment on p 167, I do not suggest that the advocated law-abiding disposition must be forceful enough *alone* to overcome dispositions associated with individual or sectorial outlooks at variance with the law. For there will often be additional motivations to comply with the law—and, particularly, the wish to avoid legal sanction—that exert influence on the actor in tandem with her law-abiding disposition.

[49] Henry Thoreau, *Walden and Civil Disobedience* (first published 1849, Paul Lauter ed, Houghton Mifflin Company 2000) 17–36, esp 18; A John Simmons, *Moral Principles and Political Obligations* (Princeton University Press 1979) 195–96, 200–01; Leslie Green, *The Authority of the State* (Clarendon Press 1988) 255–63. As regards Green's position, see comments in my 'Actions, Attitudes, and the Obligation to Obey the Law' (2013) 25 Journal of Political Philosophy 326, 343–44.

There are two principal pathways of disobedience to legal immorality under the dispositional model. The first emerges from the preconditions for adopting a law-abiding attitude and the possibility of changing that attitude when those preconditions cease to hold. The dispositional model calls for adopting and cultivating a law-abiding attitude on the condition that the legal system in question is (what I have referred to as) *reasonably just and apt to serve valuable purposes*. By this qualifying clause I mean to confine my claim to systems whose overall operation exhibits, inter alia, a reasonable level of conformity to moral standards (and, as part of this, reasonably just and fair treatment for their subjects) as well as reasonable levels of rationality, functionality, and conformity with rule-of-law principles. When the system and its organs fail to meet these standards—for example, when corruption becomes endemic among police officers, judges, and legislators, or when blatantly wrongful convictions or acquittals, disproportionate punishments, and marked disparities of sentencing become a widespread and recurring feature of the system[50]—people's trust in the law and respect for it, and, as a result, their disposition to comply with it, may significantly wane.[51] As Justice Brandeis once remarked when discussing another malpractice of government officials—wiretapping without a judicial warrant—'[i]f the Government becomes a lawbreaker, it breeds contempt for law; it invites every man to become a law unto himself'.[52] Under such conditions, the dispositional forces that otherwise impede disobedient action may weaken or even dissolve through an attitudinal change whose occurrence is entirely consistent with the model proposed here.[53]

The second pathway of disobedience lies with the overridable character of the advocated disposition. Its overridable character has already been explained.[54] What is worth highlighting at this point, however, is how override of the disposition differs from the first pathway of disobedience discussed above. First, override is not conditional on a comprehensive or overall failure

[50] See Janice Nadler, 'Flouting the Law: Does Perceived Injustice Provoke General Non-Compliance?' (2005) 83 Texas Law Review 1399, where Nadler experimentally examines, inter alia, the influence of jury mistakes on people's respect for and deference to the law.

[51] Nadler's study (ibid) empirically demonstrates a similar pattern. The experimental evidence reported there suggests that perceived injustices in the legal system lead to diminished respect for it and greater willingness to flout laws, including laws other than the particular law identified as unjust.

[52] *Olmstead v United States* 277 US 438 (1928) at 485.

[53] In such circumstances, socialization agents who otherwise have a part in cultivating law-abidance—e.g. media agencies, parents, schoolteachers, and other social role models—may also visibly become more reserved, sceptical, or resentful towards the legal and political system, thus reinforcing the process of diminishing respect for the law.

[54] See pp 136–37, 139, 143, 156.

of the legal system, but may occur as a result of a local failure or an incidental clash between a legal requirement and other compelling enough reasons. Second, the occurrence of an override does not mean that the agent's disposition to comply with law has been eliminated. It remains part of the agent's attitudinal profile, which will affect her action on other occasions, though it has yielded on the specific occasion to other, stronger forces.[55] Finally, override may occur in an instantaneous manner, unlike the typically gradual manner in which firmly embedded attitudes or dispositions change.

The possibility of attitudinal change and the overridable character of the advocated disposition mark, therefore, two distinct routes for disobedient action in response to legal immorality—if you like, two 'safety valves' of the dispositional model against legal immorality—which apply in different (though sometimes concurrently present) conditions. Of course, it does not follow from the mere existence of these 'safety valves' that they are apt to function when needed. Their likelihood to adequately function depends on a number of additional conditions, including, importantly, the specific set of cognitive and affective elements (e.g. beliefs, expectations, and sentiments) assimilated by the agent in the process of cultivating her law-abiding attitude.[56] Thus, for example, when a legal system degenerates into a seriously substandard form of governance—e.g. one that consistently disrespects basic human rights or otherwise fails to treat its subjects justly and fairly—erosion in people's disposition to comply is likely to occur only if their law-abiding attitude had been cultivated with sufficient emphasis on the (substantive and procedural) values and goods law is meant to protect and attain. It is *not* likely to occur if their disposition to comply is (wholly or mostly) the product of intense fear of punishment firmly instilled in their minds; or if it has emerged (wholly or mostly) from the inculcation of blind adulation of the 'leader' in power, a strictly authoritarian outlook, an extreme nationalist narrative that has no regard to values, rights, or reasons that stand in its way, or the like. Similarly, override of the disposition in response to legal immorality is likely to occur only if the law-abiding attitude of which it is a part has been cultivated with an appropriate level of moderation and cautioning about the limitations and fallibility of law, and in tandem with moral dispositions and

---

[55] But such incidents may nonetheless contribute to the gradual erosion of law-abiding attitudes. Empirical support for this can be found in Nadler's experimental study (n 50): as was noted, participants in the study who were exposed to laws or legal outcomes they perceived as unjust were found to be more willing to engage in law-breaking, and their willingness to do so extended beyond the particular unjust law or legal outcome in question.

[56] For a thoughtful discussion of the ways compliance with laws should optimally be promoted through civic education, see MacMullen (n 46); Ian MacMullen, *Civics Beyond Critics: Character Education in a Liberal Democracy* (OUP 2015) chs 2–3.

values that make up the broader context in which law fulfils its function. It is not likely to be overridden when it should if it came about through inculcation of strict fidelity to rules and deference to authority without more.

The very notion of a disposition to comply with the law, therefore, does not *entail* that disobedience is likely to occur when it should, but there is no reason to *reject* this notion on the grounds that it insufficiently accommodates disobedience. There is no reason to suppose that such a disposition cannot be internalized as part of an attitude that facilitates disobedience in appropriate cases. And while it remains true that such a disposition is not designed to pliably wax and wane in an attempt to mirror the best practical outcome in each situation or context of activity, if my observations to this point are correct it is the best alternative we have.

8.5. A Law-Abiding Disposition as an Actuality

I would like to digress now from a direct discussion of arguments for or against the proposed disposition, and devote some comments to a different question: to what extent do people actually have such a disposition? Why is the latter (descriptive) question relevant to the present inquiry and to my assessment of the (essentially prescriptive) claim of the dispositional model? The relevance is indirect, but not insignificant. One of my arguments in support of the dispositional model has been that for law to be able adequately to perform its beneficial social functions as a normative guide to conduct it is normally necessary that at least a significant proportion of the populace be generally disposed to comply with its requirements.[57] But now suppose that someone presented us with actual societies where, he or she argued, the population is *not* disposed to comply with the system's requirements as such or, at least, the proportion of individuals who are thus disposed is insignificant. Could such evidence indirectly discredit the foregoing argument for the dispositional model? For such evidence to be damaging, at least three conditions must hold concurrently: (1) the evidence must be convincing, such that it leads us to believe that no significant segment of the population in those societies possesses an attitudinal profile that largely matches the dispositional

---

[57] I say 'one' of my arguments mainly because the functional case for the dispositional model has both a societal dimension and an individual-agent-focused dimension, though the two are partly intertwined. What I mean here by 'an individual-agent-focused dimension' is that (when the appropriate prerequisites are met) John Doe, as an individual, has a reason to adopt the disposition because it is likely to have, over the long haul, a positive net effect on his conformity to relevant reasons for action.

model; (2) it must not be the case that, due to the sparsity of law-abiding attitudes, the extent or severity of penal measures used by the relevant legal systems is morally objectionable, economically unsustainable, or otherwise in excess of an agreeable level; and (3) it must not be the case that the rates of law compliance seen in those societies are inadequate, such that they negatively impact the law's ability to fulfil its beneficial social functions to a sufficient degree. Now, I will not discuss the application of all three conditions to specific instances, but will focus instead on the first condition, which, I will conclude, is *not* met in those instances. But these three conditions nonetheless offer an appropriate framework within which to locate and understand the relevance of empirical arguments that will feature in this section.

As may be inferred from the above, the main resource I will draw on in this section is empirical studies on the common causes of people's compliance with the law. Before I come to this body of evidence, however, I would like briefly to examine the dispositional model against the background of phenomenological observations that emerged from Chapter 5. As noted in Chapter 5,[58] the ultimate foci of empirical and phenomenological arguments are different: while the former (as far as relevant to our context) are ultimately concerned with facts about the causes of people's compliance, the latter are focused on people's conscious experience and perception. But there are also relevant links between phenomenological and empirical lines of inquiry. For one thing, people's experiences and perceptions of their own responses to legal authority can offer some indicative evidence as to the actual causes of their compliance or non-compliance. I say 'indicative'—and should add that such evidence might not have a very substantial probative weight—because, as we know, human behaviour can be shaped by subconscious or only partly conscious forces, which leave little or no phenomenological trace. That said, however, it would still seem unwarranted simply to overlook or refuse to consider the indicative input phenomenology can offer us, so long as we do not confine our field of vision to phenomenology alone.

The phenomenological evidence considered in Chapter 5 was found to have mixed content. On the one hand, it was noted that authorities (legal or other) are experienced by at least some of their subjects (whose attitude is not generally thought to be idiosyncratic) as a source of *binding* requirements.[59] When such subjects view an authority-required action as unnecessary or suboptimal on its merits, their sense or belief that they are bound by the requirement will often persist nonetheless, and will be felt or perceived as exogenous to their assessment of the balance of reasons for and against the action—as though someone 'from the outside' can rightfully bind the actor

---

[58] p 86.   [59] Section 5.2.2.

through their performative utterance qua an authority. And this force is experienced (again by *some*, but not some whose approach is generally regarded as idiosyncratic) in a manner qualitatively different from that of a mere request, a persuasive argument, or coercion without more. On the other hand, if and when the prescribed action is such that it blatantly contravenes weighty moral reasons—an action that falls below a minimum threshold standard of moral acceptability—the actor may come to see the situation in a different way.[60] An otherwise abstract and remote possibility of disobedience on moral grounds—disobedience that flows from a conviction about the immorality of the prescribed act—may then emerge and gain phenomenological salience, and may also materialize into action.[61]

I have argued that the weighing model fails to cohere with the first type of phenomenology, whereas the pre-emption thesis fails to cohere with the second.[62] The dispositional model, I suggest, adequately coheres with both types of phenomenology. This is so in virtue of two characteristics of the advocated disposition, which by now will be familiar. The first is the fact that the disposition makes its force felt in a manner not contingent on situationally applicable reasons: when the disposition has been ingrained as well as it should be, its force will generally persist independently of case-by-case assessments of the reasons for its adoption or of the merits of the action prescribed. This characteristic matches well the experienced sense of being bound to comply with what we recognize as an authority, and how this sense of normative commitment may pull in a direction different to our assessment of the balance of reasons applicable to the situation. The second characteristic is the disposition's overridability. Overridability creates a conceptual space suitable for accommodating the phenomenology of principled disobedience in response to seriously immoral directives, without forcing us to explain away the sense of normative bindingness otherwise generated by directives from the same source.[63]

I turn now from phenomenological observations to empirical evidence on common causes of law compliance. Such empirical evidence acquires special

---

[60] Section 5.2.3.

[61] Kelman and Hamilton's informative discussion of the religious and cultural roots of 'the duty to obey' and 'the duty to disobey' offers further insight into the sources and development of the dual phenomenology mentioned above (Herbert C Kelman and V Lee Hamilton, *Crimes of Obedience: Toward A Social Psychology of Authority and Responsibility* (Yale University Press 1989) 53–76).

[62] Sections 5.2.2–5.2.3 and Section 5.3.

[63] Principled disobedience, it should be added, may occur on scales wider than the scope of a particular directive, and may even reach the scale of a general revolt against the government. Such action, especially when continued over a significant period, is best subsumed under the other pathway of disobedience discussed in Section 8.4, that is, attitudinal change.

relevance in view of fairly recent expressions of scepticism by some legal theorists about the extent to which compliance with legal requirements occurs as a result of their legality.[64] Some of the most notable instances of this scepticism appeared in the form of critical responses to Tom Tyler's findings in his renowned book *Why People Obey the Law*.[65] It is appropriate therefore to begin with a brief account of Tyler's study and findings. Tyler's study is based on a large survey conducted in Chicago, whereby randomly selected respondents were asked separate questions on, first, several attitudinal variables (e.g. their sense of normative commitment to law compliance in general and their personal moral views on the content of specific laws) and, second, their behaviour when faced with various legal requirements (e.g. how frequently they break these laws). Statistical correlations between these two sets of variables were identified and analysed by Tyler in order to bear out the existence of causal links between them.

A few conceptual distinctions that feature in Tyler's analysis require mentioning and clarification before we come to his findings. The first of these is a distinction between *instrumental* motivations for compliance—which is what I have referred to here as prudential incentives, such as those associated with the risk of punishment—and *normative* motivations for compliance. Normative motivations are divided by Tyler into two subcategories: first, the agent's moral assessments of the content of specific legal requirements (which Tyler refers to as *personal morality*);[66] second, the agent's general recognition that the authority has a right to dictate behaviour (which Tyler entitles *legitimacy*, and, in order to forestall confusion with legitimacy in an objective sense,[67] I will refer to as *perceived legitimacy*). He measures perceived legitimacy by reference to two indices: first, a *sense of obligation to obey the law* (e.g. the extent to which the agent agrees with statements such as: 'people should obey the law even if it goes against what they think is right'); second, *support* for the legal system and the authorities acting on its behalf (e.g. the

---

[64] See, e.g., Laurence Claus, *Law's Evolution and Human Understanding* (OUP 2012) 65–70; and Schauer (n 22) *passim*, esp ch 5. See also Leslie Green, 'Who Believes in Political Obligation?' in Jan Narveson and John T Sanders (eds), *For and Against the State* (Rowman & Littlefield 1996) 301–17, at 311–15.

[65] Tyler (n 30).

[66] The phrase 'personal morality' can be used in a broader sense that encompasses also values attached to the operation of certain institutions or procedures, as distinct from the content of particular rules. But Tyler uses it in the sense of content-based assessments of specific legal requirements and I will do the same in discussing his study.

[67] This may be contrasted, e.g., with Raz's use of the term. When Raz speaks of 'legitimate authority', he normally refers to an authority that satisfies some justificatory conditions, as distinct from merely being viewed by people as having a right to dictate behaviour.

extent to which the agent agrees with statements such as: 'I have a great deal of respect for the police' or 'on the whole judges are honest'). For present purposes, it is specifically pertinent to bear in mind the following difference between personal morality and perceived legitimacy:[68] the former is gauged by reference to the *content of specific rules of law*, whereas the latter is gauged in a *general* way, without reference to specific rules or concrete situations in which they apply.[69]

Tyler found significant correlation between perceived legitimacy and the frequency of compliance: individuals who ascribe greater legitimacy to legal authorities less frequently violate rules of law.[70] To ascertain that this correl-ation represents a causal connection between the two variables (rather than a shared relation to a third variable), Tyler conducted a regression analysis in which other potential causal factors were controlled for.[71] The results con-firmed that perceived legitimacy makes a significant independent contribu-tion to compliance—that it is a genuine cause of compliant behaviour.[72] In a series of multiple regression analyses, which Tyler carried out in order to isolate the independent effect of different elements of perceived legitimacy,[73] people's sense of obligation to obey the law was found to be a significant con-tributor to the existing level of compliance.[74]

Another relevant finding of Tyler is that personal morality, namely subjects' assessments of the moral merit of specific legal requirements with which they are faced, is another factor exerting strong influence on their behaviour.[75] Subjects were generally inclined to act as the law requires, but they appeared more strictly to observe legal requirements that rated highly on the index of perceived moral importance, and they more frequently broke laws that rated lower on that index.[76] Thus, for example, they appeared, overall, more strictly to observe a prohibition on drunk driving than parking restrictions.[77] Prior to further analysis, it should be added that Tyler's conclusions find corroboration

---

[68] Tyler is interested in the normative/instrumental distinction at least as much as in the legit-imacy/personal morality distinction. My comments in the next couple of paragraphs will revolve mostly around the second distinction.

[69] Tyler also refers to citizens' evaluation of the quality of service received from authorities, such as the police or courts, in actual dealings they had with them in the past (Tyler (n 30) 38, 50–56). This type of variable is somewhat more specific than perceived legitimacy, but it still differs from moral assessments of the content of specific legal requirements.

[70] ibid 57.   [71] ibid 57–58.   [72] ibid 58.   [73] ibid 61.

[74] ibid 62. Tyler's findings about the role of perceived legitimacy and a general commitment to comply with the law notably echo Weber's sociological account of legal authority (which I have touched upon on pp 148–49; but see also relevant differences noted there). They also largely cohere with Robert Gerstein's sociological analysis in his 'The Practice of Fidelity to Law' (1970) 4 Law and Society Review 479.

[75] Tyler (n 30) 59.   [76] ibid 41, 44, 59.   [77] ibid 41, 44.

in several other empirical studies.[78] Thus, for example, in an empirical study conducted in the UK regarding variables affecting tax evasion, a law-abiding attitude, along with other relevant variables, was found to have a significant independent impact reflected in lower likelihood to engage in tax evasion.[79] And, as another example, empirical investigations concerning the motives responsible for drivers' and pedestrians' behaviour have identified that both their general sense of commitment to law compliance and substantive factors applying to the relevant situation—e.g. the perceived physical danger involved in violating the relevant rule, the traffic volume in the relevant surroundings, and the immediate presence of other individuals—play a role in determining how they respond to legal requirements.[80]

There are two principal respects in which the attitudinal profile identified by Tyler largely comports with the attitude advocated in this book. The first lies with his empirical finding that perceived legitimacy, and particularly subjects' sense of obligation to comply with the law, is a significant contributor to actual compliance rates. Since perceived legitimacy is defined and measured in a general manner—that is, without reference to specific rules, actions, or situations[81]—Tyler's above finding is at variance with the weighing

[78] As for the influence of perceived legitimacy on compliance, see, e.g., Don W Brown, 'Adolescent Attitudes and Lawful Behavior' (1974) 38 Public Opinion Quarterly 98; David Easton and Jack Dennis, *Children in the Political System: Origins of Political Legitimacy* (McGraw-Hill 1969); Austin Sarat, 'Support for the Legal System: An Analysis of Knowledge, Attitudes, and Behavior' (1975) 3 American Politics Quarterly 3. As for the influence of personal morality on compliance, see, e.g., Robert F Meier and Weldon T Johnson, 'Deterrence as Social Control: The Legal and Extralegal Production of Conformity' (1977) 42 American Sociological Review 292; Harold G Grasmick and Donald E Green, 'Legal Punishment, Social Disapproval and Internalization as Inhibitors of Illegal Behavior' (1980) 71 Journal of Criminal Law and Criminology 325; Matthew Silberman, 'Toward a Theory of Criminal Deterrence' (1976) 41 American Sociological Review 442; and citations in n 80 herein. See also, Jonathan Jackson et al, 'Why Do People Comply with the Law? Legitimacy and the Influence of Legal Institutions' (2012) 52 British Journal of Criminology 1051; Tom R Tyler and Jonathan Jackson, 'Popular Legitimacy and the Exercise of Legal Authority: Motivating Compliance, Cooperation and Engagement' (2014) 20 Psychology, Public Policy, and Law 78.

[79] Marta Orviska and John Hudson, 'Tax Evasion, Civic Duty and the Law Abiding Citizen' (2002) 19 European Journal of Political Economy 83, esp 93–101.

[80] Dana Yagil, 'Instrumental and Normative Motives for Compliance with Traffic Laws among Young and Older Drivers' (1998) 30 Accident Analysis and Prevention 417; Dana Yagil, 'Beliefs, Motives and Situational Factors Related to Pedestrians' Self-Reported Behavior at Signal-Controlled Crossings' (2000) 3 Transportation Research Part F 1. Regarding the influence of substantive factors on drivers' compliance, see also Louis Malenfant and Ron Van Houten, 'Increasing the Percentage of Drivers Yielding to Pedestrians in Three Canadian Cities with a Multifaceted Safety Program' (1990) 5 Health Education Research 275; David Shinar and A James McKnight, 'The Effects of Enforcement and Public Information on Compliance' in Leonard Evans and Richard C Schwing (eds), *Human Behavior and Traffic Safety* (Plenum 1985) 385–415.

[81] See Tyler (n 30) 28 (where he notes that perceived legitimacy can be measured, inter alia, by the extent to which people 'allow their external obligation to authority to override their personal self-interest or their moral views').

model's exclusive focus on the balance of reasons for action as applicable in a given situation.[82] And for the same reason, this finding is consistent with the mode of operation of a general disposition to comply with the law. It should come as little surprise, then, that Tyler himself describes the observed attitude as a 'predisposition toward following the law'.[83]

Another central aspect of compatibility between the dispositional model and Tyler's account lies with his observed effect of content-dependent moral reasons. His observation that such reasons significantly contribute to compliance rates suggests that although the influence of perceived legitimacy (and of people's sense of commitment to comply with the law) is not contingent on content-dependent reasons for or against specific actions, it also does not exclude or nullify their influence. Indeed, it may be overcome by those reasons. Such non-exclusionary commitment to comply with what the agent recognizes as authorities does not seem to chime readily with Raz's exclusionary account of authorities.[84] It coheres, however, with the disposition endorsed here which, rather than barring the influence of any reasons, merely *inclines* the agent towards compliance, and which thus remains provisional and defeasible by contrary reasons for action.

We are now in a position to consider some counterarguments of Tyler's critics. Schauer's recent critique of Tyler's study will serve as a focal reference here,[85] along with objections posed by other theorists, such as Leslie

---

[82] An objection might be raised here by someone who both supports the weighing model and believes that there are always weighty, situationally applicable reasons for action (or, to borrow Raz's terminology, first-order reasons) which point to compliance. Someone committed to these two views might say that the observed effect of people's general sense of duty to comply is a mere reflection of the weight of those first-order reasons for action. The difficulty with this argument is twofold. First, the assumption that there are always weighty first-order reasons for compliance does not seem to be correct, as demonstrated by examples such as the lonely traffic light case (see related arguments on pp 158–60). Second, even assuming that there are always such first-order reasons, it does not follow that our sense of commitment to comply with the law depends on them in the sense assumed by the weighing model. Once our sense of commitment to law compliance settles as a relatively persistent element of our attitudinal profile (as it does in the case of many people), its motivational force largely ceases to be conditional on exercises of weighting, and is, to my mind, better captured by the notion of a disposition.

[83] Tyler (n 30) 65.

[84] Three comments to forestall possible doubts at this point: (1) The fact that those agents recognized lawmakers as authorities is inferable from Tyler's attitudinal surveys (see ibid 45–50). (2) Content-dependent variables affecting compliance include people's moral views on the content of the specific rule in question and situational factors (nn 76–80 and the accompanying body text). They are not limited to an examination of the lawmaker's competence done in the domain-wide fashion envisioned by Raz's normal justification thesis (see pp 34–38). (3) I am conscious that Raz's claim is not empirical. The remark made in the body text is not intended to suggest otherwise.

[85] Schauer (n 22) 57–67. One of Schauer's principal objectives in this book is to show that an internalized commitment to comply with legal requirements in virtue of their legality is a significantly less common attitude than what many legal theorists—and most prominently HLA Hart—have

Green[86] and Laurence Claus.[87] One relevant criticism voiced by Schauer is that Tyler's account predominantly focuses on laws that people are likely to view as good laws.[88] This focus, according to Schauer, provides a limited field of vision that can hardly inform us about the extent to which people treat the fact of legality as a reason to comply with laws they *disagree* with—which, Schauer believes, is a very limited extent and far smaller than what many legal theorists have supposed. This, however, leads Schauer to a conclusion that, in at least some of his formulations, sounds like a qualification of Tyler's findings more than an objection to them. For he agrees that, when it comes to compliance with laws that people are likely to view as good laws, Tyler's research 'provides some support for the conclusion that legitimacy [which, it can be recalled, in Tyler's terminology includes a sense of obligation to obey the law] makes a difference'[89]—namely, that legitimacy as defined by Tyler increases the rate of compliance with such laws. This conclusion holds great significance because people's approval of a certain law in the abstract does not imply or guarantee that they would actually comply with it in concrete real-life situations (where it often contrasts with their immediate self-interest).[90] And, as Schauer remarks, '[i]f a sense of legitimacy will increase compliance rates under those circumstances, it is a valuable tool for policy-making purposes'.[91] Now, in terms of the present inquiry, Schauer's concession has the following implication: to accept that Tyler has correctly identified the causes of law compliance within the range of cases he has covered (though not beyond that range) is to accept that, within that range, something like the attitude advocated in this book operates and makes (along with other factors) a significant contribution to compliance. Moreover, it is not clear that Tyler's conclusions actually need to be thus qualified, for, as Tyler has pointed out in a review of Schauer's book, there is further empirical evidence that casts doubt on the thought that perceived legitimacy exerts weaker influence or plays a smaller role in shaping behaviour where the content of the rule in question enjoys a lower rate of moral approval.[92]

seemed to suppose. His critique of Tyler's empirical account forms an important part of this argument. For Tyler's response, see Tom R Tyler, 'Understanding the Force of Law' (2015) 51 Tulsa Law Review 507.

[86] Green (n 64) 311–15.   [87] Claus (n 64) 65–68.

[88] Schauer (n 22) 60–61.   [89] ibid 61.

[90] ibid, where Schauer acknowledges a similar point. See Locke's comment quoted on p 116, n 69.

[91] Schauer (n 22) 61.

[92] Tyler (n 85) 514, where Tyler refers to the results of a study reported in Tyler and Jackson (n 78). Tyler acknowledges, though, that, since there was no *general* opinion—only a less common opinion—that the rule's content has no moral force, the study is 'an admittedly imperfect natural approximation of a pure setting of the type Schauer is seeking' (Tyler (n 85) 514).

A second line of criticism, advanced by Green and Schauer, concerns Tyler's survey questions about participants' attitudes towards the law. According to this line of criticism, the statements put to participants in the survey were not fine-grained enough to bear out Tyler's conclusion about people's sense of commitment to comply with the law. Thus, for example, Green has argued that some of the statements may elicit a positive response from someone who complies with laws on the grounds of 'personal morality',[93] which, in the sense Tyler uses (and the sense I understand Green to invoke here) means moral agreement with the content of laws.[94] However, the statements Green mentions are, I think, not likely to be understood as statements about mere agreement with the content of laws, because they refer to 'the law' in general (rather than, say, 'some laws', 'good laws', 'the law, to the extent that it is morally right', or the like) and because they use terms such as 'obedience', 'obey' (rather than, say, 'conform to'), and 'respect for authority'.[95] Another argument, made by both Green and Schauer, is that some of the survey statements—e.g. the statement 'People should obey the law even if it goes against what they think is right'—do not exclude the possibility of responses based on the recognition of prudential reasons for compliance in the form of sanction.[96] This charge, however, seems to be unwarranted because most of the relevant statements include morally loaded language[97] or normative terms such as 'justified'[98] (rather than, say, 'wise' or 'prudent') or 'should'[99] (rather

---

[93] Green (n 64) 313. The statements he refers to in this connection are: 'Disobeying the law is seldom justified'; 'It is difficult to break the law and keep one's self-respect'; 'A person who refuses to obey the law is a menace to society'; and 'Obedience and respect for authority are the most important virtues children should learn'. Note that even the words 'seldom justified' in the first statement do not point to a content-dependent justification. For very few people who endorse an obligation to obey the law are likely to think that it is an absolute obligation—one that can never be overridden, come what may. The words 'seldom justified' are most plausibly understood to denote an overridable (or, as it is sometimes referred to, a prima facie) obligation, rather than a lack of obligation.

[94] Perhaps he means 'personal morality' in the sense of moral views not about the content of laws, but about qualities of the institutions or procedures from which they originate. But, even so, the general and unqualified language used in those survey statements (see the previous footnote) shows that such moral views have materialized into an attitude to the law in general. And such an attitude is entirely consonant with Tyler's findings and my claims here.

[95] See statements cited in n 93.

[96] Schauer (n 22) 60–61; Green (n 64) 313–14.

[97] For example: 'It is difficult to break the law and keep one's self-respect'; 'A person who refuses to obey the law is a menace to society'; 'Obedience and respect for authority are the most important virtues children should learn'.

[98] For example: 'Disobeying the law is seldom justified'.

[99] For example: 'People should obey the law even if it goes against what they think is right'; 'If a person is doing something and a police officer tells them to stop, they should stop even if they feel that what they are doing is legal'; 'If a person goes to court because of a dispute with another person,

than, say, 'will'). The second of these terms—'should'—requires an additional comment. 'Should' is often used in a prescriptive sense that does not depend on prudential reasons and can even conflict with them (e.g. 'people should not steal even when there is no risk of being caught or seen doing so'), but is occasionally also used in statements of advice or suggestions on prudential matters (e.g. 'you should diversify your investment portfolio'). But since law is not in the business of advising or suggesting (as indicated, inter alia, by Tyler's use of words such as 'obey' or 'disobeying' in his survey), the context gives strong and clear indication that Tyler's 'should' statements refer to the former sense of 'should', rather than the latter. And it is plausible to suppose that this is what participants in his survey understood.

Schauer proceeds to discuss empirical evidence in support of 'the conclusion of law's sanction-independent noninfluence'.[100] He starts with experimental evidence. Of the experimental studies he discusses, the one that, I think, lends the greatest amount of support to his conclusion is a study in which participants were presented with hypothetical scenarios involving a teacher acting under a blind-grading rule (which is part of a school examination policy, rather than a rule of law), and were asked to assess his actions.[101] Prior to this, participants responded to questions about their general attitudes to rule adherence on the one hand, and to ensuring that their actions produce only good outcomes regardless of the rules on the other. Overall, they attached a higher rate of importance to rule adherence. However, a seemingly different tendency appeared when participants were asked to evaluate the teacher's action in the following scenario: the teacher discovers the identity of two examinees and adjusts their marks in order to correct for an earlier mistake on his part, that is, he adds to their marks ten points which they initially lost because he had given them on the exam day a wrong handout to be used in the exam. Now, there are several grounds for questioning whether this study adequately substantiates Schauer's conclusion. I will highlight two of them.[102] First, the scenario in question provides that the teacher's actions

---

and the judge orders them to pay the other person money, they should pay that person money, even if they think that the judge is wrong'.

[100] Schauer (n 22) 64.

[101] ibid. The relevant study is Nicholas J Schweitzer et al, 'The Effect of Legal Training on Judgments of Rule of Law Violations' (paper presented to the American Psychology-Law Association, 5 March 2008). I thank Nicholas Schweitzer for providing me with the results' summary, poster, and scenarios. See also Nicholas J Schweitzer, Douglas J Sylvester, and Michael J Saks, 'Rule Violations and the Rule of Law: A Factorial Survey of Public Attitudes' (2007) 56 DePaul Law Review 615.

[102] See other points made in Yasmin Dawood, 'Coercion and the Law: Review of *The Force of Law*, by Frederick Schauer' (2015) New Rambler Review <http://newramblerreview.com/book-reviews/law/coercion-and-the-law> accessed 5 April 2017; and Tyler (n 85) 515.

took place '[a]fter the grading was done, but before submitting them [i.e. the grades] to the Principal'.[103] Although a full reading of the examination policy leaves little doubt that the rule has been broken, the framing of the policy as a blind-*grading* policy may possibly have worked to obscure that fact. Second, even setting aside the previous point, the results do not necessarily reflect indifference to the rule. They may instantiate, instead, a specific occasion of override: an instance in which participants' rule-following disposition was overridden by their recognition of the manifest injustice of the rule-directed action in those particular circumstances. As was noted earlier, however, override occurring on a particular occasion does not mean that the agent is generally indifferent to the rule, nor does it mean that the agent's disposition to follow the rule would be overridden on other occasions where it leads to a deficient or less than optimally just outcome.

Finally, both Schauer and Claus cite as evidence examples of high rates of non-compliance to certain legal rules. But there are a number of reasons to believe that this evidence does not undermine my supposition that a disposition to comply with the law forms at least a significant part, albeit not the only significant part, of what accounts for the overall level of law compliance ordinarily seen in reasonably well-functioning law-governed societies. First, in several of the cited examples although the rate of non-compliance was significant, so was the rate of compliance. Thus, for instance, a 40% parking meters scofflaw rate reported in San Francisco in 2007[104] and a 54% rate of failure to pay tax on self-reported income estimated by the Internal Revenue Service in 2007[105] mean not only that many people did not comply with these laws but also that many people did: respectively, 60% and 46%. Second, the legal requirements mentioned in some of the examples—such as a New York pet licensing requirement[106] and an Illinois Use Tax requirement[107]—may be (or may have been) less than widely known to citizens, which means that at least some of the non-compliance reported may not say much about how people tend to respond to legal requirements which they know about. Third, even conscious non-compliance with the laws in question does not necessarily mean that the actor has no disposition to comply with the law or a disposition of negligible strength. It may mean, instead, that the actor's disposition

---

[103] Schweitzer et al (n 101).   [104] Schauer (n 22) 66.   [105] ibid 67.
[106] ibid 66.
[107] Claus (n 64) 66–67. Claus notes that 'there is no excuse' for ignorance about this requirement since it is a line item on residents' state income tax returns (ibid 67). But the fact that there is no excuse for ignorance does not mean that there is no ignorance, and Illinois Department of Revenue's statement on its website that '[m]any Illinois taxpayers are unaware that a Use Tax exists in Illinois' is, I think, telling in this respect.

is not sufficiently strong to overcome *alone* (that is, when there is little or no risk of sanction for non-compliance and little or no content-based moral motivation consistent with the rule) the specific temptation of breaking *that* rule or the specific burden involved in complying with it. Such a disposition may nonetheless make the difference between compliance and non-compliance— that is, make a decisive contribution to the set of factors that together leads the actor to comply—in many other instances where one (or more) of the following applies: the sanction for non-compliance is more significant or more probable, content-based moral motivations consistent with the rule are more forceful, or the temptation/burden of breaking/complying is lesser. In other words, a disposition to comply with the law can be causally significant, and necessary for law's adequate functioning, even if it is not (or not always) causally sufficient for compliance.

If the analysis in this section is correct, Tyler's main findings stand up to the various lines of criticism considered here. And even if the criticism highlights certain limitations of his study, these are not detrimental to the supposition that the dispositional model matches by and large the attitudinal profile of at least a significant proportion of law's subjects in reasonably well-functioning law-governed societies. By the same token, the analysis in this section reveals no convincing evidence that may (indirectly) undermine the case for the dispositional model.[108]

---

[108] Once more, even if there was convincing evidence for the sparsity of law-abiding dispositions in the relevant societies, some further conditions (noted on pp 181–82) would have to be met for such evidence to negatively bear on the case for the dispositional model.

9

The Dispositional Model: Further Theoretical Issues and Concluding Remarks

In this final chapter I will discuss further theoretical issues related to the dispositional model in an attempt to cast more light on the model and lend additional support to it. I begin by considering how the dispositional model relates to a conception of rule-based decision-making, put forward by Frederick Schauer, which explains the normative force of rules in terms of a presumption (Section 9.1). I subsequently discuss the dispositional model's relationship with relevant themes in the philosophy of action and ethics, which include the distinction between state-given and object-given reasons (Section 9.2); the 'guise of the good' thesis (Section 9.3); and virtue ethics (Section 9.4). I close the chapter with general remarks on the observations made in the book (Section 9.5).

9.1. Dispositions and Presumptions

In the previous chapter, I have expressed disagreement with some of Frederick Schauer's recent claims. However, Schauer's earlier work on normativity appears to be more consistent with the model I am advocating here. In that body of work, Schauer put forward an account of rules and rule-based decision-making, according to which rules, including legal rules, exercise *presumptive* rather than conclusive force in many decision-making environments.[1] The normative force rules thus exercise, considerable though it is, remains susceptible to challenge by case-specific factors, including factors applicable within the purview of the rule in question. In this mode of operation, then, rules are to be treated by their subjects in the following manner: 'Given that result *a* is

---

[1] Frederick Schauer, 'Rules and the Rule of Law' (1991) 14 Harvard Journal of Law & Public Policy 645, 674–77; Frederick Schauer, *Playing by the Rules: A Philosophical Examination of Rule-Based Decision-Making in Law and in Life* (Clarendon Press 1991) 196–206.

Legal Directives and Practical Reasons. Noam Gur. © Noam Gur 2018. Published 2018 by Oxford University Press.

indicated by rule R, you (the rule subject) shall reach result *a*, unless or until you have a reason of great strength for not reaching result *a*.'[2] Now, the affinity between this conception and the dispositional model is that both seem to characterize the normative force of rules, or at least of some rules, as, on the one hand, operating *independently* of (what Raz calls) first-order reasons for action, but, on the other hand, remaining *overridable* by such reasons. However, there are also some important differences between the two positions, which I would like briefly to explore in this section.

The first thing to note is that dispositions and presumptions are two distinct notions, and that they differ in ways pertinent to the claim I am advancing. More specifically, dispositions of the kind discussed here are bound up with, or form an integral element of, their possessors' attitudes.[3] As was noted in Section 7.3, they can be characterized as the behavioural (or conative) element of those attitudes. Moreover, dispositions are often spoken of in connection with relatively deep-seated attitudes. When we speak of someone as having a disposition to X, or as being disposed to Y, our normal intention is to draw attention to a tendency which forms part of his or her relatively settled attitudinal profile. Presumptions, on the other hand, are *tools* or *devices* of practical deliberation.[4] As such, they may be utilized by a deliberating agent, but need not be an ingrained feature of the agent's settled mental posture. This difference manifests itself, inter alia, in the terminology we typically employ in conjunction with these two notions: we speak of presumptions as something that decision-makers 'use', 'proceed upon', 'rely on', or the like— verbs which we would not characteristically employ in connection with dispositions and attitudes. We speak of dispositions or attitudes, on the other hand, as something that agents 'possess', 'acquire', 'ingrain', or the like—verbs which we would not normally employ in connection with presumptions. The attitudinal character implicit in the notion of a disposition (and absent from the notion of presumption) forms a core element of my proposed model. And the deep-seatedness implicit in the notion of a disposition to comply with the law makes it possible to understand its relatively steadfast or fixed character— which is, in my understanding, precisely what enables it to effectively serve as a counterforce against situational biases. By contrast, little or nothing in the notion of a presumption suggests that we cannot avail ourselves of a presumption or discard it from one day to another, or even from one moment to the

---

[2] Schauer, 'Rules and the Rule of Law' (n 1) 676.

[3] Or (in the case of some dispositions) her character traits. See comments on pp 209–10.

[4] Or, in Ullman-Margalit's words, a 'method of extrication ... from unresolved deliberation processes' or a 'procedure for decision by default' (Edna Ullman-Margalit, 'On Presumption' (1983) 80 The Journal of Philosophy 143, 155).

next.[5] As such, presumptions seem to me to lack the inherent stability and motivational grip—or, if you like, the motivational stickiness—necessary for something to serve, in and of itself, as a potent, or relatively potent, bulwark against the biases discussed in this book.[6]

But some aspects of Schauer's account appear to denote a greater affinity between our positions than the above paragraph suggests. Thus, for example, he characterizes rules as '*entrenched* generalizations',[7] that is, generalizations that control decisions which come under their terms even when they (i.e. those generalizations) fail to serve their underlying justifications. By thus characterizing rules, Schauer does seem to give due manifestation and prominence to the relatively stable and fixed manner in which they are meant to guide action. So, do we substantively agree after all?[8] I believe the answer is negative. For one thing, our positions seem to differ as regards the means necessary and suitable for enabling law's generalizations to actually operate as entrenched generalizations in the decision-making of their addressees, or, put differently, about the way in which an abstract notion of 'entrenched

---

[5] This is not to deny that a decision-maker *can* make persistent use of a given presumption, and may even feel bound to use it in virtue of facts external to the presumption itself, such as a rule requiring her to do so. This may be seen, for example, when the law itself requires the decision-maker to decide in accordance with a presumption—say, a presumption that a person missing for this or that number of years is dead. The decision-maker's sense of commitment to use this presumption does not come from the presumption itself, but from the rule that requires using it and the decision-maker's attitude (and disposition) towards the rule.

[6] On similar counts, I believe that Perry's notion of 'reweighing reasons' misses something important, notwithstanding the valuable insights offered by his account (Stephen R Perry, 'Second-order Reasons, Uncertainty and Legal Theory' (1989) 62 Southern California Law Review 913, esp 932–33). What his ideas do not adequately capture, to my mind, is the role of an embedded attitudinal force that has motivational grip, such as the advocated disposition, and its connection with the domain of reasons: namely, the notion of reasons to adopt such a disposition. If we replace the dispositional model with Perry's notion of reweighing reasons—i.e. reasons to readjust the weight attached to some other reasons—it becomes appropriate to ask: is it likely in reality that an actor operating in everyday settings of activity (who lacks the disposition endorsed here) would add weight to some reasons over and above what she thinks to be their actual weight? I think the answer, in too many cases, is 'no', due to some of the same factors explored in ch 6. Of course, there remains the possibility of legal recourse to punishment or reward, but, as was argued in Section 8.2, such methods of inducement (despite their necessary contribution to general compliance) cannot constitute an adequate solution to the problem. Similarly to the comment just made about reweighing reasons, it seems to me that Perry's closely related notion of epistemically-bounded reasons (ibid 933–36, 942) falls short of capturing, and bringing to light, the attitudinal and dispositional dimension of the problem.

[7] Schauer, *Playing by the Rules* (n 1) 47–52.

[8] It might be thought that the differences highlighted in the preceding paragraph boil down to differences of focus or emphasis, in the sense that Schauer's account places the focus on rules and their intended content-independent function, whereas mine brings to the fore the mental posture that helps explain how legal rules can exert content-independent force on human behaviour. As noted in the body text, however, the difference between our positions is in fact more substantive.

generalisations' becomes an actual force shaping people's practical deliberation and actions. He sometimes appears to suggest that generalizations can be (and frequently are) entrenched through the (credible) threat of legal sanction for non-compliance.[9] Thus understood, however, 'entrenchment' of legal rules means something very different from the type of internalization I refer to in the dispositional model. 'Entrenchment', by this understanding, may reflect the subject's response to a prudential reason external to the fact of legality, and contingent on factors such as the risk of being detected, the probability of a punitive response, and the severity of punishment. Action in response to such factors does not reflect a settled attitude to legality or to the legitimacy of legal institutions in their capacity as such. In light of this, it also becomes clearer why Schauer chooses to capture the normative significance of rules by a term such as 'presumption', instead of a term denoting an ingrained attitude, such as 'disposition'.

Another possible interpretation of Schauer's position is the following. For a prescriptive generalization to become entrenched—and, thus, to operate as a rule—it must be normatively internalized. Thus, a prescriptive generalization complied with merely out of fear of sanction is not an *entrenched* generalization, though the quantum of compliant actions thus secured may be sufficient to reasonably fulfil its relevant underlying purposes. Now, when this interpretation is read in conjunction with Schauer's more recent arguments on legal coercion,[10] the upshot seems to be as follows. While rule-based decision-making does necessitate the internalization of rule-following values, it is not a form of decision-making that represents the modus operandi of law in the United States (the political community Schauer primarily focuses on).[11] There are some US laws whose *content* coincides with internalized social

---

[9] Thus, for example, when Schauer talks about the design of a decision-making environment auspicious to rule-based decision-making, he focuses first of all on strategies of inducement through punishment and reward (Schauer, 'Rules and the Rule of Law' (n 1) 693). In a similar vein, he notes: '[I]f some social system … penalizes agents for taking actions inconsistent with a set of rules even when the justifications behind those rules would be ill-served by doing so, then the agents subject to those sanctions will have prudential reasons for taking those rules *qua* rules to be reasons for action' (Schauer, *Playing by the Rules* (n 1) 123); ' … rules will at times be reasons for action for reasons that are, from the agent's perspective, prudential … ' (ibid 134).

[10] See, e.g., Frederick Schauer, 'Was Austin Right After All? On the Role of Sanctions in a Theory of Law' (2010) 23 Ratio Juris 1. See also Frederick Schauer, 'When and How (if at all) Does Law Constrain Official Action?' (2010) 44 Georgia Law Review 769; Frederick Schauer, 'The Political Risks (if any) of Breaking the Law' (2012) 4 Journal of Legal Analysis 83. These belong to a string of papers that culminated in Schauer's latest book (Frederick Schauer, *The Force of Law* (Harvard University Press 2015)).

[11] Some textual support for this interpretation can be found, e.g., in his following remark: '[T]he extreme of the civil law ideal type … , better exemplified by Bentham's aspirations than by any real civil law country, might lie at the pole of extreme decisional positivism, and a legal system pervaded

norms, but there is no general normative attitude of compliance with the law because it is the law in American society.[12] And where the law's content does not coincide with social norms, it is the sanction attached to violation (or the reward attached to compliance), rather than the fact of the requirement being a law, that causes people to comply.[13] Moreover, since Schauer does not seem to think that the US legal system was at the time he made his observations a dysfunctional system, it follows that the legal system of a large modern society can function reasonably well without its subjects responding to it in the manner of a rule-based decision-making systemically connected with the fact of its being the law—it can function reasonably well, in other words, without operating as a system of rules complied with (partly) by virtue of their legality.[14] These descriptive and evaluative claims are similar in essence to the ones I have critically discussed and rejected in Chapter 8.

Schauer's writings on rules and rule-based decision-making have been an important source of illumination for this work, and yet—on either of the alternative interpretations discussed above—there appears to be a substantive divergence between our conclusions.

9.2. State-Given and Object-Given Reasons

Surrounding the notion of reasons for attitudes are some philosophically contentious questions. One of them is whether there are independent and distinct reasons to have attitudes such as wanting or intending to perform an action (φ), that is, reasons to have these attitudes *which are not* also reasons to perform φ. This question is related to the present discussion, but is not *determinative* of its conclusion. Before I explain and substantiate this last statement, I should say a little more by way of fleshing out the question itself.

To start off with an example, the reasons I have for or against wanting or intending, say, to attend the concert tonight would normally consist (at least partly) of the reasons for or against *attending* the concert tonight. But can there also be reasons to want or intend to attend the concert tonight *other* than the reasons to do so? The question can be couched in terms of a distinction, drawn

---

by common law methods, instrumentalism, and anti-formalism, arguably instantiated in the contemporary United States, might lie at the opposite pole of minimal decisional positivism.' (Frederick Schauer, 'Positivism Before Hart' (2011) 24 Canadian Journal of Law and Jurisprudence 455, 462).

[12] Schauer, *The Force of Law* (n 10) *passim*, esp 151–53; Schauer, 'The Political Risks (if any) of Breaking the Law' (n 10) 90.

[13] Schauer, 'The Political Risks (if any) of Breaking the Law' (n 10) 86.

[14] Or, put somewhat more provocatively, without operating in the deliberation of its addressees as a system of legal rules.

by Derek Parfit, between the following two concepts: object-given reasons and state-given reasons.[15] A reason to want or intend to do φ is an object-given reason if it is provided by facts about the object of the attitude (i.e. facts about φ). Reverting to the example, a reason to want to attend tonight's concert is an object-given reason if it is provided, say, by the fact that by so doing I will be able to enjoy a sublime musical piece or watch a virtuoso performer. By contrast, a reason to want or intend to do φ is a state-given reason if it is provided by facts not about φ, but about the state of having the attitude—the state of wanting or intending to do φ. Thus, a reason to want to attend the concert tonight is a state-given reason if it is provided, say, by the fact that my wanting to attend the concert would please my wife.[16]

The question cited at the outset of this section can therefore be paraphrased in Parfit's terms as the question of whether there are state-given reasons to want or intend to act. Parfit himself has answered this question in the negative.[17] The fact that something good would result directly from the state of my wanting to attend the concert (e.g. that it would please my wife) is, if Parfit's view is assumed, not a *state-given reason to want* to attend the concert.[18] He does not deny that this type of fact is *a* reason; however, he conceptualizes it as follows: an *object-given reason to try to cause myself* to want to attend the concert.[19] Thus conceptualized, the reason stands at one remove from the relevant state of mind, and takes instead the following object: actions likely to bring it about that I have that state of mind. Parfit is not alone in holding this view. It (or a view substantially akin to it) is advocated by several other contemporary philosophers, including, for example, Allan Gibbard, John Skorupski, and Ingmar Persson.[20] Their view, however, has been met with resistance on the part of several other contemporary philosophers, such as Alfred Mele, Mark Schroeder, and Christian Piller, who have embraced state-given reasons (or close variants thereof) and have offered different arguments

---

[15] Derek Parfit, 'Rationality and Reasons' in Dan Egonsson et al (eds), *Exploring Practical Philosophy* (Ashgate 2001) 17–39, at 21–22; Derek Parfit, *On What Matters*, vol I (OUP 2011) 50.

[16] I mean here that the very fact of my wanting to attend the concert would please her, independently of whether I eventually attend it and of any feelings she may have about my eventual attendance or non-attendance.

[17] Parfit, 'Rationality and Reasons' (n 15) 24, 27; Parfit, *On What Matters* (n 15) 50–51, 420–32.

[18] Citations in n 17.   [19] ibid.

[20] Allan Gibbard, *Wise Choices, Apt Feelings: A Theory of Normative Judgment* (Harvard University Press 1990) 37; John Skorupski, *The Domain of Reasons* (OUP 2010) 54–55, 87–89; Ingmar Persson, 'Primary and Secondary Reasons' in Tony Rønnow-Rasmussen et al (eds), *Hommage à Wlodek: 60 Philosophical Papers Dedicated to Wlodek Rabinowicz* (Lund University 2017) <http://www.fil.lu.se/hommageawlodek/index.htm> accessed 25 November 2017. Some of the arguments in these texts are focused on epistemic reasons (e.g. reasons to believe something) or evaluative reasons (e.g. reasons to admire something), rather than practical reasons. But they support, *mutatis mutandis*, a similar view.

for their recognition as a distinct category of reasons.[21] This matter remains philosophically contested.

How, then, is the dispositional model situated in relation to this debate? The first thing to note is that although the model seeks to highlight a certain link between reasons and attitude, it does not take sides in the above debate—it is reconcilable with either the recognition of state-given reasons or their denial. This should become more readily observable when one brings to mind the following fact: both camps in the debate accept that attitudes such as intending or wanting to do φ may have good effects which do not reside in the value of φ or its consequences. Their disagreement is about whether the reasons associated with those good effects should be classified as (state-given) reasons to *have* the relevant attitude,[22] or (object-given) reasons to try to *bring it about* that we have it or to *cause ourselves* to have it.[23] Either of these alternative descriptions, however, is compatible with the dispositional model. This is reflected, inter alia, in the terminology the model employs: terms such as reasons to *adopt* or *cultivate* a law-abiding attitude are capacious enough to accommodate either the meaning of (state-given) reasons to have that attitude or the meaning of (object-given) reasons to try to bring it about that one has it, or to take measures conducive to its materialization, or the like.[24]

Moreover, the model *need not* be committed to one of these two alternatives for it to form a distinct and meaningful thesis. It might be thought that the centrepiece of this model—reasons to adopt a law-abiding attitude— must be characterized as state-given, rather than object-given reasons, on pain of collapsing into the weighing model. That, as will be made clear immediately, would be a mistake, albeit not an inexplicable mistake. The source of this mistake, as I see it, may be the following fact: characterizing these reasons as object-given would make it possible, in turn, to classify them as 'reasons for action' (i.e. an action or a series of actions that causes one to internalize a law-abiding attitude), rather than 'reasons for attitudes'. However—and here I clarify why I consider the above thought to be mistaken—if we recall what type of action these reasons are *for*, and what its point is, it should become apparent that they do not fit into the weighing model. For it is part of

---

[21] Alfred R Mele, 'Effective Deliberation about What to Intend: Or Striking It Rich in a Toxin-Free Environment' (1995) 79 Philosophical Studies 85; Christian Piller, 'Content-Related and Attitude-Related Reasons for Preferences' (2006) 81 Philosophy 155 (advocating a similar concept which he calls attitude-related reasons); Randolph Clarke, 'Autonomous Reasons for Intending' (2008) 86 Australasian Journal of Philosophy 191 (offering a qualified affirmation of 'autonomous reasons for intending'); James Morauta, 'In Defence of State-Based Reasons to Intend' (2010) 91 Pacific Philosophical Quarterly 208 (defending a closely related notion which he terms state-based reasons); Mark Schroeder, 'The Ubiquity of State-Given Reasons' (2012) 122 Ethics 457.

[22] See citations in n 21.   [23] Parfit, 'Rationality and Reasons' (n 15) 24.

[24] Examples of such measures were mentioned in Section 7.3.

the very 'point' of these reasons to bring the agent to internalize a conative
and motivational mechanism that operates independently of weighing and is
capable of counteracting it. And the practical outcomes ensuing from compliance with these reasons will sometimes diverge from those warranted by the
weighing model. For, as was earlier noted, according to the weighing model
our reactions to legal requirements should be based on the balance of reasons
that bear on the action required by the law, that is, reasons for and against
a concrete act of compliance in a concrete set of circumstances; whereas, on
the model advocated herein, we should internalize a certain attitude that, although generally conducive to right and desirable action, would, on occasion,
lead us to depart from the balance of applicable reasons for action. The difference between the weighing and dispositional models, therefore, does not
vanish even when the latter is cast in terms of object-given reasons.

The dispositional model, it was noted, is *reconcilable* with either the recognition or the denial of state-given reasons. Having made this observation,
however, it is worth taking notice of an *indirect* way in which the dispositional
model lends support to one of these positions, namely to the recognition of
state-given reasons. It does so by highlighting a context of practical reason
wherein the case against recognizing state-given reasons loses a fair amount
of the cogency it otherwise seems to have. This should be explained. While
some of the main objections to state-given reasons tend to focus their gaze
on attitudes towards a relatively specific and narrowly defined action or set
of actions, the dispositional model focuses on an attitude towards a normative *practice* (the legal practice)[25] containing multiple requirements regarding different actions in different spheres of life. When we concentrate
on attitudes of the former type, it is natural to suppose that the goodness
or badness of having the attitude would normally derive from the goodness
or badness of the action that is the object of the attitude. The desirability of
intending to drink a vial containing liquid x derives, in normal conditions,
from the desirability of drinking a vial containing liquid x. When we focus
on such examples, state-given reasons for attitudes appear to be not only a
redundant notion, but also one that unduly obscures the inextricable link
between reasons for having an attitude and the attitude's object. It seems to
obscure, more specifically in the case intention, the fact that the whole point
of intending to do φ is to do φ.

True, it is possible to envision situations where even an attitude towards a specific action has good or bad effects exogenous to those of the
action. That is the case, for example, in the hypothetical scenario known

---

[25] Not in the sense of an occupational or a professional field, but in a broader sense: the practice
of law as existing in one's society.

as 'the toxin puzzle'.[26] In this scenario, an eccentric billionaire offers you a million-dollar prize for *forming an intention* to drink at a later time a vial of mild toxin (which would cause a day-long pain, but would have no lasting effects). The billionaire assures you that the prize will be awarded if the relevant intention is present at a time he specifies,[27] regardless of whether in the end you actually drink the toxin. Here, the desirable effects of intending to perform a specific action clearly do not consist in the action or its consequences: you would be in the best possible position—namely, in receipt of a million dollars without drinking the toxin—by forming an intention to drink the toxin, but later changing your mind or failing to drink it for some other reason. But this type of scenario is an exceptional one, and seems like an aberration, insofar as intentions to perform specific actions are concerned.

However, when it comes to attitudes towards a *practice* of a compass as wide as that of law (even as it exists in the confines of a particular society), occasional divergences between the value of an attitude (towards the practice) and the value of an ensuing action become more readily conceivable. For law's characteristic generality means that a multiplicity of actions (in a multiplicity of situations) come under its purview—actions which vary in terms of their merits. By drawing attention to the existence and importance of attitudes towards a *practice*, therefore, the dispositional model makes it easier to envisage occasions where the value of an attitude (towards the practice) and the value of a resultant action come apart. It makes it clear that such occasions are an integral feature of our practical world, rather than a mere theoretical construction confined to unusual hypotheticals such as the toxin puzzle. And, if that is so, reasons for attitudes may deserve a conceptual category of their own after all—which is exactly what we find in the idea of state-given reasons. Against this background, then, the notion of state-given reasons is likely to appear less redundant or misleading, and more worthy of recognition, than it might otherwise appear.

9.3. The Dispositional Model and the Guise of the Good

I turn now to consider the relationship between the dispositional model and a thesis known in the philosophy of action as the 'guise of the good' thesis. This thesis can be traced back to the dialogues of Plato, and was subsequently

---

[26] Famously introduced by Gregory Kavka in his 'The Toxin Puzzle' (1983) 43 Analysis 33.
[27] He has access to advanced technology capable of verifying the presence or absence of the intention (ibid 34).

endorsed by Aristotle.[28] The latter expressed it, for example, when stating that 'everyone always acts in order to obtain that which they think good',[29] and that 'though in any case it is the object of appetite which originates movement, this object may be either the real or the apparent good'.[30] The thesis was later encapsulated in the common scholastic dictum: 'whatever is desired is desired under the appearance of the good' (*quidquid appetitur, appetitur sub specie boni*).[31] Different versions and elaborations of the thesis have been discussed in contemporary philosophy of action.[32] One version, of particular relevance in the present context, focuses on the connection between intentional actions, reasons, and good-making characteristics of those actions.[33] It says roughly this: intentional actions are actions performed for, what the actor perceives to be, reasons; and this, in turn, means that the actor perceives some good or value in the relevant action or its consequences. I said 'roughly' because this type of claim often appears in more qualified forms, but I will initially focus on the above basic form, and will attend to relevant qualifications later. Throughout I will be using generically the phrase the 'guise of the good' thesis. The context will make it clear when the intended reference is to a qualified variant of the above claim.

One way of expounding the 'guise of the good' thesis is this: suppose an agent (A) has performed an action (φ) intentionally, and you are asking A why she has performed φ. Further suppose that A's response is sincere and considered, and that she is in a sufficiently self-reflective state of mind when responding. A's reply, as envisaged by the thesis, would specify or allude to what she believes to be a (normative) reason for φ, that is, some fact which (in her view) endows φ with some value or indicates that φ is good in some way.[34]

---

[28] See, e.g., Plato's *Protagoras*, 355b–d, *Gorgias*, 467c–468d, *Meno*, 77c–78b, and *Republic*, VI, 505e, in John M Cooper (ed), *Plato: Complete Works* (Hackett Publishing 1997). See citations of Aristotle in nn 29–30.

[29] Aristotle, *Politics*, bk I, 1252a2–3, in *The Complete Works of Aristotle* (Jonathan Barnes ed, Princeton University Press 1984).

[30] Aristotle, *De Anima*, bk III, 433a27–28, in *The Complete Works of Aristotle* (n 29). See also Aristotle, *Nicomachean Ethics*, bk I, 1094a1–2, in *The Complete Works of Aristotle* (n 29), where Aristotle states that 'every action and choice is thought to aim at some good'.

[31] Or, as Aquinas put it: 'whatever man desires, he desires it under the aspect of good' (St Thomas Aquinas, *Summa Theologica* (Fathers of the English Dominican Province tr, 2nd edn, Burns, Oates & Washbourne 1927) pt I-II, q 1.6); and: 'in order that the will tend to anything, it is requisite, not that this be good in very truth, but that it be apprehended as good' (ibid pt I-II, q 8.1).

[32] For a concise survey of the debate over the thesis, see Sergio Tenenbaum, 'Guise of the Good' in Hugh LaFollette (ed), *The International Encyclopedia of Ethics* (Wiley-Blackwell 2013) 2262–71. For a recent comprehensive use of the thesis in a jurisprudential context, see Veronica Rodriguez-Blanco, *Law and Authority under the Guise of the Good* (Hart Publishing 2014).

[33] Some versions of the thesis focus not on intention, but on *desire* and its connection with perceived good.

[34] In a similar vein, see GEM Anscombe, *Intention* (2nd edn, Basil Blackwell 1963) *passim*, and esp §37.

If asked why she is carrying an umbrella, for instance, she may say something like: 'because it's going to be pouring with rain soon' (implying that the umbrella will keep her from getting drenched, which is a good thing). Her answer will be *outward*-looking, so to speak; namely, it will point to some feature of the world that she believes to be a reason to φ. It will not be *inward*-looking, that is, pointing to some state of mind that she identifies as the cause of her φ-ing—for example, 'because I want to carry an umbrella', 'because I feel like carrying an umbrella', or the like. Note that the 'guise of the good' thesis does not deny that people sometimes provide such inward-looking explanations, or other explanations that make no reference or allusion to reason (e.g. 'just because!' or 'for no special reason'). A proponent of the thesis, however, might explain such instances by saying, for example, that the agent has acted unintentionally, or is mistaken about or not fully aware of her motives, or has provided an insincere reply, or is simply conveying unwillingness to give an account of her reasons because she thinks the query is unwarranted or out of place.

How does the 'guise of the good' thesis bear on the dispositional model? And, more specifically, is the dispositional model discordant in some way with the thesis? The dispositional model, it may be said, directs its gaze (at least partly)[35] *inwards*—at an inner disposition—and to this extent it seems to be at variance with the *outward*-looking focus of the agent's explanation of her action under the 'guise of the good'. I will argue, however, that there is no inconsistency between the dispositional model and the 'guise of the good' thesis, let alone qualified variants of the thesis that feature in contemporary discourse. The first thing to note in this connection is that the 'guise of the good' thesis and the dispositional model are actually not on a collision course since they address different issues. The former makes a claim about *perceived* reasons, whereas the latter makes a claim about *real* reasons. The fact of there being a reasonably just and well-functioning legal system in place, contends the dispositional model, *is* a reason to adopt and cultivate a disposition to comply with its requirements. This claim is not about what reasons people *believe* themselves to have, but about what reasons they *actually* have.

Still, it might be suggested that if there is any significant mismatch between the dispositional model and the characteristic experience of law's subjects— namely, the phenomenology associated with their perspective—this may be a worrying sign for the dispositional model. After all, I myself earlier noted

---

[35] I say 'partly' because the model refers also to external conditions—i.e. the relevant legal system's being a reasonably just and well-functioning system—and, similarly, some of the main arguments in support of the model refer to relevant features of the world—e.g. the decisional settings in which we ordinarily operate in legally regulated contexts of activity.

that phenomenological cues should not be disregarded (even if they are no more than indicative for present purposes) and have highlighted the extent to which the dispositional model coheres with elements of our characteristic experience as law's subjects. Thus, consistency, if nothing else, requires that I consider the alleged mismatch between my model and the relevant phenomenology. Now, I take no issue with this last statement, but it is crucial to note that the potential cause for concern mentioned above hinges on two conditions: (1) whether, and to what extent, the 'guise of the good' thesis is correct, and (2) whether, and to what extent, the dispositional model is actually at odds with the phenomenology associated with the guise of the good. I will comment on these two conditions in turn.

It is beyond the scope of this book to attempt to verify or disprove the 'guise of the good' thesis. But a few words are nonetheless called for regarding the state of philosophical opinion. The thesis, it should first be emphasized, is a contentious one.[36] A large part of the criticism against it has revolved around ostensible counterexamples: actions that are, on the one hand, naturally understood as actions performed for no (real or perceived) reason, but are, on the other hand, intuitively thought of as intentional actions, or at least actions involving some degree of intentionality. Listed below are a few examples (some, but not all, of which are drawn from the literature): (1) action done out of mere habit (say, always putting on the right shoe before the left one)[37] which the actor acknowledges to be based on no reason and serving no purpose; (2) action in accordance with a superstition (say, refraining from walking under a ladder) which the relevant actor does not really believe in; (3) injurious action done for sheer malice and nothing else, evil for the sake

---

[36] Some notable objections to the 'guise of the good' thesis can be found, e.g., in Michael Stocker, 'Desiring the Bad: An Essay in Moral Psychology' (1979) 76 The Journal of Philosophy 738; J David Velleman, 'The Guise of the Good' (1992) 26 Noûs 3; Kieran Setiya, 'Explaining Action' (2003) 112 The Philosophical Review 339, esp 353–54. For some relatively recent defences of the thesis (or of qualified versions thereof), see, e.g., Joseph Raz, *From Normativity to Responsibility* (OUP 2011) 59–84; Sergio Tenenbaum, *Appearances of the Good* (CUP 2007); Matthew Boyle and Douglas Lavin, 'Goodness and Desire' in Sergio Tenenbaum (ed), *Desire, Practical Reason, and the Good* (OUP 2010) 161–201.

[37] A few clarifications: First, the example does not refer simply to putting one's shoes on, but to the action description: putting on the right shoe before the left one. Second, it is not denied that, given that the actor has a reason to put her shoes on, she has a reason to start with any *one* shoe (the reason being that it is easier than trying to simultaneously put two shoes on). But none of this entails a reason always to put on the right shoe before the left one. Third, it is not denied that some routines fulfil a beneficial function of reducing deliberation burdens and saving time, but the habit mentioned above does not seem to fulfil such a function: one could randomly begin with any shoe with no regularity, without having to deliberate on the choice and lose time in the process. Fourth, it is arguable that such actions involve a reduced form of intentionality. The gradated character of intentionality will be touched upon below.

of evil;[38] (4) knowingly irrational action performed in an outburst of anger or frustration (e.g. the actor violently throws her tennis racket to the ground after losing a match);[39] (5) taking a look at something (e.g. an event or an object) out of curiosity with the knowledge that doing so would have adverse effects and serve no good or value (e.g. peeking through the window at the aftermath of a deadly accident knowing the sight of dead bodies would do nothing but repulse the viewer and make him nauseous);[40] (6) action caused by a recurrent urge which, the actor realizes, serves no purpose (as may be the case, for example, when a wealthy kleptomaniac engages in shoplifting,[41] or when a rather compulsive but self-aware hoarder accumulates heaps of useless items in his apartment); and (7) actions such as idly stroking one's beard during a conversation (which, although people often do without attention or full attention, they may also become conscious of as they continue acting so).[42]

At least some examples in this vein have led several thinkers to take a sceptical stance towards the 'guise of the good' thesis. But their significance has also been recognized by others more sympathetic to the thesis, who have responded by incorporating several qualifications into it.[43] A few of the qualifications involve particularly significant inroads into the thesis. Thus, for instance, it has been suggested that the fifth example described above (peeking at the gruesome aftermath of an accident) should be understood as a case of action for a reason, the reason being that satisfying one's desire or urge would help one to get rid of that (nagging or distressing) desire or urge, which, on this view, can itself count as a value-endowing characteristic of the relevant action.[44] I should note, parenthetically, that I am quite uncertain as to the intuitive appeal of this suggestion: is it not more natural to say that the actor in this situation simply acts on an urge, than to say that she acts for the reason that so acting would rid her of the urge? Be that as it may, the point I wish to highlight is this: since the acting-to-rid-oneself-of-an-urge description could be extended to many instances of satisfying urges, desires,

---

[38] It may be true that many people are not capable of thus acting, but I cannot say, at least not with any confidence, that none are. For a discussion of this type of example, see, e.g., Velleman (n 36) 17–21. See contra, Anscombe (n 34) 75; Tenenbaum, *Appearances of the Good* (n 36) 251–56; Joseph Raz, 'The Guise of the Bad' (2016) 10 Journal of Ethics and Social Philosophy 1.

[39] A comparable scenario is mentioned in Gary Watson, 'Free Agency' in Gary Watson (ed), *Free Will* (2nd edn, OUP 2003) 337–51, at 342. See also Raz, *From Normativity to Responsibility* (n 36) 71, 73; Joseph Raz, *Engaging Reason: On the Theory of Value and Action* (OUP 1999) 36–44 (where it is argued that such examples do not refute the thesis).

[40] A similar example is discussed in Raz, *From Normativity to Responsibility* (n 36) 74, 82.

[41] Cf ibid 71–73.   [42] Cf ibid 70, 73.

[43] See, e.g., ibid; Raz, 'The Guise of the Bad' (n 38) 10; Boyle and Lavin (n 36) 162, 192–93.

[44] Raz, *From Normativity to Responsibility* (n 36) 82–83.

impulses, or the like—however unreasonable they are (even in the eyes of the actor)—it appears that, while the foregoing qualification allows the 'guise of the good' thesis to accommodate a wider range of cases, it also results in a significantly attenuated thesis.

Now let us put aside questions about the veracity of the thesis, and consider whether there is any phenomenological inconsistency between the thesis (or, at least, its qualified versions) and the dispositional model. I will offer three independent reasons against the thought that there is such inconsistency. The first reason arises from a qualification incorporated into the thesis by some of its prominent supporters. According to this qualification, the thesis should not be conceived of as an exceptionless thesis. It merely represents the norm or paradigm of intentional action, and, as such, allows for exceptions so long as these can be understood as departures from the norm or as non-paradigmatic cases of intentional action.[45] One type of non-paradigmatic case, for example, consists in actions done with a less-than-full degree of intentionality and agency. The intentionality and agency powers involved in an action, it has been noted, may vary in degree, and there are actions that, although plausibly classifiable as 'intentional', involve reduced degrees of intentionality and agency.[46] Insofar as such actions are done not under the guise of the good, we should regard them, according to this view, as undamaging exceptions to the thesis because they differ from its paradigm in a relevant respect.[47] Now, if this qualification is correct—as appears to me at first blush to be the case—the question may be asked: why should it not apply to acts of obedience to authority? In other words, why should it not be acknowledged that such acts are non-paradigmatic in the sense just described? After all, an act performed in obedience to authority is not an entirely self-directed and self-chosen act in every sense of these words—for, as many have accepted, there is an important (even if qualified)[48] sense in which it involves the surrender of one's personal judgement and will.[49] Of course, if 'intentionality' is understood merely as knowing that one performs this or that action (in the bare sense these words convey in ordinary

---

[45] Raz, *From Normativity to Responsibility* (n 36) 72, 79, 84, and fn 25 at 76–77; Raz, 'The Guise of the Bad' (n 38) 10; Boyle and Lavin (n 36) 192–93.

[46] Raz, *From Normativity to Responsibility* (n 36) 72–73, 84. See also Raz, *Engaging Reason* (n 39) 36–44.

[47] Raz, *From Normativity to Responsibility* (n 36) 72–73, 84.

[48] 'Qualified', inter alia, in the sense that the subject can never divest herself of the moral responsibility to oversee that she is not told to do something that falls below the threshold of moral acceptability, and to refuse when she is told to do some such thing. To this extent, no moral (and quite possibly no legal) refuge will be found in the plea 'I was only following orders'.

[49] See Raz's qualified acceptance of the 'surrender of judgement' metaphor in Joseph Raz, *The Morality of Freedom* (Clarendon Press 1986) 38–42, and references he makes there to other authors.

language) and having some form and degree of control over it, then it becomes harder to view acts of obedience as acts of reduced intentionality. But supporters of the 'guise of the good' thesis understand 'intentionality' as involving more than that—they associate it with a more robust exercise of personal agency. And since we are, *arguendo*, assuming now the correctness of their position, the question remains why not treat obedience as a non-paradigmatic case of intentionality.

An additional route of phenomenological reconciliation between the 'guise of the good' thesis and the dispositional model lies with another qualification of the thesis. According to this qualification, the thesis claims merely that 'agents see *some* good' in what they intentionally do.[50] They may do so even when believing 'that they are acting for the lesser good (or greater evil)'.[51] From this we may infer the following. Intentionally acting agents see some reason for their action. Their motivation for acting consists (at least partly) of perceived reasons. They are not, however, necessarily motivated solely by what they perceive to be reasons. The complex set of motivations affecting their action may include other forces and influences which they do not believe reflect reasons for action. Now, this qualification dovetails well with the dispositional model, for, as was highlighted earlier, the model does not advocate a law-abiding disposition that enjoys motivational exclusivity, leaving no room for other factors—including reasons for action—to exert influence on the behaviour of legal subjects. On the contrary, the envisaged disposition, as I have stressed earlier, forms just one element of a broader set of motivational factors, which may well include perceived reasons for action.[52] Thus, the foregoing qualification of the 'guise of the good' thesis, if accepted,[53] offers yet another ground for thinking that the dispositional model is phenomenologically consistent with the thesis.

A third and final ground for the above conclusion is independent of any qualification of the thesis. It simply follows from the dispositional model itself. At no point of my exposition or advocacy of the model have I suggested that the relevant disposition is entirely dissociated from ascriptions of value or good conforming to the 'guise of the good' thesis. On the contrary, I have noted in Chapter 7 that the disposition is part of an attitude that contains, inter alia, a cognitive component, that is, factual and evaluative beliefs about law and the legal system. Nor have I denied that the cognitive component

---

[50] Raz, *From Normativity to Responsibility* (n 36) 65 (emphasis added).
[51] ibid. That is the case, e.g., with akratic actions.   [52] pp 137, 167, 187.
[53] Proponents of the 'guise of the good' thesis, I think, have to adopt this qualification, because it would otherwise be difficult for them to account for intentional but akratic actions, which are a common feature of ordinary human experience.

may involve a belief that the law's requirements provide reasons for action.[54] Of course, I do not regard the content of this last belief as a full and adequate representation of law's potential normative significance. For it has been part of my argument that a theoretically sound and complete understanding of law's potential normative significance can only be attained by taking into account the attitudinal dimension of the problem. The answer to the question of how a reasonably just and well-functioning legal system bears on practical reason, my model thus contends, is *not*: the directives of such a legal system provide us with reasons to act as they require. While accepting that those directives may give rise to reasons for action (e.g. by affecting the behaviour of individuals with whom we interact, or by leading them to place reliance on our action), the model stresses that a critical part of the answer is: since, when operating in our ordinary settings of daily activity under the law, we are often prone to underestimate those reasons for action, we have a reason to adopt and cultivate an attitude capable of counteracting such biases—that is, a relatively settled and persistent (but overridable) mental posture that inclines us towards compliance with those directives (and, incidentally, may exert its influence even in some situations where compliance is not supported by the balance of reasons for action).[55] The analysis leading to this conclusion has been not only, as it were, outward-looking (that is, focused on its object of normative assessment: legal systems of the relevant description), but also inward-looking (that is, examining what type of mental posture is most likely to result in optimal action under such systems, given the agent's likely epistemic and motivational shortcomings). It is true that the latter, inward-looking perspective is not typical of the way actions are explained under the 'guise of the good'. But this is not a defect in the present analysis. If anything, it suggests that (insofar as my analysis has been otherwise cogent) the 'guise of the good' thesis offers a materially incomplete perspective for an inquiry into law's potential normative significance.

---

[54] Though I am inclined to think that it *need not* involve that belief, or exactly that belief. I would not exclude as inconceivable, for example, a subject responding to the question 'Why did you stop at the red light [referring to the desert traffic light situation]?' as follows: 'Well, there was no reason to do so in that particular situation, but I am a law-abiding citizen (for which there *are* good reasons), and that's what law-abiding citizens do.'

[55] The motivational force exerted by this attitude is not fully accounted for by the fact that the agent has the above beliefs about the law. Beliefs may be transient and/or motivationally inert, whereas our law-abider's beliefs about the law are part of an embedded attitude that is neither transient nor motivationally inert. Moreover, part of the attitude's motivational force may stem from affective, rather than cognitive, elements thereof, such as feelings of respect, pride, identification, gratitude, allegiance, and so on, towards the legal system, its institutions, its constitution, or public servants acting on its behalf (e.g. judges, magistrates, prosecutors, police officers, or jurors).

9.4. The Dispositional Model and Virtue Ethics

What is the relationship between the dispositional model and virtue ethics? Does the model imply that, when the appropriate prerequisites are met by the legal system, a law-abiding attitude becomes a virtue (in the sense used by virtue ethicists)?[56] The answer, in short, is that although there are certain similarities between the dispositional model and virtue ethical approaches, there are also significant differences between them, in view of which the dispositional model cannot be regarded as a virtue ethical argument or as an argument committed to virtue ethical assumptions. I will highlight some of the similarities and differences in turn.

The dispositional model advocates the cultivation of a certain attitude. Virtue ethics advocates the cultivation of certain character traits. Both attitudes and character traits are attributes *of an agent*. A focus on attributes of an agent, then, forms one commonality between the dispositional model and virtue ethics. And, on the other hand, it distinguishes them from moral or normative arguments that focus, not on attributes of an agent, but on her actions, or on states of affairs brought about by her actions. This is not to say that actions, or their impact on the world, are not *attributable* to agents. Even if attributable to an agent, however, they do not stand in the same relation to the agent as her character traits or attitudes do. The difference manifests itself, for example, in associated language typically used. Thus, for instance, people are often spoken of as 'having' certain character traits or attitudes ('she has the requisite temperament to become a judge', 'he has a liking for Middle Eastern cuisine'), which is a form of wording not normally used with regard to actions—we do not say that this or that person 'has' the actions performed by her.

A further, related commonality between the dispositional model and virtue ethics is their inherent connection to dispositions. A fair amount has been said here about what I mean by 'disposition', and what its role is in my advocated

---

[56] For Aristotle's aretaic approach to law-abidingness, see *Nicomachean Ethics*, bk V, 1129a30–b15, and *Politics*, bk III, 1277a25–7, b13–17, bk V, 1307b1–5, in *The Complete Works of Aristotle* (n 29). For a contemporary discussion of law-abidance as a virtue, see William A Edmundson, 'The Virtue of Law-Abidance' (2006) 6 Philosophers' Imprint 1. There are differences of content, however, between the attitude Edmundson characterizes as law-abidance and the attitude advocated herein. See more generally in the context of virtue and law, Lawrence B Solum, 'Virtue Jurisprudence: Towards an Aretaic Theory of Law' in Liesbeth Huppes-Cluysenaer and Nuno MMS Coelho (eds), *Aristotle and The Philosophy of Law: Theory, Practice and Justice* (Springer 2013) 1–31; Amalia Amaya, 'Virtue and Reason in Law' in Maksymilian Del Mar (ed), *New Waves in Philosophy of Law* (Palgrave Macmillan 2011) 123–43; Kimberley Brownlee, 'What's Virtuous about the Law?' (2015) 21 Legal Theory 1.

model. As regards virtue ethics, the relevance of dispositions can be readily appreciated: a virtue (such as courage, benevolence, integrity, humility, and so on) is an excellent character trait;[57] and a character trait, in turn, is an inner disposition (or a complex cluster of dispositions) 'to notice, expect, value, feel, desire, choose, act, and react in certain characteristic ways'.[58] All virtues, then, consist of dispositions (though not all dispositions are virtuous). Now, from the fact that virtue ethics and my advocated model share a relation to the idea of a disposition, some further, more specific commonalities follow: for example, they share the modality characteristic of dispositions (namely, the fact that p's disposition to φ does not imply that p is φ-ing, has φ-ed, or will ever φ, but only that she φ-es, or tends to φ, under certain conditions). And, finally, the dispositions endorsed by virtue ethics have other attributes that, even if not present in all dispositions, are present in the disposition advocated in this book, such as their relative deep-seatedness and relative motivational persistence in the face of contingencies,[59] their typically defeasible influence on action, and the fact that cultivation and habituation typically play a part (even if not the same part) in their formation.

As noted above, however, there are also significant *dis*similarities between the dispositional model and virtue ethics, which rule out the possibility of assimilating the former into the latter. First, although deep-seatedness was listed above among the features of similarity, there is a difference in the *degree* of deep-seatedness of, on the one hand, the advocated law-abiding attitude, and, on the other hand, character traits (the centre of attention of virtue ethics). Character traits are particularly deep-seated attributes of their possessors. When describing someone, for example, as kind, honest, or courageous person, or as vicious or a liar, we typically refer to attributes that, as it were, go all the way down—as such, they tend to be firmly fixed characteristics of that person's psychological make-up. Their degree of deep-seatedness and fixedness is typically *higher* than that which is necessary, and which is advocated here, in relation to a law-abiding attitude.[60]

---

[57] Rosalind Hursthouse and Glen Pettigrove, 'Virtue Ethics' in Edward N Zalta (ed), *Stanford Encyclopedia of Philosophy* (2016) s 1.1 <https://plato.stanford.edu/entries/ethics-virtue> accessed 2 July 2017.

[58] ibid.

[59] Which is not to say that they have similar *degrees* of deep-seatedness and motivational persistence—see relevant comment in the body text that follows.

[60] And it is also, I think, higher than the *characteristic* degree of deep-seatedness and fixedness of a law-abiding attitude. If this is right, a likely reason is that some of the most critical formation stages of our personal character tend to precede the formation of our law-related attitudes. Law typically only begins to enter our mental horizon a bit later, when the nucleus of our personality is already well into the process of its formation. And although law bears some *relation* to notions that play an earlier formative role—e.g. right and wrong, and authority—this relation does not place law-related attitudes on a par with our deepest and most basic characteristics as persons.

Second, the primary question taken up in this book is different from the focal questions of virtue ethics. My primary question has been: In what way can law bear on our practical reasons? Or, what kind of practical reasons can it give rise to? As implied by 'practical reasons', this question is asked with an ultimate view to the performance of right and desirable actions.[61] And this remains true even if, as has emerged from the analysis, an adequate answer must take into account not just reasons for action, but crucially also reasons for adopting certain attitudes and dispositions that would be conducive to right and desirable actions under the law. By way of comparison, the focal questions of a virtue ethical inquiry are: What sort of person should I be? How should I live? (Or some variants of these questions.) Unlike my inquiry, then, a virtue ethical inquiry treats the question of how one ought to *be* as *prior* to the question of what actions one should perform (even if it maintains that the virtuous person will normally act as she should). To couch this comparison in somewhat more figurative terms, there is a difference in the direction of inquiry between my account and a virtue ethical account: the latter builds, as it were, from the inside out (that is, from character to actions) whereas mine proceeds from the outside in (that is, from actions to attitudes).[62]

Intimately connected to the preceding point is another, third difference between the dispositional model and virtue ethical arguments. No claim has been made here to the effect that a law-abiding attitude is virtuous (in the virtue ethical sense of the word), and no part of my account implies a commitment to such a claim. The line of reasoning which led me to endorse this attitude (when certain prerequisites are met by the relevant legal system) was an *instrumentalist* line of reasoning:[63] namely that it is an attitude that (when those prerequisites are met) tends to make its possessors likelier to act as they should when faced with legal requirements. I have not advocated a law-abiding attitude as something valuable in and of itself, but merely as a means that can indirectly (through its interaction with another 'mediator': law) promote right or desirable action. Contrast this with virtues—such as honesty, modesty, or friendliness—as conceived of by virtue ethicists: their role and significance in ethics is seen, on this approach, not as purely instrumental or merely derivative, but as fundamental or basic.[64] They are seen as a primary and constitutive part of human flourishing and well-being.

---

[61] pp 2–3.

[62] I borrow this figure of speech (i.e. inside out vs outside in) from Edmundson (n 56) 6.

[63] But see relevant clarification made in the final paragraph of this section.

[64] Michael Slote, *From Morality to Virtue* (OUP 1992) xiv, 89. See also James Griffin's characterization of virtue ethics in James Griffin, *Value Judgement: Improving Our Ethical Beliefs* (Clarendon Press 1996) 113.

I wish to close this section with two clarifications. The first focuses on a distinction between virtue *ethics* and virtue *theory*, and its relation to my position. In the preceding two paragraphs I have distinguished the dispositional model from the former, but not from the latter. Virtue theory encompasses a wide range of character-focused arguments, including ones that do *not* ascribe moral priority to their advocated character traits. Arguments of the latter type may endorse certain character traits, for example, on purely instrumentalist grounds, such as their tendency to generate good consequences[65] (or, in some variants, their tendency to generate good consequences in the form of maximum utility).[66] The instrumentalist nature of my argument for the dispositional model is, therefore, compatible with virtue theory. Having said that, even virtue theory is a category under which I would be quite reluctant to subsume my model, if only because 'virtues', as noted earlier, tend to connote, and are mostly associated with, character traits more deep-seated and more firmly fixed than the type of law-abiding attitude advocated herein.

The second clarification, which stems from the first, concerns the particular sense in which my reasoning is instrumentalist. The instrumentalist nature of my reasoning should not be mistaken for a commitment to a consequentialist assessment criterion for the moral merit of an action. I have argued that— *given* that a legal system meets certain moral and other prerequisites, which I have defined in terms capacious enough to accommodate different moral outlooks[67]—a law-abiding disposition is likely to be conducive to right and desirable action in response to legal requirements. I have not embarked upon a discussion of the deeper moral grounds underpinning the moral merit or demerit of any of the actions such a system requires or forbids: for example, whether their moral merit or demerit is ultimately predicated upon (i) their good or bad consequences, (ii) deontological grounds, (iii) both their consequences and deontological grounds, or (iv) either consequentialist or deontological grounds (depending on the context of regulation[68] and the type of conduct regulated[69]). Such questions were effectively put to one side when I stipulated, in the broad terms I did, the moral prerequisite to be satisfied

---

[65] See, e.g., Julia Driver, *Uneasy Virtue* (CUP 2001) esp ch 4; Ben Bradley, 'Virtue Consequentialism' (2005) 17 Utilitas 282.

[66] See, e.g., Henry Sidgwick, *The Methods of Ethics* (first published 1874, Hackett Publishing 1981) bk III, ch XIV, s 1. See also Bentham's account of dispositions in Jeremy Bentham, *A Fragment on Government and An Introduction to The Principles of Morals and Legislation* (first published 1776, Wilfrid Harrison ed, Basil Blackwell 1948) ch XI, esp s 2.

[67] pp 135, 138.

[68] For example, criminal law, environmental regulation, financial regulation, etc.

[69] For example, whether an act has been legally prohibited because of its tendency to harm people other than the actor or its potential to harm the actor herself.

by a legal system. They cannot and need not be addressed in the context of this book.

9.5. Concluding Remarks

I close with some general remarks on the observations made in this book. Although a few of these remarks will involve partial restatement of earlier claims, they are generally not made in the way of a summary of my arguments or conclusions. My comments fall into three clusters that largely correlate the three parts of the book.

Part I has revealed a moral difficulty that afflicts the move between, on the one hand, the ultimate Razian rationale of recourse to (legitimate) legal authorities—namely, facilitating conformity with reasons—and, on the other hand, the idea of pre-emptive reasons. Although reliance on a legal authority that is better placed to decide than we are will help us to better conform to relevant reasons, *pre-emptive* (or exclusionary) reliance on it, I have argued, is a notion that does not withstand moral scrutiny. The reason can be encapsulated, in very brief form, in the combined effect of the following three considerations. (1) The fallibility of even competent and informed authorities[70] means that even such authorities may, on occasion, direct their subjects to morally wrong actions. Moreover, the generality of rules means that even good rules may, under certain contingencies, point their subjects to morally objectionable actions. (2) In some of these cases, the gravity and the manifest nature of the immorality involved will be such that, as moral agents, we should refuse to go along with it—such that it must compel disobedience. (3) Such cases do not lend themselves to exhaustive specification in advance through detailed descriptions of all the circumstances in which they arise. And while the Razian can try to provide for them through broadly defined limitations on legitimate authority or the scope of its exclusionary force, the actual demarcation of those limiting categories—and their applicability or inapplicability to particular cases—will depend on the weight of reasons for and against compliance, which is not a criterion that pre-emptive or exclusionary reasons can coherently depend on.

In Part II, the weighing model, an antithesis to Raz's position, has been critically examined. One of the central observations made in the course of this discussion concerns the normative relevance of a certain, partly cognitive

---

[70] Including those whose comparative competence and information render them generally apt to direct the relevant subjects to better conform to reasons in the domain in question.

and partly motivational problem.[71] Drawing on empirical work in psychology,[72] I have argued that an important part of the justification for using legal forms of social ordering lies in their structural suitability to address practical problems that involve the operation of some common situational biases.[73] The most immediate conclusion I have drawn from this argument is that the weighing model fails to provide a normative framework within which law could adequately fulfil its conduct-guiding function. But the argument from situational biases has wider significance for questions about the justification of law, the occasions for its appropriate use, and the normative force we can ascribe to certain legal systems (namely, systems that meet the moral and other prerequisites stated in Section 7.1). One noteworthy effect of the argument, which emerged in the course of the discussion, is that it readjusts the focus of epistemic grounds for legitimacy in the following way: since the argument revolves around structural features of law and common situational biases, it de-emphasizes the justificatory significance of a test that compares the authority and each individual subject in terms of attributes such as personal or professional knowledge, understanding, and skills in a specific domain. The level of prominence assigned to the latter type of test in the Razian strand of thought is one that, if I am correct, exceeds its due share in the explanation of why law binds us when it does[74]—by which I mean that it exceeds its due share even in the epistemic part of the story.[75]

---

[71] The problem I am referring to here consists in certain biases, but I do not suggest that *all* biases, or even all biases discussed here, have partly motivational origins.

[72] Psychology was drawn upon here in a manner confined and instrumental to my specific purposes. For a discussion of other potential ways in which psychology could inform jurisprudence, see Dan Priel, 'Jurisprudence and Psychology' in Maksymilian Del Mar (ed), *New Waves in Legal Philosophy* (Palgrave Macmillan 2011) 77–99.

[73] Which include self-enhancement bias, self-serving bias, hyperbolic or myopic discounting, availability bias, and a meta-bias known as the bias blind spot.

[74] For some comments of Raz in the vein of the above-described test, see, e.g., Raz, *The Morality of Freedom* (n 49) 70, 73–74, 77–78, 80, 99–100, 104; Joseph Raz, *Ethics in the Public Domain: Essays in the Morality of Law and Politics* (rev paperback edn, Clarendon Press 1995) 347, 350; Joseph Raz, 'The Problem of Authority: Revisiting the Service Conception' (2006) 90 Minnesota Law Review 1003, 1033–34. Compare my reservations about the Razian test with other lines of criticism against it voiced, e.g., in Scott Hershovitz, 'Legitimacy, Democracy, and Razian Authority' (2003) 9 Legal Theory 201; Thomas Christiano, 'The Authority of Democracy' (2004) 12 Journal of Political Philosophy 266; Kenneth E Himma, 'Just Cause You're Smarter Than Me Doesn't Give You a Right to Tell Me What to Do' (2007) 27 Oxford Journal of Legal Studies 121. See also James Sherman, 'Unresolved Problems in the Service Conception of Authority' (2010) 30 Oxford Journal of Legal Studies 419 (where Sherman offers a constructive critique of Raz's service conception). For relevant Razian defences, see, e.g., Raz, 'The Problem of Authority' (n 74); Daniel Viehoff, 'Debate: Procedure and Outcome in the Justification of Authority' (2011) 19 Journal of Political Philosophy 248.

[75] This qualification is called for particularly because Raz, apart from endorsing the individually-applied-and-domain-specific comparative test I am questioning here, has also made the following

I am not suggesting, of course, that domain-specific substantive knowledge and understanding do not matter for lawmaking. Nor am I denying that where lawmakers are not even *reasonably* informed about, or reasonably apt to understand, the domains of activity they regulate, their operation may undermine the law's normative force. But to acknowledge this much is not to say that, in the range of instances situated above that threshold, individual comparisons of substantive knowledge and understanding of specific domains are the epistemic paradigm that underpins the explanation of why law binds us when it does.[76] The normative implications of this point have been more fully discussed earlier in the book,[77] where it was seen that the foregoing difference in epistemic focus can, in turn, make a significant difference, of size and shape, to the scope of normative legitimacy of a legal system.

Another part of the significance of the argument from situational biases lies in its simultaneous connection with both cognitive and motivational problems. This connection serves to dispel the thought that our subject matter can be insulated from motivational questions. The point was noted earlier in the book,[78] but merits further attention here. To begin with, in the eyes of someone oblivious to the relevance of biases, it might appear that motivations influencing the agent are an issue extraneous to a discussion of practical reason.[79] Reasons for or against an action (in the sense we are concerned with) are a normative beast, so to speak—they bear on what we *should* or *should not* do.[80] What the agent is or is not *motivated* to do, it might be thought,[81]

---

statement: 'In fact, in my view, political authorities are justified primarily on the grounds of coordination, though these are mixed with considerations of expertise' (Joseph Raz, 'Facing Up: A Reply' (1989) 62 Southern California Law Review 1153, 1164. See also ibid 1180; Raz, *The Morality of Freedom* (n 49) 30–31, 56; Raz, *Ethics in the Public Domain* (n 74) 349).

[76] In at least one place, Raz cites some epistemic considerations that appear closer to those I have focused on (Raz, *The Morality of Freedom* (n 49) 75), but the overall picture emerging from his work, and his piecemeal view of the scope of governmental authority, denote a strong emphasis (as far as epistemic factors are concerned) on domain-specific substantive expertise.

[77] pp 127–29, 168–69.   [78] pp 125–27.

[79] More precisely, this may be their impression if they do not assume a desire-based/internalist theory of reasons (see p 10, n 37).

[80] There are some conceptual questions about reasons that I am glossing over here for the purpose of presenting the above point of view (see body text and notes on pp 9–10). What is material to the position I am describing is the assumption that reasons for action are a normative kind, such that they can apply to someone even if he or she is not motivated to do what they are a reason for.

[81] See proviso in n 79. I set aside the fact that the thought stated above tends to be associated with specific, and not uncontested, meta-ethical assumptions. For relevant critical discussions in current jurisprudential discourse, see, e.g., Maksymilian Del Mar, 'The Natural and the Normative: The Distinction, not the Dichotomy between Facts and Values in a Broader Context' in Sanne Taekema, Bart van Klink, and Wouter de Been (eds), *The Development of Law: Creating Legal Facts and Norms Through Interdisciplinary Research?* (Elgar 2016) 224–41, esp at 230–36; Shivprasad Swaminathan, 'Projectivism and the Metaethical Foundations of the Normativity of Law' (2016) 7 Jurisprudence 231; Sylvie Delacroix, 'Law and Habits' (2017) 37 Oxford Journal of Legal Studies 660.

is beside the point when practical reason is at issue. This thought might operate as a tacit assumption that turns the attention away from motivational problems. And we also saw it (or, at least, what can be interpreted as a similar thought) invoked in the form of an explicit argument.[82] Now, while it can be readily agreed that motivations and reasons for action are two distinct notions that ought not to be conflated, the thought that the agent's motivations *do not bear* on her practically relevant reasons is, I think, erroneous.[83] A preliminary point to recall in this regard is that, apart from reasons for or against an action, we have other practically relevant reasons: we have, for example, reasons to adopt some modes of reasoning rather than others, such as the fact that some are more conducive to correct decisions than others. Biases are, of course, highly pertinent to such reasons, because if one mode of reasoning is more amenable to bias than another mode of reasoning, that is a reason to prefer the former over the latter. But, and this step concludes my point, biases—or, at least, some biases—are not a purely *cognitive* phenomenon: some of them, including some of those relevant here, are linked with both motivational and cognitive factors.[84] They have cognitive effects, such as influencing our perception of reasons for action and their weight. But their sources and triggering conditions are partly motivational—as is the case, for example, when self-interest motivations manifest themselves in the form of a self-serving bias. Here, then, are motivational factors that make their impact felt (in a cognitive form) right at the heart of what has been our topic of inquiry.

---

[82] pp 125–26, where I quote from Joseph Raz, 'Postema on Law's Autonomy and Public Practical Reasons: A Critical Comment' (1998) 4 Legal Theory 1, 12. Some other comments of Raz, however, suggest a different, or more qualified, approach to the relevance of motivational factors: see, e.g., Raz, *The Morality of Freedom* (n 49) 75.

[83] That is, it is erroneous even from the perspective of theories about reasons that are not desire-based/internalist theories.

[84] See, e.g., Tom Pyszczynski and Jeff Greenberg, 'Toward an Integration of Cognitive and Motivational Perspectives on Social Inference: A Biased Hypothesis-Testing Model' in Leonard Berkowitz (ed), *Advances in Experimental Social Psychology*, vol 20 (Academic Press 1987) 297–340; Ziva Kunda, 'The Case for Motivated Reasoning' (1990) 108 Psychological Bulletin 480; Peter H Ditto and David F Lopez, 'Motivated Skepticism: Use of Differential Decision Criteria for Preferred and Nonpreferred Conclusions' (1992) 63 Journal of Personality and Social Psychology 568; David Dunning, 'On the Motives Underlying Social Cognition' in Norbert Schwarz and Abraham Tesser (eds), *Blackwell Handbook of Social Psychology*, vol 1 (Blackwell 2001) 348–74; Erica Dawson, Thomas Gilovich, and Dennis T Regan, 'Motivated Reasoning and Performance in the Wason Selection Task' (2002) 28 Personality and Social Psychology Bulletin 1379; Emily Balcetis and David Dunning, 'See What You Want to See: The Impact of Motivational States on Visual Perception' (2006) 91 Journal of Personality and Social Psychology 612; David Dunning, 'Motivated Cognition in Self and Social Thought' in Mario Mikulincer and Phillip R Shaver (eds), *APA Handbook of Personality and Social Psychology*, vol 1 (American Psychological Association 2015) 777–803.

But does it really matter from the perspective of practical reason, it might be asked, whether a cognitive error originates from a motivational source or from another source? Implicit in the analysis I have pursued in this book is a positive answer: the partly motivational origins of the type of errors mentioned above matter a great deal. Most pertinently, they are part of the reason why the model put forward and defended in Part III of the book is one that incorporates what I have called the attitudinal or dispositional dimension—namely, why my proposed model involves a mechanism with motivational purchase and persistence such as a well-settled (but overridable) disposition. Since the *problem* is partly motivational, its *solution* must be one that incorporates a motivationally resistant mechanism.[85] Now, what has already been said in the book by way of explaining this model, distinguishing it from other alternatives, and advocating it, need not be reiterated. But two further comments are worth making. First, the dispositional model, it bears noting, serves to highlight a deficiency in a Razian thesis that has so far not been directly scrutinized here, namely the normal justification thesis.[86] Let me explain. The legitimacy condition stated in the normal justification thesis is a binary condition. It is binary in the sense that it refers to two alternative modes of reasoning: (1) the agent 'accepts the directives of the alleged authority as authoritatively binding and tries to follow them'[87] (an alternative which, by Raz's understanding, means acceptance of the directives as pre-emptive reasons); or (2) the agent tries 'to follow the reasons which apply to him directly'[88] (a mode of reasoning consistent with what I have referred to as the weighing model). The normal and primary way to establish (legitimate) authority, according to the thesis, is by showing that the person over whom authority is supposed to be exercised is likely better to conform with reasons that apply to her by recourse to alternative 1 than by recourse to alternative 2. However, when the dispositional model is brought to mind, a critical problem about the normal justification thesis comes to the surface: its comparative test is incomplete,[89] since alternatives 1 and 2 are not the only relevant alternatives.[90] This binary character of

---

[85] I have also discussed the role of punishment and reward practices and the role of moral dispositions, and have argued that, notwithstanding their essential roles, they cannot provide an adequate substitute for the attitude and disposition advocated here. See Sections 8.2 and 8.3.

[86] What I mean is that the thesis *itself* has not been scrutinized here. I did, however, express reservations about the way Raz *applies* the thesis, namely about his piecemeal approach to its application.

[87] Raz, *The Morality of Freedom* (n 49) 53.

[88] ibid.

[89] On pp 102–03 I have rejected a somewhat different dichotomy, whereby the supposed alternative to pre-emption is one in which authoritative directives make no normative difference.

[90] A similar objection is raised by Shapiro (Scott J Shapiro, 'Authority' in Jules L Coleman and Scott J Shapiro (eds), *The Oxford Handbook of Jurisprudence and Philosophy of Law* (OUP 2002) 382–439, at 409), though he understands Raz's second alternative as involving a subject who 'completely

the test would not be particularly problematic, of course, if other alternatives were evidently inferior to alternatives 1 and 2. But that is not the case, and, if I am correct to make the observations I have made in this book, there exists a better alternative in the form of the dispositional model.[91]

A second and final comment reverts to what I have called the attitudinal (or dispositional) dimension of the problem. Part of what I have sought to do in this book, and particularly in Part III, is to demonstrate that this dimension of the problem merits greater attention than it has been given so far. Past discussions of our topic have, for the most part, focused on law's normative significance in terms of (first-order) reasons to act as it requires and/or (second-order) reasons that exclude some opposing reasons.[92] I have not denied that the operation of law sometimes, or even often, brings into play reasons of the former type, those called by Raz first-order reasons. What I have called attention to, however, is another—less direct, but, as I see it, highly significant—way in which law, reasons, and actions connect when certain prerequisites of legitimacy are met. The link I have highlighted is less direct in that the reasons it consists of are not reasons for or against any legally required act, but reasons to adopt a certain attitude towards the law—a law-abiding attitude, as I have referred to it—whose conative component is a relatively settled (but overridable) disposition to comply with legal requirements. The foregoing link can be schematically represented thus: a reasonably just and well-functioning legal system→reasons (that favour certain attitudes and dispositions)→a law-abiding attitude that disposes its possessor to comply with legal requirements→actions. The disposition at the heart of this model, as has been illustrated, is not a mere motivational reflection of

---

ignores' an authoritative directive and 'deliberates in its absence' (ibid). Raz may mean here a more inclusive weighing process that takes account of reasons for action that the directive brings into play.

[91] I am conscious that the range of alternatives I have considered and commented on in the book (i.e. the weighing, pre-emption, and dispositional models, as well as other alternatives such as Schauer's presumptive conception of rules) is not exhaustive of all the conceivable alternatives. However, even after taking into account other alternatives that I could not discuss here, the dispositional model is the one I find most appealing.

[92] It is worth recalling that exclusionary or pre-emptive reasons are not reasons about attitudes. Exclusionary reasons, as explicated by Raz in several places, are reasons against *acting for* some reasons (see, e.g., Joseph Raz, *Practical Reason and Norms* (2nd edn, Princeton University Press 1990) 39; Raz, 'Facing Up' (n 75) 1156–57). They are not reasons to adopt this or that settled and standing mental posture, which is the sense of 'attitudinal' I am referring to here. Thus, as was noted earlier, whether an agent has complied with a pre-emptive reason to φ is a question of what reasons she was acting for in φ-ing (assuming she has φ-ed), not a question of what settled attitudinal profile she has, or what measures she has taken to change it. Incidentally, recall another respect in which the dispositional model differs from the pre-emption thesis, namely the non-exclusionary, overridable character of the advocated disposition.

applicable reasons for action.[93] But nor is it a force detached from the domain of reasons, a force exogenous to the sequential link just charted. It is an integral element of the sequential link, connected, on the one hand, with reasons (i.e. the reasons to adopt it) and, on the other hand, with actions (i.e. the actions that would ensue from it, if adopted).

Although the legal philosophical literature includes prominent references to attitudes and dispositions,[94] within the discourse on law's interaction with practical reason not much has been said on reasons vis-à-vis them. Attitudes and dispositions, in other words, have not been usually discussed in this context as something *regarding which* we have reasons—not even in the qualified formulations favoured by deniers of state-given reasons, such as reasons to take measures conducive to the formation of certain attitudes, or reasons to try to bring it about that we have certain attitudes.[95] My observation of the relevance and significance of such reasons has emerged from an inquiry focused on the legal domain. But, when considering the wider context of our practical lives and the role played by attitudes in it, I find this outcome of the inquiry anything but surprising. Attitudes—and reasons that favour some of them, and disfavour others—seem to play a ubiquitous role in our practical lives. Employers take account of attitudes (of job applicants or employees) when deciding whom to hire, promote, or dismiss. Counselling psychologists, rehab centres, advertising agencies, and social campaigns are in large part about influencing or changing attitudes. Many, if not all, international and ethnic conflicts have part of their explanation in people's attitudes, which are also key to their resolution. And there are multiple other examples in this vein that come to mind. What such examples suggest is not only that attitudes pervade our lives and make a substantial practical difference in many spheres of activity, but also that we have reasons of great importance in relation to attitudes—such as reasons to adopt, maintain, nurture, or change certain attitudes and concomitant dispositions. If I am right to draw the conclusions I have drawn in this book, such reasons are key to an adequate understanding of the normative significance of reasonably just and well-functioning legal systems. I hope to have lent here some measure of support to their fuller integration in jurisprudential thought and discourse.

---

[93] On this point, and for other arguments to the effect that the dispositional model is not reducible to the weighing model, see pp 156–60.

[94] To mention two: Jeremy Bentham, *Of Laws in General* (HLA Hart ed, Athlone Press 1970) 16, 18, 109; HLA Hart, *The Concept of Law* (3rd edn with an introduction by Leslie Green, OUP 2012) 57, 85, 102, 137, 201–02.

[95] It is worth recalling here that my proposed model is not committed to the idea of state-given reasons (even if it lends some indirect support to it). The model is reconcilable with a conceptualization of reasons such as those mentioned in the body text as object-given reasons. See Section 9.2.

Bibliography

Abel RL, 'Torts' in Kairys D (ed), *The Politics of Law: A Progressive Critique* (3rd edn, Basic Books 1998) 445–70

Adams NP, 'In Defence of Content-Independence' (2017) 23 Legal Theory 143

Ainslie G, 'Specious Reward: A Behavioral Theory of Impulsiveness and Impulse Control' (1975) 82 Psychological Bulletin 463

Ainslie G and Haendel V, 'The Motives of the Will' in Gottheil E et al (eds), *Etiologic Aspects of Alcohol and Drug Abuse* (Charles C Thomas 1983) 119–40

Alexander L, 'Law and Exclusionary Reasons' (1990) 18 Philosophical Topics 5

Alexander L, 'The Gap' (1991) 14 Harvard Journal of Law & Public Policy 695

Alexy R, *The Argument from Injustice: A Reply to Legal Positivism* (Paulson SL and Paulson BL trs, Clarendon Press 2002)

Alicke MD et al, 'Personal Contact, Individuation, and the Better-Than-Average Effect' (1995) 68 Journal of Personality and Social Psychology 804

Alvarez M, *Kinds of Reasons: An Essay in the Philosophy of Action* (OUP 2010)

Alwin DF, Cohen RL, and Newcomb TM, *Political Attitudes over the Lifespan: The Bennington Women after Fifty Years* (University of Wisconsin Press 1991)

Amaya A, 'Virtue and Reason in Law' in Del Mar M (ed), *New Waves in Philosophy of Law* (Palgrave Macmillan 2011) 123–43

Anscombe GEM, *Intention* (2nd edn, Basil Blackwell 1963)

Aquinas T, *Summa Theologica* (Fathers of the English Dominican Province tr, 2nd edn, Burns, Oates & Washbourne 1927)

Archer A, 'Moral Rationalism without Overridingness' (2014) 27 Ratio 100

Aristotle, *De Anima; Nicomachean Ethics; Politics* in *The Complete Works of Aristotle* (Barnes J (ed), Princeton University Press 1984)

Armitage CJ and Conner M, 'Efficacy of the Theory of Planned Behavior: A Meta-Analytic Review' (2001) 40 British Journal of Social Psychology 471

Armstrong D, Martin CB, and Place UT, *Dispositions: A Debate* (Routledge 1996)

Arnett JJ, 'Adolescents' Uses of Media for Self-Socialisation' (1995) 25 Journal of Youth and Adolescence 519

Austin J, *The Province of Jurisprudence Determined and the Uses of the Study of Jurisprudence* (first published 1832, Hackett 1998)

Babcock L and Loewenstein G, 'Explaining Bargaining Impasse: The Role of Self-Serving Biases' (1997) 11 Journal of Economic Perspectives 109

Balcetis E and Dunning D, 'See What You Want to See: The Impact of Motivational States on Visual Perception' (2006) 91 Journal of Personality and Social Psychology 612

Baumhart R, *An Honest Profit: What Businessmen Say About Ethics in Business* (Holt, Rinehart and Winston 1968)

Bell DA, *Race, Racism and American Law* (6th edn, Aspen Publishers 2008)

Bentham J, *A Fragment on Government and An Introduction to The Principles of Morals and Legislation* (first published 1776, Harrison W ed, Basil Blackwell 1948)

Bentham J, *Of Laws in General* (Hart HLA ed, The Athlone Press 1970)

Bix BH, 'The Nature of Law and Reasons for Action' (2011) 5 Problema 399

Blass T, 'Understanding Behavior in the Milgram Obedience Experiment: The Role of Personality, Situations, and Their Interactions' (1991) 60 Journal of Personality and Social Psychology 398

Bohner G and Wanke M, *Attitudes and Attitude Change* (Psychology Press 2002)

Bond E, *Reason and Value* (CUP 1983)

Boyle M and Lavin D, 'Goodness and Desire' in Tenenbaum S (ed), *Desire, Practical Reason, and the Good* (OUP 2010) 161–201

Boynton G, Patterson SC, and Hedlund RD, 'The Structure of Public Support for Legislative Institutions' (1968) 12 Midwest Journal of Political Science 163

Bradley B, 'Virtue Consequentialism' (2005) 17 Utilitas 282

Bradley GV, 'Response to Endicott: The Case of the Wise Electrician' (2005) 50 The American Journal of Jurisprudence 257

Brinkley D, *Rosa Parks: A Life* (Penguin 2000)

Broome J, 'Normative Practical Reasoning' (2001) 75 Proceedings of the Aristotelian Society 175

Broome J, 'Reasons' in Wallace RJ et al (eds), *Reason and Value: Themes from the Moral Philosophy of Joseph Raz* (Clarendon Press 2004) 28–55

Brown DW, 'Adolescent Attitudes and Lawful Behavior' (1974) 38 Public Opinion Quarterly 98

Brown JD, 'Evaluations of Self and Others: Self-Enhancement Biases in Social Judgments' (1986) 4 Social Cognition 353

Brown SR, 'Consistency and the Persistence of Ideology: Some Experimental Results' (1970) 34 The Public Opinion Quarterly 60

Brownlee K, 'What's Virtuous about the Law?' (2015) 21 Legal Theory 1

Chang R, 'Can Desires Provide Reasons for Action?' in Wallace RJ et al (eds), *Reason and Value: Themes from the Moral Philosophy of Joseph Raz* (OUP 2004) 56–90

Choi S and Fara F, 'Dispositions' in Zalta EN (ed), *Stanford Encyclopedia of Philosophy* <http://plato.stanford.edu/entries/dispositions> accessed 2 November 2017

Christiano T, 'The Authority of Democracy' (2004) 12 Journal of Political Philosophy 266

Clarke D, 'Exclusionary Reasons' (1977) 86 Mind 252

Clarke R, 'Autonomous Reasons for Intending' (2008) 86 Australasian Journal of Philosophy 191

Claus L, *Law's Evolution and Human Understanding* (OUP 2012)

Cohn ES and White SO, *Legal Socialization: A Study of Norms and Rules* (Springer-Verlag 1990)

Coleman J, *The Practice of Principle* (OUP 2001)

Cotterrell R, *The Sociology of Law: An Introduction* (2nd edn, OUP 1992)

Crenshaw K et al (eds), *Critical Race Theory: The Key Writings That Formed the Movement* (The New Press 1995)

Crisp RJ and Turner R, *Essential Social Psychology* (2nd edn, Sage 2010)

Cross KP, 'Not Can, But Will College Teaching Be Improved?' (1977) 17 New Directions for Higher Education 1

Crowe J, 'Clarifying the Natural Law Thesis' (2012) 37 Australian Journal of Legal Philosophy 159

Dagger R, *Civic Virtues: Rights, Citizenship, and Republican Liberalism* (OUP 1997)

Dan-Cohen M, 'Decision Rules and Conduct Rules: On Acoustic Separation in Criminal Law' (1984) 97 Harvard Law Review 625

Dancy J, *Practical Reality* (OUP 2003)

Dare T, 'Raz, Exclusionary Reasons, and Legal Positivism' (1989) 8 Eidos 11

Dawood Y, 'Coercion and the Law: Review of The Force of Law, by Frederick Schauer' (2015) New Rambler Review http://newramblerreview.com/book-reviews/law/coercion-and-the-law accessed 5 April 2017

Dawson E, Gilovich T, and Regan DT, 'Motivated Reasoning and Performance in the Wason Selection Task' (2002) 28 Personality and Social Psychology Bulletin 1379

Del Mar M, 'The Natural and the Normative: The Distinction, not the Dichotomy between Facts and Values in a Broader Context' in Taekema S, van Klink B, and de Been W (eds), *The Development of Law: Creating Legal Facts and Norms Through Interdisciplinary Research?* (Elgar 2016) 224–41

Delacroix S, 'Law and Habits' (2017) 37 Oxford Journal of Legal Studies 660

Delgado R and Stefancic J (eds), *Critical Race Theory: The Cutting Edge* (3rd edn, Temple University Press 2013)

Dicey AV, *Lectures on the Relation Between Law and Public Opinion in England During the Nineteenth Century* (2nd edn, Macmillan 1914)

Dickson J, *Evaluation and Legal Theory* (Hart Publishing 2001)

Dickson J, 'Is Bad Law Still Law? Is Bad Law Really Law?' in Del Mar M and Bankowski Z (eds), *Law as Institutional Normative Order* (Ashgate 2009) 161–83

Ditto PH and Lopez DF, 'Motivated Skepticism: Use of Differential Decision Criteria for Preferred and Nonpreferred Conclusions' (1992) 63 Journal of Personality and Social Psychology 568

Dormandy K, 'Epistemic Authority: Preemption or Proper Basing?' (2017) Erkenn, https://doi.org/10.1007/s10670-017-9913-3

Driver J, *Uneasy Virtue* (CUP 2001)

Dunning D, 'On the Motives Underlying Social Cognition' in Schwarz N and Tesser A (eds), *Blackwell Handbook of Social Psychology*, vol 1 (Blackwell 2001) 348–74

Dunning D, 'Motivated Cognition in Self and Social Thought' in Mikulincer M and Shaver PR (eds), *APA Handbook of Personality and Social Psychology*, vol 1 (American Psychological Association 2015) 777–803

Dunning D, Meyerowitz JA, and Holzberg AD, 'Ambiguity and Self-Evaluation: The Role of Idiosyncratic Trait Definitions in Self-Serving Assessments of Ability' (1989) 57 Journal of Personality and Social Psychology 1082

Dunning D et al, 'Why People Fail to Recognize Their Own Incompetence' (2003) 12 Current Directions in Psychological Science 83

Dworkin R, *Taking Rights Seriously* (rev paperback edn with a reply to critics, Duckworth 1978)

Dworkin R, *Law's Empire* (Fontana 1986)

Dworkin R, 'Thirty Years On' (2002) 115 Harvard Law Review 1655

Eagly AH and Chaiken S, 'The Advantages of an Inclusive Definition of Attitude' (2007) 25 Social Cognition 582

Easton D and Dennis J, *Children in the Political System: Origins of Political Legitimacy* (McGraw-Hill 1969)

Edmundson WA, 'Rethinking Exclusionary Reasons: A Second Edition of Joseph Raz's "Practical Reason and Norms"' (1993) 12 Law and Philosophy 329

Edmundson WA, *Three Anarchical Fallacies: An Essay on Political Authority* (CUP 1998)

Edmundson WA, 'The Virtue of Law-Abidance' (2006) 6 Philosophers' Imprint 1

Ehrenberg KM, 'Critical Reception of Raz's Theory of Authority' (2011) 6 Philosophy Compass 777

Ehrenberg KM, *The Functions of Law* (OUP 2016)

Ehrlinger J, Gilovich T, and Ross L, 'Peering Into the Bias Blind Spot: People's Assessment of Bias in Themselves and Others' (2005) 31 Personality and Social Psychology Bulletin 680

Endicott T, 'The Subsidiarity of Law and the Obligation to Obey' (2005) 50 The American Journal of Jurisprudence 233

Enoch D, 'Reason-Giving and the Law' in Green L and Leiter B (eds) *Oxford Studies in Philosophy of Law*, vol 1 (OUP 2011) 1–38

Enoch D, 'Authority and Reason-Giving' (2014) 89 Philosophy and Phenomenological Research 296

Essert C, 'A Dilemma for Protected Reasons' (2012) 31 Law and Philosophy 49

Fagan J and Tyler TR, 'Legal Socialization of Children and Adolescents' (2005) 18 Social Justice Research 217

Farnsworth W, 'The Legal Regulation of Self-Serving Bias' (2003) 37 UC Davis Law Review 567

Finnis JM, 'The Authority of Law in the Predicament of Contemporary Social Theory' (1984) 1 Notre Dame Journal of Law, Ethics & Public Policy 115

Finnis JM, 'Law as Co-ordination' (1989) 2 Ratio Juris 97

Finnis JM, *Natural Law and Natural Rights* (2nd edn, Clarendon Press 2011)

Fishbein M and Ajzen I, 'Attitudes Towards Objects as Predictors of Single and Multiple Behavioral Criteria' (1974) 81 Psychological Review 59

Fishbein M and Ajzen I, *Belief, Attitude, Intention, and Behavior: An Introduction to Theory and Research* (Addison-Wesley 1975)

Fishbein M and Ajzen I, 'Attitude–Behavior Relations: A Theoretical Analysis and Review of Empirical Research' (1977) 84 Psychological Bulletin 888

Flathman RE, *The Practice of Political Authority: Authority and the Authoritative* (University of Chicago Press 1980)

Fodor JA, *Psychosemantics* (MIT Press 1987)

Foot P, *Virtues and Vices* (Clarendon Press 2002)

Friedrich J, 'On Seeing Oneself as Less Self-Serving Than Others: The Ultimate Self-Serving Bias?' (1996) 23 Teaching of Psychology 107

Fuller LL, *The Morality of Law* (2nd edn, Yale University Press 1969)

Gamson WA, Fireman B, and Rytina S, *Encounters with Unjust Authority* (Dorsey Press 1982)

Gans C, 'Mandatory Rules and Exclusionary Reasons' (1986) 15 Philosophia 373

Gardner J, *Law as a Leap of Faith* (OUP 2012)

Gauthier D, 'Afterthoughts' in MacLean D (ed), *The Security Gamble: Deterrence Dilemmas in the Nuclear Age* (Rowman and Allanheld 1984) 159–61

Gauthier D, 'Rethinking the Toxin Puzzle' in Coleman JL and Morris CW (eds), *Rational Commitment and Social Justice: Essays for Gregory Kavka* (CUP 1998) 47–58

Gerstein R, 'The Practice of Fidelity to Law' (1970) 4 Law & Society Review 479

Gibbard A, *Wise Choices, Apt Feelings: A Theory of Normative Judgment* (Harvard University Press 1990)

Goslin DA (ed), *Handbook of Socialization Theory and Research* (Rand McNally 1969)

Graham PA, ' "Ought" and Ability' (2011) 120 The Philosophical Review 337

Grasmick HG and Green DE, 'Legal Punishment, Social Disapproval and Internalization as Inhibitors of Illegal Behavior' (1980) 71 Journal of Criminal Law and Criminology 325

Green L, *The Authority of the State* (Clarendon Press 1988)

Green L, 'Who Believes in Political Obligation?' in Narveson J and Sanders JT (eds), *For and Against the State* (Rowman & Littlefield 1996) 301–17

Greenawalt K, *Conflicts of Law and Morality* (paperback edn, OUP 1989)

Greenberg M, 'How Facts Make Law' in Hershowitz S (ed), *Exploring Law's Empire: The Jurisprudence of Ronald Dworkin* (OUP 2006) 225–64

Griffin J, *Value Judgement: Improving Our Ethical Beliefs* (Clarendon Press 1996)

Grusec JE and Hastings PD, *Handbook of Socialization: Theory and Research* (Guilford Press 2007)

Gur N, 'Are Legal Rules Content-Independent Reasons?' (2011) 5 Problema 175

Gur N, 'Actions, Attitudes, and the Obligation to Obey the Law' (2013) 25 Journal of Political Philosophy 326

Gur N, 'Form and Value in Law' (2014) 5 Jurisprudence 85

Guttel E and Harel A, 'Matching Probabilities: The Behavioral Law and Economics of Repeated Behavior' (2005) 72 University of Chicago Law Review 1197

Hammond M, Howarth J, and Keat R, *Understanding Phenomenology* (Basil Blackwell 1991)

Hare R, *Moral Thinking: Its Levels, Method and Point* (Clarendon Press 1981)

Hart HLA, 'Are there any Natural Rights?' (1955) 64 Philosophical Review 175

Hart HLA, *The Concept of Law* (3rd edn with an introduction by Green L, OUP 2012)

Heinz WR, 'Self-Socialization and Post-Traditional Society' in Settersten RA and Owens TJ (eds), *Advances in Life Course Research: New Frontiers in Socialization* (Elsevier 2002) 41–64

Herrnstein RJ, 'Rational Choice Theory: Necessary but Not Sufficient' (1990) 45 American Psychologist 356

Hershovitz S, 'Legitimacy, Democracy, and Razian Authority' (2003) 9 Legal Theory 201

Heuer U, 'Reasons for Actions and Desires' (2004) 121 Philosophical Studies 43

Heuer U, 'Reasons and Impossibility' (2010) 147 Philosophical Studies 235

Himma KE, 'Law's Claim of Legitimate Authority' in Coleman J (ed), *Hart's Postscript: Essays on the Postscript to the Concept of Law* (OUP 2001) 271–309

Himma KE, 'Just Cause You're Smarter Than Me Doesn't Give You a Right to Tell Me What to Do' (2007) 27 Oxford Journal of Legal Studies 121

Hobbes T, *Leviathan* (first published 1651, Tuck R ed, CUP 1991)

Horwitz MJ, *The Transformation of American Law, 1780–1860* (Harvard University Press 1977)

Hume D, *A Treatise of Human Nature* (first published 1740, Selby-Bigge LA and Nidditch PH eds, Clarendon Press 1978)

Hunter R, 'The Power of Feminist Judgments?' (2012) 20 Feminist Legal Studies 135

Hursthouse R and Pettigrove G, 'Virtue Ethics' in Zalta EN, *Stanford Encyclopedia of Philosophy* (2016) <https://plato.stanford.edu/entries/ethics-virtue> accessed 2 July 2017

Hurd HM, 'Challenging Authority' (1991) 100 Yale Law Journal 1611

Jackson J et al, 'Why Do People Comply with the Law? Legitimacy and the Influence of Legal Institutions' (2012) 52 British Journal of Criminology 1051

Kahle LR and Berman JJ, 'Attitudes Cause Behaviors: A Cross-Lagged Panel Analysis' (1979) 37 Journal of Personality and Social Psychology 315

Kant I, *Critique of Practical Reason; Groundwork of the Metaphysics of Morals; The Metaphysics of Morals* in Kant I, *Practical Philosophy* (Gregor MJ ed and tr, CUP 1996)

Katz D and Stotland E, 'A Preliminary Statement to a Theory of Attitude Structure and Change' in Koch S (ed), *Psychology: A Study of a Science*, vol 3 (McGraw-Hill 1959) 423–75

Kavka GS, 'The Toxin Puzzle' (1983) 43 Analysis 33

Kekes J, '"Ought implies Can" and Two Kinds of Morality' 34 Philosophical Quarterly 459

Kelman HC and Hamilton VL, *Crimes of Obedience: Toward A Social Psychology of Authority and Responsibility* (Yale University Press 1989)

Kilham W and Mann L, 'Level of Destructive Obedience as a Function of Transmitter and Executant Roles in the Milgram Obedience Paradigm' (1974) 29 Journal of Personality and Social Psychology 696

Kirby KN, 'Bidding on the Future: Evidence Against Normative Discounting of Delayed Rewards' (1997) 126 Journal of Experimental Psychology: General 54

Kirby KN and Herrnstein RJ, 'Preference Reversals due to Myopic Discounting of Delayed Reward' (1995) 6 Psychological Science 83

Klosko G, *The Principle of Fairness and Political Obligation* (Rowman & Littlefield 1992)

Kramer MH, *In Defense of Legal Positivism* (OUP 1999)

Kramer MH, 'On the Moral Status of the Rule of Law' (2004) 63 Cambridge Law Journal 65

Kruger J, 'Lake Wobegon Be Gone! The "Below-Average Effect" and the Egocentric Nature of Comparative Ability Judgments' (1999) 77 Journal of Personality and Social Psychology 221

Kruger J and Dunning D, 'Unskilled and Unaware of It: How Difficulties in Recognizing One's Own Incompetence Lead to Inflated Self-Assessment' (1999) 77 Journal of Personality and Social Psychology 1121

Kunda Z, 'The Case for Motivated Reasoning' (1990) 108 Psychological Bulletin 480

Kyritsis D, *Where Our Protection Lies: Separation of Powers and Constitutional Review* (OUP 2017)

LaPiere RT, 'Attitudes vs. Actions' (1934) 13 Social Forces 230

Larwood L and Whittaker W, 'Managerial Myopia: Self-Serving Biases in Organizational Planning' (1977) 62 Journal of Applied Psychology 194

Lichtenstein S et al, 'Judged Frequency of Lethal Events' (1978) 4 Journal of Experimental Psychology: Human Learning and Memory 551

Locke J, *Two Treatises of Government* (first published 1689, Laslett P ed, CUP 1967)

Maccoby EE and Jacklin CN, *The Psychology of Sex Differences* (Stanford University Press 1974)

MacKinnon C, 'Feminism, Marxism, Method and the State: Toward Feminist Jurisprudence' (1983) 8 Signs 635

MacKinnon C, *Feminism Unmodified: Discourses on Life and Law* (Harvard University Press 1987)

MacMullen I, 'Educating Children to Comply with Laws' (2013) 21 Journal of Political Philosophy 1

MacMullen I, *Civics Beyond Critics: Character Education in a Liberal Democracy* (OUP 2015)

Maguire B, 'The Value-Based Theory of Reasons' (2016) 3 Ergo 233

Maio G and Haddock G, *The Psychology of Attitudes and Attitude Change* (Sage 2009)

Malenfant L and Houten RV, 'Increasing the Percentage of Drivers Yielding to Pedestrians in Three Canadian Cities with a Multifaceted Safety Program' (1990) 5 Health Education Research 275

Marcus RB, 'Some Revisionary Proposals about Belief and Believing' (1990) 50 Philosophy and Phenomenological Research 133

Markwick P, 'Law and Content-Independent Reasons' (2000) 20 Oxford Journal of Legal Studies 579

Markwick P, 'Independent of Content' (2003) 9 Legal Theory 43

Martin M, *Judging Positivism* (Hart Publishing 2014)

Martin W, 'Ought but Cannot' (2009) 109 Proceedings of the Aristotelian Society 103

Marwell G, Aiken MT, and Demereth N, 'The Persistence of Political Attitudes Among 1960s Civil Rights Activists' (1987) 51 Public Opinion Quarterly 359

McAdams RH, *The Expressive Powers of Law: Theories and Limits* (Harvard University Press 2015)

McKitrick J, 'Dispositional Pluralism' in Damschen G et al (eds), *Debating Dispositions: Issues in Metaphysics, Epistemology and Philosophy of Mind* (Walter de Gruyter 2009) 186–203

McPherson-Frantz C, 'I AM Being Fair: The Bias Blind Spot as a Stumbling Block to Seeing Both Sides' (2006) 28 Basic and Applied Social Psychology 157

Meier RF and Johnson WT, 'Deterrence as Social Control: The Legal and Extralegal Production of Conformity' (1977) 42 American Sociological Review 292

Mele AR, 'Effective Deliberation about What to Intend: Or Striking It Rich in a Toxin-Free Environment' (1995) 79 Philosophical Studies 85

Messick DM, 'Social Interdependence and Decision Making' in Wright G (ed), *Behavioral Decision Making* (Plenum 1985) 87–109

Messick DM and Sentis KP, 'Fairness and Preference' (1979) 15 Journal of Experimental Social Psychology 418

Mian E, 'The Curious Case of Exclusionary Reasons' (2002) 15 Canadian Journal of Law and Jurisprudence 99

Milgram S, *Obedience to Authority: An Experimental View* (Pinter & Martin 2005)

Millar A and Navarick DJ, 'Self-Control and Choice in Humans: Effects of Video Game Playing as a Positive Reinforcer' (1984) 15 Learning and Motivation 203

Moore MS, 'Authority, Law, and Razian Reasons' (1989) 62 Southern California Law Review 827

Moran D, *Introduction to Phenomenology* (Routledge 2000)

Morauta J, 'In Defence of State-Based Reasons to Intend' (2010) 91 Pacific Philosophical Quarterly 208

Mossman MJ, 'Feminism and Legal Method: The Difference it Makes' (1987) 3 Wisconsin Women Law Journal 147

Mumford S, *Dispositions* (OUP 1998)

Mumford S and Anjum RL, 'Dispositional Modality' in Gethmann CF (ed), *Lebenswelt und Wissenschaft: Deutsches Jahrbuch für Philosophie*, vol 2 (Meiner 2011) 468–82

Murphy MC, *Natural Law in Jurisprudence and Politics* (CUP 2006)

Nadler J, 'Flouting the Law: Does Perceived Injustice Provoke General Non-Compliance?' (2005) 83 Texas Law Review 1399

Orviska M and Hudson J, 'Tax Evasion, Civic Duty and the Law Abiding Citizen' (2002) 19 European Journal of Political Economy 83

Orviska M and Hudson J, 'Quiet in the Cathedral: Who is the Law Abiding Citizen?' (2006) 23 Homo Oeconomicus 129

Owens D, 'Rationalism About Obligation' (2008) 16 European Journal of Philosophy 403

Parfit D, 'Rationality and Reasons' in Egonsson D et al (eds), *Exploring Practical Philosophy* (Ashgate 2001) 17–39

Parfit D, *On What Matters*, vol I (OUP 2011)

Parks R and Haskins J, *Rosa Parks: My Story* (Penguin 1992)

Parks R and Reed GJ, *Quiet Strength: The Faith, the Hope, and the Heart of a Woman Who Changed a Nation* (Zondervan Publishing House 1994)

Perry SR, 'Second-order Reasons, Uncertainty and Legal Theory' (1989) 62 Southern California Law Review 913

Persson I, 'Primary and Secondary Reasons' in Rønnow-Rasmussen R et al (eds), Hommage à Wlodek: 60 Philosophical Papers Dedicated to Wlodek Rabinowicz (Lund University 2017) <http://www.fil.lu.se/hommageawlodek/index.htm> accessed 25 November 2017

Peter F, 'Political Legitimacy' in Zalta EN (ed) Stanford Encyclopedia of Philosophy <https://plato.stanford.edu/entries/legitimacy/> accessed 15 December 2017

Piller C, 'Content-Related and Attitude-Related Reasons for Preferences' (2006) 81 Philosophy 155

Piller C, 'Kinds of Practical Reasons: Attitude-Related Reasons and Exclusionary Reasons' in Miguens S, Pinto JA, and Mauro CE (eds), *Analyses* (Porto University 2006) 98–105

Pink T, *The Psychology of Freedom* (CUP 1996)

Plato, *Gorgias; Meno; Protagoras; Republic* in Cooper JM (ed), *Plato: Complete Works* (Hacket Publishing 1997)

Pogarsky G and Babcock L, 'Damage Caps, Motivated Anchoring, and Bargaining Impasse' (2001) 30 Journal of Legal Studies 143

Portmore DW, 'Are Moral Reasons Morally Overriding?' (2008) 11 Ethical Theory and Moral Practice 369

Postema GJ, 'Positivism, I Presume? . . . Comments on Schauer's "Rules and the Rule of Law"' (1991) 14 Harvard Journal of Law & Public Policy 797

Preston CE and Harris S, 'Psychology of Drivers in Traffic Accidents' (1965) 49 Journal of Applied Psychology 284

Priel D, 'Jurisprudence and Psychology' in Del Mar M (ed), *New Waves in Legal Philosophy* (Palgrave Macmillan 2011) 77–99

Prior EW, *Dispositions* (Aberdeen University Press 1985)

Pronin E, Gilovich T, and Ross L, 'Objectivity in the Eye of the Beholder: Divergent Perceptions of Bias in Self Versus Others' (2004) 111 Psychological Review 781

Pronin E, Lin DY, and Ross L, 'The Bias Blind Spot: Perception of Bias in Self Versus Others' (2002) 28 Personality and Social Psychology Bulletin 369

Pyszczynski T and Greenberg J, 'Toward an Integration of Cognitive and Motivational Perspectives on Social Inference: A Biased Hypothesis-Testing Model' in Berkowitz L (ed), *Advances in Experimental Social Psychology*, vol 20 (Academic Press 1987) 297–340

Radbruch G, 'Five Minutes of Legal Philosophy (1945)' (2006) 26 Oxford Journal of Legal Studies 13

Radbruch G, 'Statutory Lawlessness and Supra-Statutory Law (1946)' (2006) 26 Oxford Journal of Legal Studies 1

Rawls J, 'Legal Obligation and the Duty of Fair Play' in Hook S (ed), *Law and Philosophy* (New York University Press 1964) 3–18

Raz J, *The Morality of Freedom* (Clarendon Press 1986)

Raz J, 'Facing Up: A Reply' (1989) 62 Southern California Law Review 1153

Raz J, *Practical Reason and Norms* (2nd edn, Princeton University Press 1990)

Raz J, *Ethics in the Public Domain: Essays in the Morality of Law and Politics* (rev paperback edn, Clarendon Press 1995)

Raz J, 'Intention Without Retrieval' in Marmor A (ed), *Law and Interpretation* (Clarendon Press 1995) 155–76

Raz J, 'Intention in Interpretation' in George RP (ed), *The Autonomy of Law* (Clarendon Press 1996) 249–86

Raz J, 'Why Interpret?' (1996) 9 Ratio Juris 349

Raz J, 'Postema on Law's Autonomy and Public Practical Reasons: A Critical Comment' (1998) 4 Legal Theory 1

Raz J, *Engaging Reason: On the Theory of Value and Action* (OUP 1999)

Raz J, 'Reasoning with Rules' (2001) 54 Current Legal Problems 1

Raz J, 'The Problem of Authority: Revisiting the Service Conception' (2006) 90 Minnesota Law Review 1003

Raz J, *The Authority of Law: Essays on Law and Morality* (2nd edn, OUP 2009)

Raz J, *Between Authority and Interpretation: On the Theory of Law and Practical Reason* (OUP 2009)

Raz J, 'On Respect, Authority, and Neutrality: A Response' (2010) 120 Ethics 279

Raz J, *From Normativity to Responsibility* (OUP 2011)

Raz J, 'The Guise of the Bad' (2016) 10 Journal of Ethics and Social Philosophy 1

Raz J, 'Value and the Weight of Practical Reasons', in Lord E and Maguire B (eds), *Weighing Reasons* (OUP 2016) 141–56

Raz J (ed), *Authority* (New York University Press 1990)

Regan DH, 'Law's Halo' (1986) 4 Social Philosophy and Policy 15

Regan DH, 'Authority and Value: Reflections on Raz's Morality of Freedom' (1989) 62 Southern California Law Review 995

Regan DH, 'Reasons, Authority, and the Meaning of "Obey": Further Thoughts on Raz and Obedience to Law' (1990) 30 Canadian Journal of Law and Jurisprudence 3

Reicher SD, Haslam SA, and Smith JR, 'Working Toward the Experimenter: Reconceptualizing Obedience Within the Milgram Paradigm as Identification-Based Followership' (2012) 7 Perspectives on Psychological Science 315

Rodgers HR and Lewis EB, 'Political Support and Compliance Attitudes: A Study of Adolescents' (1974) 2 American Politics Research 61

Rodgers HR and Taylor G, 'Preadult Orientations Toward Legal Compliance: Notes Toward a Theory' (1970) 51 Social Science Quarterly 359

Rodriguez-Blanco V, *Law and Authority under the Guise of the Good* (Hart Publishing 2014)

Rosenberg MJ and Hovland CI, 'Cognitive, Affective, and Behavioral Components of Attitudes' in Rosenberg MJ et al (eds), *Attitude Organization and Change: An Analysis of Consistency Among Attitude Components* (Yale University Press 1960) 1–14

Rundle K, *Forms Liberate: Reclaiming the Jurisprudence of Lon L Fuller* (Hart Publishing 2012)

Sarat A, 'Support for the Legal System: An Analysis of Knowledge, Attitudes, and Behavior' (1975) 3 American Politics Quarterly 3

Sarat A, 'Legal Obligation: A Survey Study' (1977) 9 Polity 384

Sarat A, 'Studying American Legal Culture: An Assessment of Survey Evidence' (1977) 11 Law and Society Review 427

Sartre J-P, *Essays in Existentialism* (The Citadel Press 1965)

Scanlon TM, *What We Owe to Each Other* (Harvard University Press 1998)

Schauer F, *Playing by the Rules: A Philosophical Examination of Rule-Based Decision-Making in Law and in Life* (Clarendon Press 1991)

Schauer F, 'Rules and the Rule of Law' (1991) 14 Harvard Journal of Law & Public Policy 645

Schauer F, 'Was Austin Right After All? On the Role of Sanctions in a Theory of Law' (2010) 23 Ratio Juris 1

Schauer F, 'When and How (if at all) Does Law Constrain Official Action?' (2010) 44 Georgia Law Review 769

Schauer F, 'The Political Risks (if any) of Breaking the Law' (2012) 4 Journal of Legal Analysis 83

Schauer F, *The Force of Law* (Harvard University Press 2015)

Schleidgen S (ed), *Should We Always Act Morally? Essays on Overridingness* (Tectum 2012)

Schroeder M, 'The Ubiquity of State-Given Reasons' (2012) 122 Ethics 457

Schweitzer NJ, Sylvester DJ, and Saks MJ, 'Rule Violations and the Rule of Law: A Factorial Survey of Public Attitudes' (2007) 56 DePaul Law Review 615

Schweitzer NJ et al, 'The Effect of Legal Training on Judgments of Rule of Law Violations' (paper presented to the American Psychology-Law Association, 5 March 2008)

Schwitzgebel E, 'A Dispositional Approach to the Attitudes: Thinking Outside of the Belief Box' in Nottelmann N (ed), *New Essays on Belief: Constitution, Content and Structure* (Palgrave 2013) 75–99

Schwitzgebel E, 'Belief' in Zalta EN (ed), *Stanford Encyclopedia of Philosophy* <http://plato.stanford.edu/entries/belief> accessed 2 November 2017

Sciaraffa S, 'On Content-Independent Reasons: It's Not in the Name' (2009) 28 Law and Philosophy 233

Setiya K, 'Explaining Action' (2003) 112 The Philosophical Review 339

Shapiro SJ, 'Authority' in Coleman JL and Shapiro SJ (eds), *The Oxford Handbook of Jurisprudence and Philosophy of Law* (OUP 2002) 382–439

Shapiro SJ, *Legality* (Harvard University Press 2011)

Sherman J, 'Unresolved Problems in the Service Conception of Authority' (2010) 30 Oxford Journal of Legal Studies 419

Shinar D and McKnight AJ, 'The Effects of Enforcement and Public Information on Compliance' in Evans L and Schwing RC (eds), *Human Behavior and Traffic Safety* (Plenum 1985) 385–415

Shiner RA, 'Exclusionary Reasons and the Explanation of Behaviour' (1992) 5 Ratio Juris 1

Sidgwick H, *The Methods of Ethics* (first published 1874, Hackett Publishing 1981)

Silberman M, 'Toward a Theory of Criminal Deterrence' (1976) 41 American Sociological Review 442

Simmonds NE, *Central Issues in Jurisprudence: Justice, Law and Rights* (Sweet and Maxwell 2002)

Simmonds NE, *Law as a Moral Idea* (OUP 2007)

Simmons AJ, *Moral Principles and Political Obligations* (Princeton University Press 1979)

Skorupski J, *The Domain of Reasons* (OUP 2010)

Slote M, *From Morality to Virtue* (OUP 1992)

Slovic P, *The Perception of Risk* (Earthscan 2000)

Smith M, 'Is There a Prima Facie Obligation to Obey the Law?' (1973) 82 Yale Law Journal 950

Smith M, *The Moral Problem* (Blackwell 1994)

Snyder M and Swann WB, 'When Actions Reflect Attitudes: The Politics of Impression Management' (1976) 34 Journal of Personality and Social Psychology 1034

Sokolowski R, *Introduction to Phenomenology* (CUP 2000)

Solnick JV et al, 'An Experimental Analysis of Impulsivity and Impulse Control in Humans' (1980) 11 Learning and Motivation 61

Solum LB, 'Virtue Jurisprudence: Towards an Aretaic Theory of Law' in Huppes-Cluysenaer L and Coelho NMMS (eds), *Aristotle and The Philosophy of Law: Theory, Practice and Justice* (Springer 2013) 1–31

Soper P, *The Ethics of Deference: Learning From Law's Morals* (CUP 2002)

Spaak T, 'Legal Positivism, Law's Normativity, and the Normative Force of Legal Justification' (2003) 16 Ratio Juris 469

Stavropoulos NE, 'Why Principles?' (2007) Oxford Legal Studies Research Paper 28/2007 <https://papers.ssrn.com/sol3/papers.cfm?abstract_id=1023758> accessed 5 September 2017

Stocker M, 'Desiring the Bad: An Essay in Moral Psychology' (1979) 76 The Journal of Philosophy 738

Streumer B, 'Reasons and Impossibility' (2007) 136 Philosophical Studies 351

Stroud S, 'Moral Overridingness and Moral Theory' (1998) 79 Pacific Philosophical Quarterly 170

Sunshine J and Tyler TR, 'The Role of Procedural Justice and Legitimacy in Shaping Public Support for Policing' (2003) 37 Law and Society Review 513

Sunstein CR, 'On the Expressive Function of Law' (1996) 144 University of Pennsylvania Law Review 2021

Sunstein CR, *Risk and Reason: Safety, Law and the Environment* (CUP 2002)

Svenson O, 'Are We All Less Risky and More Skillful Than Our Fellow Drivers?' (1981) 47 Acta Psychologica 143

Swaminathan S, 'Projectivism and the Metaethical Foundations of the Normativity of Law' (2016) 7 Jurisprudence 231

Talbot B, 'The Best Argument for "Ought Implies Can" is a Better Argument Against "Ought Implies Can"' (2016) 3 Ergo 377

Tapp JL and Kohlberg L, 'Developing Senses of Law and Legal Justice' (1971) 27 Journal of Social Issues 65

Tapp JL and Levine FJ, 'Legal Socialization: Strategies for Ethical Legality' (1974) 27 Stanford Law Review 1

Taub N and Schneider EM, 'Women's Subordination and the Role of Law' in Kairys D (ed), *The Politics of Law of Law: A Progressive Critque* (3rd edn, Basic Books 1998) 328–55

Tenenbaum S, *Appearances of the Good* (CUP 2007)

Tenenbaum S, 'Guise of the Good' in LaFollette H (ed), *The International Encyclopedia of Ethics* (Wiley-Blackwell 2013) 2262–71

Thompson L and Loewenstein G, 'Egocentric Interpretations of Fairness and Interpersonal Conflict' (1992) 51 Organizational Behavior and Human Decision Processes 176

Thoreau H, *Walden and Civil Disobedience* (first published 1849, Lauter P ed, Houghton Mifflin Company 2000)

Tobin DD et al, 'The Intrapsychics of Gender: A Model of Self-Socialization' (2010) 117 Psychological Review 601

Tosi J, 'A Fair Play Account of Legitimate Political Authority' (2017) 23 Legal Theory 55

Tur RH, 'Defeasibilism' (2001) 21 Oxford Journal of Legal Studies 355

Tushnet M, 'A Marxist Analysis of American Law' (1978) 1 Marxist Perspectives 96

Tushnet M, 'The Critique of Rights' (1993) 47 SMU Law Review 23

Tversky A and Kahneman D, 'Availability: A Heuristic for Judging Frequency and Probability' (1973) 5 Cognitive Psychology 207

Tversky A and Kahneman D, 'Judgment under Uncertainty: Heuristics and Biases' (1974) 185 Science 1124

Tyler TR, *Why People Obey the Law* (with a new afterword by the author, Princeton University Press 2006)

Tyler TR, 'Understanding the Force of Law' (2015) 51 Tulsa Law Review 507

Tyler TR and Huo YJ, *Trust in the Law: Encouraging Public Cooperation with the Police and Courts* (Russell Sage Foundation 2002)

Tyler TR and Jackson J, 'Popular Legitimacy and the Exercise of Legal Authority: Motivating Compliance, Cooperation and Engagement' (2014) 20 Psychology, Public Policy, and Law 78

Ullman-Margalit E, 'On Presumption' (1983) 80 The Journal of Philosophy 143

Velleman JD, 'The Guise of the Good' (1992) 26 Noûs 3

Viehoff D, 'Debate: Procedure and Outcome in the Justification of Authority' (2011) 19 Journal of Political Philosophy 248

van der Vossen B, 'Assessing Law's Claim to Authority' (2011) 31 Oxford Journal of Legal Studies 481

Waldron J, 'Why Law—Efficacy, Freedom, or Fidelity?' (1994) 13 Law and Philosophy 259

Waluchow WJ, 'Authority and the Practical Difference Thesis: A Defense of Inclusive Legal Positivism' (2000) 6 Legal Theory 45

Watson G, 'Free Agency' in Watson G (ed), *Free Will* (2nd edn, OUP 2003) 337–51

Weber M, *The Methodology of the Social Sciences* (Shils EA and Finch HA eds and trs, Free Press 1949)

Weber M, *The Theory of Social and Economic Organization* (Parsons T ed, Henderson A and Parsons T trs, Free Press 1964)

Weber M, *Economy and Society: An Outline of Interpretive Sociology* (Roth G and Wittich C eds, University of California Press 1978)

Wicker AW, 'Attitudes versus Actions: The Relationship of Verbal and Overt Behavioural Responses to Attitude Objects' (1969) 25 Journal of Social Issues 41

Williams B, *Moral Luck* (CUP 1981)

Wilson TD and Kraft D, 'Why Do I Love Thee?: Effects of Repeated Introspections about a Dating Relationship on Attitudes toward the Relationship' (1993) 19 Personality and Social Psychology Bulletin 409

Winston GC and Woodbury RG, 'Myopic Discounting: Empirical Evidence' in Kaish S and Gilad B (eds), *Handbook of Behavioral Economics*, vol 2B (JAI Press 1991) 325–42

Wolf U, 'Cyber-Crime: Law Enforcement Must Keep Pace With Tech-Savvy Criminals' (2009) <http://www.govtech.com/dc/articles/Cyber-Crime-Law-Enforcement-Must-Keep-Pace.html?page=1> accessed 10 April 2017

Yagil D, 'Instrumental and Normative Motives for Compliance with Traffic Laws among Young and Older Drivers' (1998) 30 Accident Analysis and Prevention 417

Yagil D, 'Beliefs, Motives and Situational Factors Related to Pedestrians' Self-Reported Behavior at Signal-Controlled Crossings' (2000) 3 Transportation Research Part F 1

Index

Lightning Source UK Ltd.
Milton Keynes UK
UKHW020215170123
415479UK00003B/79